YOUR INTRODUCTION TO
PSYCHOLOGY

YOUR INTRODUCTION TO
PSYCHOLOGY

BY KJELL RAAHEIM AND JOHN RADFORD

J. W. Cappelens Forlag a·s – Oslo
Sigma – London

Illustrations delivered by:
Rune J. Andersson: p. 154–157–165–169.
Bulls Pressetjeneste: p. 19.
Geir Bølstad: p. 175.
JWC-archive: p. 17–18–21–23–40–63–71–76–84–86–91–92–150–166.
JWC-design dep.: p. 48–50–53–69–98–99–121–128.
Piet Hein: p. 183.
Sigurd Myrer: p. 143.
NTB: p. 11–24–33–61–111–119–130–148–152.
Gloria Shayler: p. 68–155.
Samfoto:
p. 12–13–16–34–36–39–42–44–47–49–62–64–66–72–73–75–85–87–94–95–97–
109–110–115–117–122–123–126–129–138–140–141–142–145–147–149–
153–168–172–177–178–180–182.
Helge Sunde: p. 9.
Steinar Torvbråten: p. 171.

© UK: Sigma Forlag Distribution
    25 Jellicoe House
    4 Osnaburgh Street
    London NW1 3AY

This book is partly based on *Innføring i generell psykologi*, Cappelen 1979 by
Karl Halvor Teigen and Kjell Raaheim.

Printed by a.s Joh. Nordahls Trykkeri, Oslo 1984

Cover design by Olsvik & Svenningsen a·s, Oslo

ISBN 82-02-09988-9

Contents

We want to say hello

We have called this book *Your Introduction to Psychology*. We have the idea that you, the reader, are someone who has heard or thought about some psychological questions, and would like to find out a bit more. Perhaps you have been interested or annoyed by something a psychologist has said, or has been reported as saying, in the papers or on television.

Many books called "Introduction to. . ." are really textbooks. This is not. We have not tried to be complete, and we have not written with an examination in mind. In each chapter we have tried to explain the sort of problems that arise in studying some aspect of human behaviour, and the sort of answers that psychologists try to give. We have ended each chapter with what we call Psychology in Action, where we give some examples of research and applications of psychology as they are going on in the 1980s. They are not conclusive findings, but current work.

We have in our minds what does tend to happen when one is introduced as a psychologist. "Oh, that's all a lot of nonsense – just common sense really", or "I blame all this delinquency on you psychologists and sociologists", or "I suppose you can tell what I'm thinking". Such remarks are not confined to casual conversations at parties.

Or, more seriously: "I've never quite understood what psychology actually is, can you explain it simply?". The answer might be along the lines of: "Well, the sorts of questions psychology is concerned with are. . .; and the sort of work that is being done now is. . .". This book, we hope, gives that kind of answer.

Over the last twenty years or so psychology has become quite a popular subject to study. Indeed in the USA it has been at times the most popular of all college subjects. That has not been matched in the UK, but there has been a notable increase in degree courses. Psychology was introduced as a GCE "A" level subject in 1970. Three girls at Framlingham High School, Suffolk, examined by one of the present authors, were the very first candidates. There are now some thousands each year at "A" level and A/O level. This growth still leaves, indeed perhaps has resulted in, a large number of enquiries about the subject.

Psychology has always been, and still remains, quite a small profession. The current membership of the British Psychological Society, the professional body in the UK, is around 10,500 compared with, for example, about 63,000 doctors and 23,000 dentists.

But the influence of psychology as a science has been, it seems to us, far greater than this might suggest. Considered in historical terms, human beings seem to think about themselves very differently now from the way they did, say 150 years ago. And this has partly been due to the development of those sciences that systematically study man and his behaviour, of which psychology is one. A particularly notable one, we believe, because it uses experiment, in its widest sense, as above all the preferred method of investigation.

We cannot say that all the effects have been good, nor all the results foolproof. But that cannot be claimed for any science. What matters is that we keep an open mind, that we seek to understand and explain, that we try to be more objective and less prejudiced. What cannot be denied is the effect that psychological theories and findings, good or bad, have had for better or worse. As one of us has put it, there can be very few individuals, in western society at least, who have not experienced child-rearing, education, job selection and training, the social services, propaganda and advertising, health care or the penal system. All these are directly or indirectly based on ideas about human beings and how they work.

Society itself is shaped by beliefs about behaviour. Some of these are supported by evidence, some are not. Sometimes evidence has never been sought, again it may be distorted or misused. Some awareness of such factors must be part of any tolerably adequate education today.

Acknowledgements
Mrs Irene Morris and Mrs Estelle Ingram both typed parts of the manuscript with great efficiency. Ms Gloria Shayler provided the illustrations on pages 68 and 155. Mrs Juliet Rydland prepared the final version of the manuscript. Our thanks to all of them.

CHAPTER ONE

Psychology as a Science. The History of Psychology

Introduction

Literally, psychology means teachings about the soul. The word is of Greek origin, *psyche* means soul and *logos* means line of teaching. The way psychology has developed however, it is neither a question of the soul, as the word is used in religious and philosophical connections, nor of any particular line of teaching. It would be more correct to say that we have to do with a many-sided research area, which consists of a long series of different questions about the way human beings, and sometimes animals, behave and how they experience the world.

Within a broad context, these are questions like: Why do we experience the world as we do? What is it that determines my actions? What is it that makes people so

Psychology aims at explaining both human and animal behaviour, normal as well as deviant, and adjustment as well as conflict. The experience of the individual is also of central importance, although more difficult to get hold of. What do you think is going on in the minds of the two characters in this picture?

different? What is the relationship between thought and emotions? It is not so easy to answer questions like these, and perhaps even more difficult to ascertain whether a proposed answer is correct. We are therefore obliged to split up the questions, in order to deal with more specific conditions. The question of why people are different from each other, cannot be answered in the same way irrespective of which people we are talking about. That grown ups and children are different from each other has another explanation than has the differences between people from varying cultures. Differences between siblings (brothers and sisters) must be explained in still other ways. Nor can the question be asked without making clear which differences we want to explain. Is it, for instance, the differences in language, in emotional reactions, or in intelligence? In similar fashion, other questions have to be broken down to make it possible to deal with them in a reasonable way. "Why do we experience things the way we do?" – *Which things?* – "What is it that determines my actions?" – *Which actions?* To be able to formulate questions which could be given reasonably exact answers, psychology has gradually moved a long way from the more general, naive way of questioning, natural for anyone who, for the first time, starts wondering about what lies "behind" peoples' behaviour. So we can find researchers engaged in the study of the specific conditions for experiencing visual illusions, for memorizing lists of isolated syllables, for the solution of puzzles etc. None of them seems to be trying to tackle the more fundamental problems of life. Psychological researchers have frequently been criticised for giving indirect and evasive answers when important and pressing questions are brought up. Such critique is only partly justified. If they had tried to answer

very complex and imprecise questions in a simple and authoritative way, we would have greater reason to become alarmed. The history of science abounds in attempts to give clearcut, universal solutions to intricate questions, but sooner or later they have proved to be wrong. To enlarge our psychological knowledge, it seems unavoidable that we must go through a process of sharpening and specifying our questions as much as possible.

What psychology is not

There is hardly another field about whose content and value there are so many different ideas and conflicting opinions. Let us take a look at two very common misunderstandings.

The first is the conception that the subject matter of psychology is to discuss phenomena partly beyond the normal run of events, something one has to turn to if it is difficult to explain human behaviour in the usual way. The extract below from a newspaper is an example of this.

«I cannot explain this»

I cannot explain what happened in the second half. It must have something to do with psychology. We'll have to discuss the matter and after a bit we will be able to see it in perspective.

It is when behaviour becomes unusual and very peculiar that we feel the need to explain it. What is it that makes twenty young people sit for days perched on poles in the sea? Perhaps the behaviour becomes more understandable when you are told that they are taking part in the Dutch pole-sitting championship. But do you accept this as a sufficient explanation?

From a psychological point of view, it would be equally important to explain why the football team in question did well in the first half, as it is to explain why they didn't make it in the second. In the same way it will be of equal importance to be able to explain why a student goes to school in the normal way each day for a hundred days, as it is to explain why he is not present on the hundred and first; or that a teacher is able to keep going for 20 years, as it is to explain why he has a breakdown in his 21st year.

Not only can we see a tendency to look for "psychological" explanations in the face of the deviant or seemingly inexplicable phenomenon. Also, many people have an expectation that the "psychological" explanation should come from a different level to that of every day life. For instance, that it should deal with unconscious processes or hidden forces in mental life. To a certain extent some of the

psychological schools and in particular psychoanalysis, have helped to confirm such expectations. Within general psychology however, there is no tendency to prefer more fanciful explanations above more straightforward ones. To say that a person acts the way he does because of habit is just as good a psychological explanation as to say that the behaviour is due to an "unconscious fear" or is given some other subtle reason.

Psychology thus may be too narrowly conceived, but in other contexts it might also be given too broad boundaries. We see examples of this where another popular misconception is concerned, namely the one that psychology should be in a position to give the most authoritative answers to all questions concerning the behaviour of human beings. In fact, it doesn't seem reasonable that a mother with many years' experience in the bringing up of children should brush all her experience aside be-

11

To understand the life situation of this individual, it must be considered from different angles. Not just a psychological one but also a medical, a legal, a political and a social one.

cause of some remark from a psychologist. But statements from so-called experts are sometimes regarded as far more important than conclusions drawn from the experience of every day life.

Psychology is only one among several sciences that have to do with the human being as their field of study. Among the natural sciences we might mention physiology and medicine, which both deal with the human body and its functions in normal conditions and in illness. In biology and zoology, man is compared to other species. In geography and anthropology we study how the human race has spread out all over the world, different ways of life and how people cope with different physical environments. The social sciences study humans as members of society. History as well as the study of literature may give us important insights into the destiny of individual human beings. Even religion and law deal with humans, and can offer perspectives upon higher as well as lower human needs.

A complete understanding of a person's behaviour cannot neglect any of these fields of knowledge. For instance, no amount of psychological expertise can make up for missing knowledge of such factors as the person's biological, historical or cultural background. How a certain person would succeed in a new career might, in some cases, be better predicted by one who knows the field of work thoroughly, than by a psychologist with a thorough knowledge of the person in question. The smile of the Mona Lisa might be interpreted more adequately by an art historian with a knowledge of Leonardo da Vinci's special style of portraiture than by a psychologist who tries to draw conclusions about Mona Lisa's (or Leonardo's) personality and emotional life. Psychology gives us no simple key which alone can open up for us deeper insights into human nature.

What is going on here? Can you describe what is happening without interpreting it?

Psychology and the basic rules of science

We have already referred to psychology as a science. This may give the impression that psychologists are in possession of a great store of exact knowledge. If we approach psychology with such an expectation, we will quite likely be disappointed. The multitude of questions, theories and viewpoints will in any case tell us that psychology is far from being a close-knit system resting upon indisputable facts. How is this compatible with our description of psychology as a science?

The answer lies in the fact that "scientific" or "not scientific" is not merely a question of truth and falsehood. To be scientific is rather a question of having to follow certain methodological procedures, or "rules of the game", which we hopefully and reasonably expect will help us to come closer to the truth. Prophecies and miracle cures do not follow this set of rules, and can accordingly not be accepted as scientific, even if they should happen to be true, because we do not understand how they work. Instead of explaining the background for their advice, the soothsayers and quacks typically try to keep their methods secret. The scientific nature of a subject, therefore does not lie in which statements are made, but in the attempt to substantiate these statements, and the willingness to change or discard them if they should turn out to be untenable.

One basic claim of all scientific procedure is the claim of *objectivity*, which implies that the researcher should try to find out what really is the case, regardless of his own personal opinions and preferences. It follows that he has to make use of methods that are open to public inspection, and might be followed by others who want to check his results. Intuition and revelation are therefore not entitled to be accepted as

13

scientific ways of enlarging one's knowledge.

Also, it should be made clear what is *observation* and what is *interpretation* of this observation. An example might clarify this. John B. Watson, the founder of Behaviourism, made in the 1920's a pioneering investigation of the original emotional reactions of infants. One of these is, according to Watson, anger or rage, which can be observed in a baby whose arms and legs are held tightly. Now even Watson, the proponent of an objective psychology, is in this case guilty of mixing together observation and interpretation. What one really can *observe* is the screaming and the stiffening of the muscles; that the baby is trying to get loose, and the emotion "anger" is our interpretation of what is going on (which may be true or false).

Objectivity and the difference between observation and interpretation however, is not an all-or-none affair. We cannot always say that a research finding either is objective or based on a subjective or arbitrary procedure; nor is it always easy to draw a distinction between observation and interpretation. The question of objectivity cannot be settled independently of the kind of phenomena we are investigating and the methods we have at our disposal.

For a result to qualify as "scientific", it must be possible to repeat it, that means another researcher using the same method must be able to find the same as in the original investigation. This has been called the criterion of *reproducibility*. A procedure that leads to reproducible results is termed *reliable*.

One of the reasons why phenomena like telepathy and extrasensory perception have been difficult to place within psychological science, has to do with their lack of reproducibility. While many people have experienced, or heard of such phenomena, they do not show up with any regularity when one tries to investigate them more closely; and until we are able to develop methods that make possible a reliable study of these phenomena, they cannot be given a secure place within the realm of science.

While a reproducible finding or a reliable method may serve as a sort of guarantee that our observations are trustworthy, we are not entitled to believe that our interpretation of the observations must be the correct one. If we find in a series of trials that a person is able to guess which figure another person is thinking of, consistently better than chance, we have reason to claim this as a fact, worthy of further investigation. But it might be too hasty to conclude that we now have evidence of an extra-sensory phenomenon. Thus reliability is only a part of the research story, the other part being the question of validity: whether what we have observed, really is what we believe it to be. One of the most famous of early psychological investigations was that of Clever Hans. Clever Hans was a horse who seemed to be able to do mathematics, giving his answers by pawing the ground. The psychologist Otto Pfungst showed that it was really his owner who was working out the answers. Hans would stop pawing at a minute cue, unnoticed by onlookers, given by his master. When the master was not there, Hans could no longer do sums. What the onlookers had seen was a very clever bit of learning for a horse, but it was not mathematics.

The validity of our interpretations is not something that can be decided by any simple method. There is no simple standard of validity. What we have to do is to get an overview over as many interpretations as possible, and then try to find or

14

create situations where different interpretations would lead one to expect different observations. Thus the results from further studies will help us to decide which interpretation is the correct one. Let us again take an example.

It is well known that a blind person can develop a very accurate "feeling" of obstacles in his path. This is often described as some sort of "facial vision", and has been interpreted as an extreme sensitivity to air streams against the skin of the face. To test the validity of this interpretation, an experiment was undertaken in which the faces of the blind were covered with cloth. Still they had no difficulties in sensing a hindrance, as for instance a wall ahead. On the other hand the blind subjects became unable to orient themselves when their *ears* were blocked. Also the task became more difficult if the floor had a carpet and the subjects were prevented from making any sound. Apparently their method of orientation was dependent upon echoes from the wall. This interpretation was convincingly confirmed when the *experimenter* went into the room equipped with a microphone, while the blind subject was sitting with earphones in a room next door. Now the blind subject was able to tell when the experimenter approached one of the walls.

The psychological experiment

We have already given some examples of how experiments are used to test the validity of hypotheses. By an experiment we mean an artificial prepared situation where the researcher himself tries to bring about the phenomenon he wants to study. There are a number of advantages in such a procedure. Firstly, the experiment affords good control over the conditions of observation. We know when we are going to observe and what we are looking for. Secondly, we don't have to wait for a similar situation to arise in real life, but can create situations that would almost never appear in a natural way. Take for instance the situation above where the blind and sighted persons were linked by radio. Thirdly, in an experiment, we can limit the situation in such a way that a number of interpretations will be automatically ruled out. In the ideal case one tries to keep all important conditions constant, apart from the factor or factors singled out for study. If the results vary with the variation in these factors, we have reason to believe that we have a clue to how the phenomenon should be explained.

Referring to the above experiment we might say when we find that the sense of orientation varies as the possibility of listening to an echo varies, while other conditions are eliminated or held constant, it is reasonable to assume that for the blind, hearing is a decisive factor in the ability to avoid obstacles. Because of its methodological advantages the experiment has been allotted a central place in psychological research, and it is no accident that this method to many people is the mark of scientific psychology. Of course, critics will point to the fact that psychological experiments seem to create as many problems as they intend to solve. For one thing, experimenting with humans is something quite different from experimenting with balls running down an inclined plane.

In contrast to steel balls, people will be affected by the fact that they are being observed and are taking part in a research project. For instance, they will be interested in knowing what the experimenter is looking for and what he expects the participants to do. The American psychologist Robert Rosenthal claims that the

Not all aspects of human life can be studied experimentally.

experimenter's expectancy will exert a subtle but often decisive influence on the subjects' behaviour, increasing the chances of confirming the research hypothesis. This so-called Rosenthal effect (or experimenter expectancy effect) may show itself without the subjects being aware of it, and even when the experimenter himself has no intention of giving away clues as to which results he is expecting to find. After all, human beings should not have more difficulty in taking hints than Clever Hans! In addition, the very fact that the experimental situation is an artificial one makes it possible to question the representativeness and usefulness of the results. To what extent are we entitled to consider the results of investigations like these typical of human behaviour in general? It is also true that quite a lot of psychological questions (including some of the most interesting ones) are of such a nature that – for practi-

cal or ethical reasons – they do not lend themselves easily to experimental study. Some examples are the causes of mental illness and the role of heredity and environment in the development of abilities and personality traits. One reason to use *animals* in psychological research, is to be able to study experimentally topics that would entail rather drastic interventions. Animal research has also been performed extensively by psychologists wanting to study basic psychological processes, as for instance learning, in its most simple and uncomplicated form. In both cases, we however face a great problem of generalization. To what extent can results from the animal laboratory be relied upon when the question is to explain human behaviour? It is of little help to know that the results are objective and collected in a reliable way if their validity is limited to a particular species. As a conclusion so far we must say that there are no specific procedures that would guarantee the scientific value of research. To study memory non-experimentally by merely collecting anecdotes about memory wizards or absentminded professors would clearly be unscientific, but it might be just as unscientific to draw conclusions about human motivation solely on the basis of research with say rats. To be scientific means that we constantly try to utilize the most suitable methods available and that we collect results from a variety of sources. To rely exclusively on one particular "foolproof" method is to depart from the scientific approach and engage in *pseudo science* instead.

And we must accept what investigations show, not rely on belief. An example of this is *phrenology,* the theory that you can describe someone's personality accurately by feeling the shape of their head. Phrenology had a long run, over a hundred years, before research showed conclusively that the brain does not have bits set aside for "faculties" of aggression or loving or what

not; and in any case the shape of the skull does not mirror the formation of the brain. Phrenology was originally a perfectly good theory; but if it persists today it is in defiance of the facts. It is no longer science but pseudo science. The same goes for many other cults on sale to a gullible public.

Brief outline of the history of psychology

Throughout all ages, human beings have asked questions about human nature. Attempts to bring these questions together and answering them in a more systematic way are of more recent origin. Despite its Greek roots, the name "psychology" is an invention of the late 16th century, and it did not emerge as a separate field of study (independent of philosophy) until nearly three hundred years later. Roughly we might divide the history and pre-history of psychology into four periods.

A psychological experiment from the age of the Vikings. According to the story, after the battle of Hjørungavåg, the defeated Vagn and his men were sitting on a log, waiting to be executed. Torkjel cut off the head of the first man with his great axe. The next man said: «I have a needle in my hand. If I am still conscious after my head is off I'll stick the needle in the ground». They cut off his head and the needle fell to the ground. As far as we know the experiment has never been repeated, but the results seem convincing: consciousness presupposes that the head is in its place.

De anima

·VETRICVLVS· ·II·VETRICVLVS· ·III·VETRICVLVS·

Mediaeval illustration to a thesis about the soul (*De Anima*) by Albertus Magnus. It was thought that different parts of the soul were located in the ventricles (hollow spaces) of the brain.

1. Pre-history: Antiquity and the Middle Ages

The earliest scholarly treatise about the soul was written by the Greek philosopher Aristotle (384–322 BC). Aristotle poses a set of questions about the nature of the soul and its relationship to the body. He makes a comparison between the soul of humans, the soul of animals and the soul of plants, and discusses the different parts or faculties of the soul. This was, for Aristotle, a way of identifying the essential ways in which various sorts of living things differ from each other. In other works of Aristotle there are scattered fruitful observations and speculations about human emotions, reactions, habits, and thoughts. Aristotle, essentially a biologist, sought to explain why living beings behave as they do, and in particular towards what ends they strive, rather than giving a purely mechanical or physiological account.

As was the case with most other disciplines, psychology in the next 2000 years was strongly influenced by Aristotle, to the extent that his views could be reconciled or re-interpreted to fit in with the dogmas of Christianity. It is typical of psychology in this period that the soul is conceived as a real substance, something almost concrete. On the one hand the soul is co-existent with life, permeating and sustaining the living body, on the other hand it merges into the spiritual and divine sphere of reality. Thus it became important to distinguish between higher and lower strata of the soul. A further distinction was made between two types of powers or faculties of the soul, those having to do with ideas and knowledge, and those having to do with motives and feelings. We thus have a group of lower, pre-intellectual abilities of sensation, memory and imagination, which can be contrasted with the higher ones, reason and understanding. Similarly, lower forms of emotional life, like "desire", "affects", and "passions" are contrasted with the power of will. Similar ways of dividing up mental life are still in use, but we no longer talk about a fixed number of separate and clearly discriminable mental powers.

2. From 1600 to about 1850

With the Renaissance liberation from old philosophical and religious dogmas, and the growth of science, we find the beginnings of an empirical psychology from the 17th century onwards. The French philosopher René *Descartes* (1596–1650) made an influential contribution by maintaining that he would not trust other ideas than those he could conceive in such a clear and distinct way that there was no room for doubt. By this criterion, the most basic and reliable fact turned out to be his own consciousness. "I think, therefore I am." The soul itself cannot be experienced directly, but the existence of one's own consciousness can be verified by anyone. From Descartes down to our century, psychology has almost invariably been defined as *the study of consciousness*.

That this study should be undertaken in an objective way and according to the rules of natural science, is made clear in a famous passage from the Dutch philosopher *Spinoza,* one of Descartes' successors: "I shall consider human actions and desires in exactly the same manner, as though I were concerned with lines, planes, and solids." Many psychologists now regret that, after Descartes, mind and body were considered two quite separate things, rather than as two aspects of the whole person.

Within British empiricism, philosophers

What to Descartes was the most obvious of all truths, is not equally obvious to everybody.

from John Locke at the end of the 1600's to James Mill at the beginning of the 1800's tried to analyse consciousness systematically. In contrast to Descartes, they wished to found their knowledge on evidence rather than on intuition. Taking the science of their day as a model, they made an attempt to identify the elementary units of consciousness, and to discover how these parts in turn were related to each other. It seemed to them that mental life in its entirety was composed of "ideas", which ultimately could be derived from sensory experience. We cannot think of anything without some kind of mental image, and cannot imagine anything without using previous experiences as our point of departure. This holds true even if I try to imagine something new or non-existent, which by closer analysis can be shown to consist in a new *combination* of previously sensed elements. The continuity of mental life is due to the fact that ideas tend to combine, or be associated with each other. Aristotle long ago had pointed to the tendency of memories to be connected to each other in a lawful way. Thus an idea will make me recall something I have experienced on the same occasion or in the same place ("contiguity"), something similar, or something contrasting. These so-called *laws of association* were now established as basic laws of consciousness, governing thoughts and feelings as well as memories. It is obvious that this is rather like a sort of chemistry, with ideas as the elements which combine and re-combine according to certain rules. One or other of the physical sciences has often been taken as a model for mental life, the most recent example being computers. The leading principle: to derive higher mental processes from lower ones, and try to understand complex phenomena from their elementary constituents, has kept re-occurring in

the history of psychology ever since.

Although much was written on psychological topics in this period, psychology itself was viewed as a branch of philosophy; "moral philosophy", as the discipline was called in Britain. Psychological thinkers certainly showed more of ingenuity and argumentation than genuine interest for scientific observation and method. The empirical basis of the "empiricists" was in most cases limited to unsystematic observations and illustrative examples.

3. Psychology becomes a science

Not until the second part of the 19th century did psychology become separated from philosophy and gain the status of a science on its own. It was physiology, then a rather young and rapidly expanding science, that showed the way. Experimental methods had been developed to investigate sense organs as well as the nervous system and its functioning, and had produced results that also were relevant for psychology. In Germany in particular, a number of brilliant researchers were occupied with the study of the senses. One of the main questions was: which external, physical events are *stimuli* for our sensory experiences? The question must of course be specified further. What are the stimuli for the experience of colours? What are the physical counterparts of the different dimensions of sounds (pitch, loudness etc.)? Do our experiences mirror the physical properties of stimuli or are they rather determined by the properties of our sense organs?

In his "Law of the specific sense energies" Johannes Müller maintained that the connection between the sense organs and the brain must be responsible for the "quality" of our experience. An irritation of the auditory nerve will lead to an experience of noise, a similar irritation of the tongue might give an impression of taste, whereas on the surface of the skin it would be felt as touch or tickling. Pressure to the eye ball leads to impressions of colour, and so on. What we experience is thus not a direct reproduction of the qualities of real objects, but is strictly speaking more informative of our nervous system than of the things that influence it.

Another central question had to do with the quantitative rather than the qualitative aspect of sense perception. How intense has a stimulus to be in order to be detected? What is the smallest difference between two stimuli that will allow us to experience them as different? Gustav T. *Fechner,* who hoped that the answer to such questions could help to solve the old philosophical problem of the relationship between the mind and the body, between the psychological and the physical, called this field of research *psycho-physics.* He developed a series of experimental and statistical methods to be able to examine this relationship in an exact, quantitative way. Inspired by sense physiology and by Fechner's pioneering work *Wilhelm Wundt* in 1879 founded the first laboratory for experimental psychology in Leipzig. This year is often regarded as the birth year of scientific psychology. The research that was performed in this laboratory by Wundt himself and by his numerous collaborators and students from several countries, became the model for psychology in the re-

Towards the end of the 19th century there was a surge of interest in unconscious processes, hypnosis, and extrasensory phenomena, which were however very seldom investigated with satisfactory scientific controls. This picture from the 1880s is entitled «A soirée in clairvoyance».

mainder of this period, which lasts into the first decade of our own century.

Although methods were different, psychology was still defined as the study of consciousness, whose content: sensations, images and associations now were brought into the laboratory. A colleague of Wundt, Hermann *Ebbinghaus,* investigated the laws of association in a series of experiments that are regarded as the basis for modern research in memory (1885).

Ebbinghaus' procedure offers a good illustration of how old and familiar theoretical questions could be approached using new scientific methods. Ebbinghaus started out to construct lists of nonsense syllables, consisting of three letters like VOP TAF HOM DEB RIF, which had the advantage of being relatively homogeneous and easy to quantify. Using himself as a subject, Ebbinghaus read the lists aloud at even speed until he could repeat them once without any errors. He could now on the basis of a long series of experiments draw "learning curves", showing progress as a function of number of repetitions, as well as "memory curves" (or curves of forgetting) showing recall of the original material as a function of time. At the same time he systematically investigated the effect of list length, extra repetitions, and relearning of apparently forgotten material.

It is tempting to blame the pioneer work of Ebbinghaus for being simply "too scientific". Intending to study "pure" memory he had constructed a situation so deviant from everyday life, that it might be of limited value if we want information about the ordinary workings of the memory process. The same objection might be raised against the laboratory studies of Wundt and Fechner, and for that matter also against quite a bit of more recent experimental psychology. It seems that we are up against a fundamental dilemma of research. The more we try to study a phenomenon in an exact and well controlled way, the more we might feel that we are taking it out of its natural context, at the risk of seeing it wither, like a cut flower. Perhaps we cannot study sea water without taking an isolated "sample", but at the same time we have to admit that what we are splashing around in the bucket is far from being anything like the ocean itself!

4. The 20th century.
Behaviourism and psychoanalysis

Around the turn of the century dissatisfaction grew with the traditional definition of psychology as "the study of consciousness".

For one thing it seemed that the introduction of scientific methods had not contributed to any great agreement as to what consciousness was all about. For instance, there was a fierce debate between those who claimed that thinking always depends upon images, and those who found evidence for so-called "imageless thoughts". Appeals to introspection – the observation of one's own content of consciousness – did not settle the issue. This method was apparently not reliable and objective enough for scientific purposes.

Secondly, it became evident that consciousness itself is rather limited, and perhaps not even the most important part of our total mental life. Fechner had suggested that one might look upon mental life as an iceberg, where the part above the surface might look impressive but at the same time be only a fraction compared to the masses below sea level. Thus very much of what determines our thoughts, feelings and acts, may be unavailable to introspection.

The third and perhaps most telling criticism against the psychology of consciousness came from those who were inspired by Darwin's theory of evolution. From an evolutionary perspective, the task of psychology is to study the mechanisms of human as well as animal adaptation and the abilities that make us survive in the struggle of life. What counts in this connection must be what one does, rather than what one feels; behaviour rather than consciousness. When human beings are regarded as biological organisms on a level with other animals, introspection cannot any longer be the chief method of study. Around 1900, animals began to be used in psychological research to elucidate questions of more general psychological interest. Especially famous are the studies of learning by Thorndike in the U.S.A. and by Pavlov in Russia.

Behaviourism. The most prominent representative of the emerging behavioural research was the American *John B. Watson* (1875–1958), who in 1913 declared that psychology from now on should be a completely objective study of behaviour. A psychologist should, no more than a natural scientist, concern himself with his subjects' private experiences and opinions. What was to be explained was their publicly observable behaviour only (hence the label "Behaviourism"). Explanations were to avoid concepts tainted by "subjectivism", "mentalism", "mysticism" and similar "mediaeval superstitions". What strictly can be observed is *stimuli* confronting the organism and *responses* made to these stimuli. The ultimate goal of psychology must be to predict from a given stimulus how the organism will react, and from a given response to conclude which stimuli

The results of introspection (self-observation) depend very much on who makes the observation.

Sigmund Freud the originator of psychoanalysis is probably for most people the best known figure in the history of psychology.

even beggar-man and thief, regardless of his talents, penchants, tendencies, abilities, vocations and race of ancestors."

However, it soon became clear that psychology could not be limited to study S–R connections without considering how the person *interpreted* the stimuli and what he *intended* by his responses. The attractive, sweeping simplicity of Watson's views were in course of time replaced by more complicated models worked out by the later behaviourists. In our days we can witness a certain renewed interest in simple and powerful behaviouristic formulations, as those proposed by *B. F. Skinner* (see next chapter).

The behaviouristic school has brought us quite a long way from the original meaning of the term psychology. As a historian of psychology jokingly exclaims: "Pity poor psychology! First it lost its soul, then went out of its mind, and finally lost consciousness. No wonder that it now has trouble with behaviour!"

Psychoanalysis. To many people the founder of modern psychology is neither Wilhelm Wundt nor John B. Watson, but Sigmund Freud. Freud (1856–1939) had a medical education, and worked as a neurologist in Vienna. He was neither engaged in analysing the components of consciousness, nor studying S–R connections, but trying to understand nervous symptoms that did not make sense from a purely physiological point of view. For example, compulsions to repeat meaningless actions, unexplained fainting, inability to have a normal sex life. Pursuing this task he was led not only to investigate the most inaccessible regions of his patients' mental life, but towards a psychological method to treat their nervous illnesses. He developed a theory of the causes of the psycho-neuroses which gradually broadened into a

have been present, Watson announced.

Thus the old doctrine of the association of ideas was replaced by a theory of associations between Stimuli and Responses. Accordingly, Behaviourism is often described as an S–R psychology.

The merit of behaviourism was to direct the attention of psychologists to concrete acts and how these are dependent upon the external situation (or the environment). Behaviourism made an especially important contribution to the psychology of learning. On the other hand, the uniqueness of the individual tended to be neglected, as development was considered to be a rather mechanical product of environmental stimulation.

Watson claimed that he would be able to train any normal infant "to become any type of specialist I might select – doctor, lawyer, artist, merchant-chief and, yes, comprehensive theory of personality and child development, and finally branched into speculations about the nature of art, culture and religion. Psychoanalysis has accordingly sometimes been regarded as a philosophy of life rather than a psychological theory.

Freud's point of departure was a quite simple one. His work with neurotic patients had convinced him that the individual himself possesses the key to his own problems, and that it is possible to disclose knowledge, memories, wishes and pent-up feelings which the person hitherto was unaware of. Through interpretation of dreams, the method of free association (where the patient is asked to let his thoughts run freely and report whatever comes to mind), and untiring patience on the part of the psychoanalyst, hitherto unconscious material can be brought into the open. To Freud, man appeared as a being with restricted capacity for self awareness and self control, originally ruled by affects and passions which civilisation only partly succeeds in curbing. In the depths of the human soul, a perpetual battle is going on between the "primitive" and the "controlling" forces, with varying outcome, ranging from open conflict to successful defence.

To Freud the *unconscious mental forces* were of more fundamental importance than conscious mental life, *elementary biological drives* (especially sexuality and aggression) more than rational and acceptable reasons for behaviour, and *childhood and upbringing in the first years of life* were considered more important explanations of behaviour than the life situation of the grown-up person. None of these points was totally new, but Freud built them into a theory which constituted a new view of human personality. He argued for instance that the unconscious part of personality is not only very comprehensive, but stands also in sharp contradiction to our conscious self, which actively tries to defend itself through repression and other "defense mechanisms". In his theory of the instincts (or drives) he particularly stressed their flexibility and changeability. An aggressive impulse which cannot be given direct outlet may for instance be re-directed against a scape-goat, or even be transformed into its opposite as over-demonstrative kindness. In contradiction to the traditional view of childhood as an innocent period of life, Freud spoke of varieties of "infantile sexuality", which from an adult point of view would be described as pretty perverse. An infant responds to stimuli, regardless of whether it is conventionally "right" or "wrong" to do so.

Freud has been criticised for using his neurotic patients as models for a general theory of personality, including that of the mentally healthy person. This has of course the advantage of pointing to the fact that the step from mental health to mental illness is indeed a short one. Maladjustment is quite as human and explicable as adjustment. On the other hands, a preoccupation with maladjustment might paint a far too pessimistic picture of human nature. Nor has Freud's view of mental illnesses and their treatment gone uncriticised. Even among Freud's original followers there were conflicting opinions. Best known among the dissenters are *Carl G. Jung* and *Alfred Adler* who, each in his own way, built further upon some of Freud's ideas and discarded others.

After an initial struggle, Freud's ideas began to be taken seriously, but it has proved much more difficult to integrate them into general psychology. Many of Freud's ideas have been adopted, at least in modified form, but many more are still controversial. Attempts to test the theory experimentally have met with mixed success. Perhaps Freud's real importance is giving us a new perspective from which to view human behaviour.

Psychology today

Behaviourism and psychoanalysis are only two, although very prominent and influential traditions that have left their marks upon modern psychology. Other psychological schools, like *functionalism,* the *Gestalt* movement, *existential* and *phenomenological* psychology have offered alternative perspectives upon the methods and subject matter of psychology, but will not be presented here. The brief sketch of the two movements presented above should nevertheless suffice to give you an idea of the scope of modern psychology when it comes to the questions of what is studied, which methods are being used and which kinds of theories are presented. The situation of today is however not characterized by opposing schools. Some theories have been modified, reworked and perhaps revised so as to incorporate elements from formerly contrasting theories. Others have been replaced by more specialised models, and new approaches are continually tried out. It does not appear that psychology has settled in a definite mould, even if the days of grand, conflicting systems are over. Its methods range from well controlled laboratory experiments, aided by advanced technical equipment to free observations of people in their natural surroundings, as for instance in a working group.

Investigators may study a quite circumscribed problem, as for instance the conditions of motion perception in the visual field. Such a study will almost certainly follow the rules of experimental work, described in a previous section, and build upon findings and principles already discussed in the first psychological laboratories. But psychologists of today also feel free to approach more complex problems with methods that are more uncertain and where the results to begin with only give a vague idea of where the answer might be. An example of this might be the task of investigating the necessary conditions for mental health and normal personality development.

It has been asserted that psychology today is not one discipline but rather a cluster of related disciplines. We could take this as an indication that psychology is still a young science that has not developed its final form, but it might also be an expression that its subject matter: human experience and behaviour – is so complex and many-sided that numerous approaches are both allowable and desirable. With this in mind, it is perhaps not so strange that the man in the street occasionally complains that "different psychologists are saying different things". Maybe they are answering different questions?

In this book we are going to give a few examples of this many-sided subject, and will often deal with topics where all of us have a good measure of practical experience, and therefore can contribute both to posing the questions and to evaluating the answers.

"The best way to learn English is through the discipline of Latin." So Lord Strabolgi is quoted as stating in the House of Lords, 28 January 1981.

There is not a shred of evidence to support this amazing remark. Indeed what we know of the process of learning, (see Chapter two), tells us that we can dismiss it as nonsense. Parliament, and public life generally, are full of those who are ever ready to pronounce on matters of human behaviour with the certainty of ignorance. It is not just that they are unaware of the evidence; they appear not to realise that there is such a thing.

Lord Strabolgi's remark might well have been made in 1881, not 1981. The first psychological laboratory had been opened by Wilhelm Wundt only two years before. In 1869 Francis Galton showed in his extraordinarily innovative book *Hereditary Genius* that human abilities are not mystical and inexplicable; they can be investigated objectively, empirically, and mathematically. This idea was inspired by the publication ten years before of *The Origin of Species* by Galton's cousin Charles Darwin. Galton's book, frequently reprinted, was perhaps just as epoch-making, and is even more readable today.

To give just a glimpse of Galton: amid a welter of serious scientific questions he wondered whether prayer is as effective as some suppose. Of all human lives, he argued, those of the royal family are prayed for most – a routine in every church on Sundays. Do they therefore live longer than average? The figures showed they did not.

Although perhaps amusing now, this little example illustrates the essence of psychology: the application of a scientific approach to human behaviour. Many of the problems of behaviour are very old indeed. Every society has the task of teaching children, and every advanced civilisation, certainly back to the Greeks of the 6th century BC, has speculated on the most effective way to learn. Some questions seem quite fundamental to any understanding of ourselves. To what extent are we determined by our genetic inheritance, and to what extent shaped by society? How do the mind and the body interact? Can we really be said to possess free will? Much of the history of psychology consists of gradually bringing such philosophical puzzles within the realm of scientific enquiry. By no means all have yielded to this, and some perhaps never will. But it is perhaps not too grandiose to claim that the painstaking effort is part of a characteristically human attempt to understand ourselves a little better, to have a little more control over our own future.

While the fundamental issues are often very old, the day-to-day problems of psychology are often quite novel. This is particularly true with the ever-accelerating changes in technology. At the moment of writing, legislation is being hurried through to censor or ban "video nasties". Neither censorship nor violence is new, but videos are. Part of the argument is that a very high proportion, nearly half, of children aged seven to sixteen have seen a horrific video film in the UK, as shown by a questionnaire survey. But two psychologists, Guy Cumberbatch and Paul Bates, took the same questionnaire into schools, with one crucial difference. They substituted some fabricated film titles for real films. 68% of children, they found, claimed to have seen films that do not exist. The original questionnaire was such that, they said: "Frankly, we found it embarrassing to waste the time of children and teachers on it.» (*The Times,* 30 March 1984).

Of course experts disagree. Peter Sutcliffe, the "Yorkshire Ripper" found sane at his trial after long argument, has now (1984) been found to suffer from severe psychiatric illness. It may be that his condition deteriorated in prison. But disagreement of experts is unavoidable. What matters in science is the way in which we seek to resolve the disagreement. Is it by resort to folklore and custom; or to authority; or to reasoned argument; or to evidence? The appeal to reason, but above all to evidence, is what characterises science.

A persistent belief has been that the eldest child differs from brothers and sisters in some significant way. Of course such a child has for a time a unique experience, and a special position often recognised by society, as legal heir for example. Research has been reported which seems to show that first-borns more often become astronauts, Nobel prize-winners, prime ministers and presidents; they have higher IQs and do better at school. However Cecile Ernst and Jules Augst (1983) of the University of Zurich, analysed 1500 studies of the effects of family position. They conclude that birth order has little or no effect. One of the main problems is that in most industrial countries parents of large families tend on the whole to have less money, less education, and lower IQs than those of smaller families. Thus the lower down the birth order, approximately speaking, a child is, the less privileged the

home she or he comes from. This may not be an end to the matter, of course: but we must base our view on the best evidence available, not on a theory or even on one or two studies.

In many ways psychology exemplifies the influential view of science propounded by Sir Karl Popper. Popper has argued that science necessarily proceeds by forming a hypothesis, a theory, about how things are, and looking for evidence that would disprove this. As long as no such evidence is found, it makes sense to continue to hold to the theory. When it is found, as it always is eventually, we must modify or discard the theory and substitute a better one. Or to put it in his own formula: Problems – Theories – Criticisms – Problems. This is very much what psychologists do. And indeed the psychological processes underlying the method have been studied, by Peter Wason and others (Chapter 4).

We mentioned earlier some of the misconceptions about psychology, such as the idea that it is mainly concerned with abnormal behaviour. Another is that there is something called "the psychological approach", especially to delinquency or crime, which is essentially a woolly, ineffective attempt to "understand" the wrongdoer rather than apply what is needed, usually efficacious punishment. Of course this is nonsense. Punishment, reward and anything else that affects behaviour, are all equally psychological. The question is, which works best?

Kathleen Fisher reports (1984) on effective programmes to deal with one particular form of juvenile crime, fire-setting or arson. Obviously this is behaviour which can have extremely dangerous and costly consequences. It was disturbing when, in

28

the late 1970s, it was reported that arson in the United States had increased over three-fold (325%) in the last ten years. As the authorities began to get alarmed, a preventive programme had already begun. It built on the work of Kenneth Fineman, an assistant clinical professor of medical psychology at the University of California. Working closely with the Fire Service, he concentrated on young arsonists. Although not definitely proved, many investigators believe that arson nearly always begins in childhood: adults don't just suddenly take it up. Fire fascinates many children. One study showed that 45% of kindergarten children had played with matches and 21% had started fires. But why should some of these go on to serious crime? "One thing firesetters seem to have in common," states Fineman, "is that, during their formative years, they were never appropriately educated about fire safety. They were allowed free rein. Nobody ever corrected them, nobody ever said 'no'." This is consistent with a review of research by Robert Vreeland and Marcus Waller, who rather frequently found an absent or inattentive father in the family, one with a negative attitude. As one counsellor put it: "The father would come in and say things like, 'can't you do something with this kid, like lock him up?'."

From this background a number of similar programmes have been developed – there are currently about 100 in 32 states. Typical is that in San Francisco, called Firehawks. Essentially it involves pairing an individual child (it is nearly always a boy) who has started a fire with a working fireman. The arrangement is voluntary, but when it works the firefighter acts as a substitute father, at least in respect of attitude to fire. He may explain basic rules of fire safety at first, but mostly the two just eat together, go to watch sport, or do homework. The fireman is available to the boy, including at the fire station. This sort of arrangement lasts for about a year. Reports show that it is almost 100% effective, in that the boys do not set further fires.

This is a "psychological" approach that seems to be less expensive and to work better than the previous methods: either shocking the child by showing dramatic effects of fires, or up to six months in a residential treatment centre. Of course, the long-term results have yet to be observed.

Equally psychological are investigations into human factors in warfare: factors as diverse as map-reading, officer selection and loss of sleep. For example, the Army Personnel Research Establishment at Farnborough, Hampshire, has been researching for several years into the need for sleep under battle conditions (reported by Rodney Cowton, Defence Correspondent of *The Times,* 14 November 1983). The Falklands conflict in 1982 was in some ways a "typical" modern conventional battle: a few weeks of intensive activity under harsh conditions. Hence experiments such as one in which three platoons went on a nine-day exercise, living out in bad weather in Northumberland. One platoon was not allowed to sleep, another was allowed 1½ hours sleep every 24 hours, the third 3 hours a day. The men were volunteers and could drop out if they wished; of course they would not be able to do so in action. Men in the first platoon ceased to be militarily effective after the third night and gave up after the fourth. The second group were effective for six days, and about half carried on to the end of the exercise. The third group nearly all finished and remained effective throughout.

This and other experiments have shown that mental factors and mood are more affected than physical ability, while even very tired men can concentrate enough to shoot accurately, even though the speed of their reactions slows down markedly.

Work such as this shows how a psychological approach interacts with many other approaches in real life problems. Let us give one more example of such problems, that of chronic pain. Despite modern advances in surgery and drugs, distressing pain often persists for long periods when the cause is either not known or cannot be directly treated: for example in limbs paralysed after a stroke, which in a number of cases is irreversible. Bruno J Urban of the Pain Clinic at Duke University Medical Center, North Carolina, in a review of different approaches (1982) stresses: "Multi-disciplinary evaluation and treatment of chronic pain are typically required." Pain is clearly something that is both physical and mental. Many people have had the experience of receiving a minor injury in a game, or while swimming, yet not feeling pain until later.

Acute pain can be treated medically by analgesics, but for chronic pain these are less useful because patients can become habituated so that the effect decreases, or addicted, or suffer side effects. Other, more effective medical means include injecting an anaesthetic block to a neural pain pathway. Electrical stimulation of the nerves can help in some cases and, more rarely, surgery. But even in these cases it is clear that psychological factors often great-ly affect the outcome. For example, the suffering of many chronic pain patients often seems more related to individual reactions and circumstances than to the physical cause. Many such patients can benefit from behavioural programmes which help them to view pain more objectively, to manage it better, to become more active and less passive. Urban suggests that this is often the best first approach, rather than immediately using physical means. Further, it is frequently found that depression is accompanied by worse experience of pain. Relieving depression by antidepressant drugs or perhaps by psychotherapy can help. Psychology also contributes to the understanding and treatment of pain by developing more accurate ways of assessing the individual experience of it, and by showing the complexity of its causes and their interaction. For example, headache: rarely a simple matter yet, according to research, often treated as such by physicians.

Once again, there is nothing new about pain. What are new are the methods of understanding, explaining, and treating. It hardly matters whether we call these medical or physiological or psychological: each approach depends on the others.

In trying to study human beings, including ourselves, in a scientific way, we are concerned both with what works and with why it does so. But equally we cannot avoid two other sorts of questions. One is what sort of thing *ought* to be done. Every scientist faces this problem. Should physicists help to produce nuclear bombs? Should psychologists aid military efficiency? But in the case of psychology it is more complex, because we can hardly separate what works from what ought to be done.

Those people who are concerned about law and order in society sometimes call vociferously for heavier punishments. This may be justifiable, or not, on all sorts of moral grounds; and it may work, or not; but we cannot infer one from the other. As psychologists we want to look at the evidence.

The other sort of question concerns the assumptions we make about human nature itself. At various times we have regarded ourselves as possessed of eternal souls, as just another species of animal, as rather complicated machines. The last is popular in its most modern version with the rise of information science and the development of artificial intelligence. Men and machines seem to be getting closer, artificial joints and heart pacemakers are almost commonplace and robot dancing a current fad. Already machines can almost see, read, and talk: will the next generation really think? And where does that place us? These too are practical problems for psychology in action.

CHAPTER TWO

Learning, Memory, and Forgetting

Introduction

One of the most important characteristics of human beings is their spectacular ability to accumulate knowledge and make use of experience. As one biologist has put it, we are born with an almost life-threatening lack of genuine instincts. Still we are capable of surviving in a world far more complicated and unpredictable than the world of most animals. But this is only after a long period of apprenticeship: As we know, human beings have a longer period of upbringing (in relation to their total life span) than members of any other species. Nearly all human activity presupposes learning.

In modern psychology, *learning* is a central and very comprehensive topic. In everyday speech, "learning" applies especially to the systematic acquisition of new skills, capabilities, and knowledge. In psychology, the concept is broadened to cover all modifications of behaviour and ways of thinking that are due to past activity and experience. Bad habits of work or a distaste for classical music can be a result of learning just as much as fluency in a foreign language or the art of playing the piano. Only behavioural changes that are transient or mainly due to non-psychological influences (like biological growth, illness and brain damages) fall outside of the psychology of learning.

Memory consists in retaining what has been learnt in such a way that one can show it or repeat it later on. Not necessarily after a long span of time; memory is also

a question of keeping in mind what happened just a few seconds ago. Accordingly, some theorists distinguish between *short term* and *long term memory*. In the latter case it is a question of what we can remember after hours, days, or years. *Forgetting* is, of course, the opposite of remembering. Something has been learnt at an earlier point of time, which at the present moment we are unable to remember. We can show the relationship between the concepts by the following simple equation:

What we remember – What we have forgotten

= What we have learnt

The equation is perhaps not as simple as it looks. We sometimes hear people complain that they have "forgotten" something which was never really learnt in the first place. Simple arithmetic shows that poor performance might have two reasons: We have either forgotten much or we have learnt very little:

What we remember =

What we have learnt – What we have forgotten

With most people complaining of bad memory it is really the learning that has failed.

We can point out two sides of memory. Firstly, we believe that there is more in memory than what is available on a given occasion. We can say "I do remember it"

Memory
Learning – Retention – Recall/Demonstration of what we have learnt

even if "it does not come to my mind just now". We are here referring to the *retention* or the *storing* of the material, and we are using the word "remember" to indicate that the material is in there, somewhere, among all the other things in the store

The limits to what can be learned are very flexible, even for an animal. Nevertheless a circus act such as this would not be possible if the bear did not have a natural balancing ability to build on.

room. Secondly, we might come to use the same word to explain the very fact that we cannot find the material at present. "I can't remember it just now" means that I am unable to *recall* what I have learnt before, again inferring that the material is still in the store room, to be found later on perhaps.

Learning and memory then may be looked upon as one continuous process with three different phases. We see that learning and memory are two sides of the same entity. It is not possible to study one of the two without presupposing the other. Memory implies that something has been learnt, and learning as such cannot be studied without at the same time having someone show that something is remembered. Whether a psychological experiment is to be called an experiment on learning or one on memory is mainly a question of definition. Normally the difference would be that in a learning experiment, one looks at the material to be learned and the way learning is taking place, whereas in an experiment on memory one is more engaged with the question of the different conditions influencing the availability of what has been learnt and the possibility of recalling it.

Learning – a passive or an active process?

Sit quietly and listen! This is a remark we have heard in many learning situations and it may give the impression that learning merely means quietly receiving something. In the educational theory of the past,

Education today tries to achieve the active participation of the students. The open school system and the language laboratory both do this in different ways.

34

teaching was looked upon as a kind of filling up with knowledge, where a person who already had the knowledge, the teacher, gave some demonstration in such a way that the listeners, the students, only had to receive. When the Roman teacher of rhetoric Quintilian wanted to stress the point that teaching had to be adjusted to the capacity of the student, he did it with the following words. "Jars with narrow openings cannot be filled if too much is poured in at once, but they will easily fill up if one pours with a gentle even hand, or maybe even drop by drop."

Today a passive model of learning would be looked upon as quite insufficient. This we clearly see when it is a question of attaining skills. No one can learn to play a violin without having touched the bow or swim without getting wet. When the learning of habits or the unlearning of bad habits is concerned, it seems that we very easily forget this. We often use very much energy in explaining to ourselves or to other people what we ought to have done or what we should not have done instead of making sure that the activity one wants to learn is in fact performed. In particular when it comes to a question of getting new knowledge, we behave as if it was only a question of placing ourselves in the right situation by for instance just reading a number of pages in a text book, without any reflection on what this might mean, or what we are going to do with the information we receive.

Through the influence of behaviourism, the psychology of learning has profited by a demonstration that what is going to be learned is some *activity* that can only be learned through the activity itself. A student does not learn what he reads but what he does with what he reads. We might look with the deepest sympathy at the student who asked his teacher the following question "How am I to sit still when you want me to follow what you say?"

Experiments have shown for instance that if we have only one hour at our disposal to learn a certain amount of material it would pay off to use most of the time for some activity with the material instead of just reading it over and over again. The activity may be of different kinds as for instance, writing notes, trying to reproduce part of the text etc. In one particular experiment where the subjects had to learn a list of syllables, the best results were obtained when 80 per cent of the time was spent *not* looking at the list, the subjects instead actively trying to reproduce the syllables. The passive intake of the material always must be reduced to a minimum, even though one naturally must allow oneself the time to at least read through the list or the book, as the case may be.

It may seem as if we want to maintain that nothing much can be learned by just listening or reading something from books, but then we must be aware of the fact that reading and listening are themselves activities which usually are accompanied by a great amount of thinking and reasoning. To ask someone to listen well is thus not the same as to ask the person to take a passive, receiving attitude. If the request is to have an educational function, it has also to be a demand for some activity and in effect come to mean "Think about it."

The importance of activity also shows itself in the relationship between learning and motivation. One of the most important tasks a teacher has is to induce motivation in the students. If the students have the will to learn and interest in the material to be learned, it may seem that the process of learning almost goes automatically. A student who has difficulties in remembering poetry from a text book may be able to recall the lyrics of a large number of pop

Practical skills have to be learned through practice. What is the role of the instructor here? Should he demonstrate, explain, help, or stay in the background?

music songs. Another who is not very clever in remembering dates from history may be able to keep a very accurate record of what has happened in the last 20 years of soccer.

The secret of motivation lies in its resulting in activity. We do something with the material, look it up, are aware of it, repeat it to ourselves, think about it and talk about it in many connections.

But neither motivation nor activity gives any guarantee that the learning process will go as it ought to. If the motivation has been added from the outside by for instance a promised gift or by a threat of punishment, the attention and with that the activity might be directed towards these outside conditions so as to make the learning suffer. The student who is given the choice between working hard with a difficult curriculum in mathematics or having to repeat one year in school (a choice that may be real enough in some countries) might naturally become motivated, but his motivation might perhaps be directed towards finding a way away from it all.

If we are promised a greater reward if we do well, our efforts may be directed towards being clever at the exam rather than to working hard with what has to be learned.

An activity may also run the risk of having a bad influence if it contains something wrong or if it is irrelevant and has very little to do with what is going to be learned. Asking all sorts of question in trying to please the teacher might be a way of reducing one's chances of really grasping what he is talking about.

We learn from our mistakes, it is said, but very often we unfortunately only learn to repeat the errors. This may sometimes lead to the result that our achievements become steadily poorer. If we take a break in our learning efforts we might in some cases do better than before when after a while we start again. One of the reasons why it normally is an advantage to distribute the learning over a period of time is that we escape the disadvantage of repeatedly rehearsing the same errors. We get an opportunity of simply forgetting some of the errors from one attempt to the next.

Activity then does not mean activity at any price. In some forms of programmed teaching the activity of the students is secured by having the student continually fill in words that are omitted in the text. This may make us more attentive but our. . . . . may sometimes perhaps not be directed towards the material we are going to. . . . . . If the. . . . . . . is not properly arranged the whole affair may perhaps come to be judged as a silly game rather than a serious. . . . .

Learning – an unavoidable process?

We usually look upon learning as something only happening at certain times of the day when we officially are asked to learn as for instance in school, or when training for a particular purpose. However, in psychology, we would not sharply distinguish between situations of learning and the situations where no formal learning is taking place. If we think of learning as being closely connected with some activ-

ity or other, there should constantly exist a basis for learning, since some activity is almost always going on. Learning may, however, very often take other directions than what we want. Even when we try to run away from our problems we learn something: not to solve the problems but how to escape them. A student who never listens to what the teacher has to say is also learning something, namely to avoid being taught and someone who never opens his mouth to say anything becomes gradually more skilful in keeping his mouth shut.

Quite a lot of our habits and even more of our bad habits seem to have come about in such an automatic way. We have perhaps never done anything in particular to get them, but one day it seems they have come to stay. Psychologists disagree when it comes to the question of to what extent learning can be described as an automatic process. At one extreme we find those who argue that every repetition of some kind of behaviour necessarily leads to an increased tendency to perform this act. As the American psychologist William James said many years ago:

"The drunken Rip van Winkle in Jefferson's play excuses himself for every fresh dereliction by saying I won't count this time! Well! He may not count it, and a kind Heaven may not count it; but it is being counted none the less. Down among his nerve-cells and fibres the molecules are counting it, registering and storing it up to be used against him when the next temptation comes. Nothing we ever do is, in strict scientific literalness, wiped out."

A similar point of view is seen within the theory of classical conditioning. According to this theory any activity (response) would be tied together with the stimuli that act upon the organism at a certain time. By a sufficient number of repetitions, these new stimuli would elicit the response even if S and R originally had nothing to do with each other. Let us here take a look at one of the best known experiments in psychology.

It derived from some even more famous experiments by the Russian physiologist Ivan Pavlov, in which he sounded a bell just as meat powder was given to a dog. After a number of trials, the dog would salivate to the sound of the bell alone. While this now sounds rather obvious, for Pavlov the interest lay in using such experiments to investigate the working of the nervous system: he maintained to the end of his life he was doing physiology, not psychology.

For J. B. Watson, however, the *conditioned reflex* seemed to offer just the unit of learning needed by his new objective psychology.

Watson demonstrated how it is possible to condition a fear reaction to what is originally a neutral or positive stimulus. He let a 9 month old boy Albert play with a white rat each day. The animal did not create any fear in the child, but then one day Watson frightened Albert by banging a steel rod with a hammer just when the boy reached out for the animal. After a few combinations of this (rat plus frightening sound) the sight of the rat alone was enough to elicit a strong fear reaction.

Not all studies of conditioning have been as successful as the one with Albert. Indeed in some connections we might be struck by the astonishing resistance of the human being to making use of experience. Developmental and educational psychologists have shown how difficult it can be for a child to learn something in an area where the child does not yet have the basic concepts and thus has not any frame into which he could put his experience. The Swiss psychologist Jean Piaget refers to these frames, or ways of organising experience, as "schemes" or "schemata". Psy-

choanalysts in a similar way have demonstrated that an experience that cannot be reconciled with the picture a person has of himself becomes overlooked, repressed or changed. Even the drunkard in William James's example would probably as long as he could, stick to the opinion that he is the master of his alcohol consumption, even if time and again he finds that he is in fact governed by it. Studies of alcoholics do in fact show that they frequently "explain away" any sign that they are no longer able to control their drinking. Also the very optimistic person always believes that everything will go well in spite of the fact that he constantly experiences the opposite. We perhaps also know of people who make up their minds on the basis of a single experience and who thereafter become immune to new and contradictory information.

Learning is thus not only dependent on repetition of certain experiences and activities. It is also a question of the susceptibility of the individual, which in turn would depend on how these experiences are interpreted. In one case a participant in an experiment for conditioning where a light signal was given immediately before a slight electric shock to his hand still hadn't learnt to withdraw his hand when he heard the sound after several hundred trials. Being questioned about it, he explained that he had believed that it was all a kind of competition to endure pain.

Feedback and reinforcement of behaviour

If we are blindfolded and asked to draw lines of exactly 10 cm each, it is doubtful whether we would improve in our attempts irrespective of the number of trials. An early American learning psychologist E. L.

38

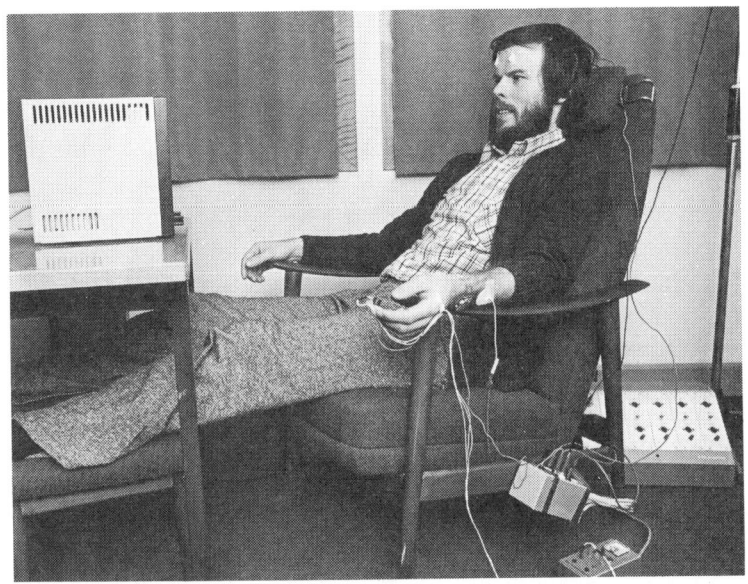

Biofeedback. The subject is looking at a screen giving continuous information about different physiological functions, allowing him in some cases to control reactions which he normally could not, such as heartrate.

Thorndike, in his time performed just such an experiment, with the aim of showing that activity and repetition were not enough to bring about the desired result of learning. To be able to make use of the experience or training, it is necessary that we in some way get information about the results; that we get *feedback* as it is called. The term is taken from *cybernetics* (the study of the regulating and selfregulating mechanisms in nature and technology) and is used in psychology in describing the influences on behaviour of the outcome of, among other things, the learning process.

In many forms of training of skill, such feedback comes almost automatically. A child learning to ride a bicycle is "told" by the results of the efforts which movements are correct and which will be unsuccessful. Attempts at going against the law of gravity or other physical laws would immediately and very firmly be denied by the bicycle itself. At other times it may be more difficult to judge whether one is on the right track. The art of teaching a skill lies in aiding the learner to discriminate be-

tween the right and wrong movements. Today the use of video may give the learner an opportunity to see himself in action and profit from studying the different moves.

Also when it comes to such a complicated thing as knowing oneself we are dependent on feedback from our social environment. If we keep our thoughts and emotions to ourselves, we get little opportunity to learn from others and from their reaction to what we think and mean. It then becomes very important that our surroundings react in a natural and consistent way. We might easily become confused if what is welcomed one day is reacted to rather negatively the next.

If we lack feedback, positive or negative, for what we are doing we very easily become insecure. (With "positive feedback" we refer to "signals" that increase the strength of a response, whilst "negative feedback" is what weakens the tendency to act in a particular way.) It has further been shown that additional feedback may bring about learning in areas which one previously thought were outside human control. By means of electronic equipment one is able to give continuous information to a person about his blood pressure, heart beat, muscle tension and brain activity and thereby enable the person, to a certain extent at least, to learn to regulate these functions. This method, called bio-feed-back, has proved itself to be promising in the treatment of certain illnesses as for instance, epilepsy and migraine.

Information or reinforcement?

Up till now we have talked about feedback as if it only consisted in giving information to the one who is learning. Some information one might choose either to take notice of or to ignore. But many learning psychologists hold that what happens after a response has a much more automatic and immediate influence on learning, a fact we have mentioned earlier. Thorndike formulated the Law of Effect which he held was basic to all learning. According to this law, any stimulus-response connection which has a positive effect on the organism automatically becomes strengthened.

Within modern behaviouristic learning theory, such an effect of feedback is called *reinforcement*. The idea is that certain consequences of behaviour such as rewards, confirmation etc., have a direct importance for whether the behaviour is learned.

B. F. Skinner has called this form of learning *operant conditioning*. That is a conditioning where the response is not elicited by the stimulus to which it is connected, as it is in classical conditioning, but where the response is dependent on what one has achieved with it previously. The response is any action that *operates* on the environment with a certain effect: an effect that makes the response more likely to occur in the future.

With animals it is often food that is used as the "reinforcing agent". The experimenter may for instance, give a pigeon some corn each time it lifts its foot. After a short while, the pigeon might spend all of his time jumping about on one leg. One of the most striking examples of the principle of reinforcement and its power we have is the so-called superstitious behaviour. Skinner has demonstrated that if one gives pigeons, for example, a reinforcement each 15 seconds, irrespective of what the pigeons are doing at the moment, they will later on come to develop a very strange stereotyped form of reaction. While one would jump about, another might go around with its neck stretched stiffly forward, a third may be standing still or perhaps very energetically moving its wings. The reinforcements have in effect, nothing to do with what they are really doing, but since they are only repeating what they happened to be doing the first time they were reinforced, they would never discover that their behaviour could have been different. It is tempting to draw parallels with some forms of irrational behaviour among human beings and Skinner does not refrain from transferring his results with pigeons and rats to the area of human learning.

There is a great deal of disagreement, however, about how automatic such rein-

Boy, have I got this guy conditioned! Every time I press the lever he drops food in.

forcement really is. Derek Blackman, a British psychology professor, gives an example of how he himself came to play the role of the pigeon. Some students had decided to condition his behaviour when he was lecturing. They agreed to let a female student smile and nod each time the professor looked in her direction or moved towards that side of the room. By the end of the lecture he was directing all his activity to this particular part of the room and looked as if he was only speaking to this particular person, without being aware of the reason why he did so. We might perhaps take this as an example of how reinforcement also may have some automatic influence on the behaviour of humans, but it is unlikely that Professor Blackman would have behaved in the same way if he had known of the students' plan.

Irrrespective of how we come to conceive of feedback there is little doubt that this is an important means of shaping behaviour and influencing learning.

Immediate and delayed feedback

A mother who finds her two year old son engaged in investigating the electric plug with some pointed object would probably not wait to let the child discover the effect for itself, she would rather take the matter in her own hands and give the necessary feedback in an angry voice.

If the mother, instead of giving such immediate feedback, had seen it as her task only to remove the boy and to let the father when he later comes home take over the teaching of how to deal with electric equipment, the result of the experience might not have been the same. A delayed feedback from the father of a similar type to the one used by the mother at the moment the incident took place would perhaps result in nothing more than the boy's attempts to avoid his father in the afternoon. We are thus running the risk that the boy is not able to see the connection between the feedback and the behaviour in question, but that he by being given his feedback starts to behave in an unwanted way.

In a similar way, many forms of inappropriate behaviour might be learned as a result of short-sighted positive results. The immediate and pleasant feeling after a glass of alcohol might mean more to all one's drinking habits than the physical unpleasantness and regrets the day after. Being caught while doing something wrong has a much stronger effect than any punishment following months later.

Precise or imprecise feedback

If one wants to steer learning it is necessary that the information given is relatively detailed and precise. A written essay being handed back to the student with the comment "not too good" or "some improvement" in itself gives no basis for learning and when this as a rule is rather delayed feedback the matter is even worse. What we need to know is what is not so good and in which way we are improving. The reason why some people never learn is perhaps the same. The information comes too late and is not precise enough.

Indeed experiments have shown that students asked to solve written problems have had an advantage if they can give themselves quick and precise feedback. In one group the number of solutions was increased by 50% when students had been asked to formulate to themselves as precisely as possible what was really the difficulty in each case.

Gambling often involves the principle of intermittent reinforcement, but in a lottery one may never win yet continue to try one's luck. Human beings are more subtle than rats, or are they more foolish?

Continuous or intermittent reinforcement

Skinner tells that he was once in the middle of a series of experiments in his laboratory when he ran out of food for the rats he was using. Instead of breaking up the experiment he decided to ration the food: when previously the rats had received a reward each time they gave the correct response, they now only got the food now and then. To his great surprise Skinner discovered that the frequency of reaction increased!

This phenomenon has since been investigated systematically. It is found that intermittent reinforcement is far better than continuous when it comes to maintaining behaviour; in particular when the reinforcement is given randomly. This also holds true for many human learning situations. Many people will keep up some activity that has not proved of any particular value in the past as for instance participating in games for money, because sometimes it might end well. Bingo, and fruit machines, are more or less systematically based on this principle, and often produce extremely persistent behaviour. To explain the currently even more popular space invader games, however, is more complex, since reinforcement depends on skill as well as chance.

If good and bad luck had not been unsystematically mixed in life we would perhaps much sooner become wiser from our misfortunes. On the other hand, if all of our good deeds were regularly rewarded some unexpected setback might much more easily have made us lose faith.

Positive and negative information

The example of intermittent reinforcement seems to suggest that one single positive experience may have greater importance than a series of negative ones when it comes to maintaining behaviour. But how is it when we are trying to learn something new?

Let us assume that two students, independently of each other, are going to translate a passage from a foreign language and are facing a word neither of them knows. Both have to guess and by chance. A guesses right whereas B makes the wrong guess. If now A is told that he is right and B is told that he is wrong, who do you think will have learnt the most?

In this case the person who has only received a No would have less chance to learn something since he has not received sufficient information to be able to know what he *should* have answered. Very often one is as wise as before after having made the mistake.

If A and B had only two answers to choose between, the value of information of a Yes and a No answer would objectively be the same. Subjectively speaking the two kinds of information might nevertheless be different. B who guessed a No would at least have to take the time to draw the conclusion X is wrong, therefore Y must be correct. On top of that, B is later entering into learning with a handicap, up to now he has only performed in the wrong way, not yet having presented the correct answer (Compare the section about activity). To know that one has made a mistake on top of everything might make one feel embarrassed and thus less motivated to try again (See next section about punishment). Research has also shown that most people have difficulties in correctly interpreting negative information. (See chapter Six.)

Despite all the disadvantages of the negative reactions, most of us behave as if the most important thing in tuition and upbringing is to make people aware of the errors they are making. As a child we would as a rule receive more noes than yeses. As a student we are more frequently told what is incorrect. This is perhaps not so strange since it is usually the errors we have to do something about, and of course the errors are what people around us very easily see. It seems as if we are caught in a hopeless paradox. The less we have learned the more errors we make and the more errors we make the less we learn.

It might be objected to this that a No answer also has its importance. It points to the necessity of doing something else, even if in itself it does not tell what this is going to be. It is possible though to combine it with positive information by saying "Don't do this; do that instead".

Some of the more modern educational schemes (compare programmed teaching) may in fact be criticised because they give too few possibilities to make mistakes. This may make students less attentive, and neither would they reach a full understanding of which type of errors they would have to try to avoid. In a text book on Chess the Swedish Grand Master Ståhlberg says, quite in contradiction to all theories of reinforcement, "remember we learn more from our mistakes than from our victories. Therefore it is important that one studies one's lost games with greater attention than those we have won."

When we so often do not learn from our mistakes, it is perhaps because we lack the objectivity and the patience of the chess master to analyse our lost games.

Punishment

In former times punishment in school was considered necessary and a natural part of the learning process. Dr. Samuel Johnson accounted for his mastery of Latin and Greek with the reply "My master whipped me very well". It was a common belief that knowledge could not be kept unless it was "knocked in". Modern learning psychology has perhaps gone to the other extreme. It is argued, by for instance Skinner, that punishment does not contribute to learn-

ing. Admittedly, we sometimes refrain from doing what we have been punished for, but this does not necessarily mean that it has been forgotten or unlearned, it is rather a question of inhibition. The impulse to act in some way is as great as before and there is perhaps a fair chance that we would resume the activity later on.

In spite of all this, most of us can give examples from our own experience of how punishment can be both effective and appropriate. This happens in particular when the punishment is not given us by another person, but comes about as a consequence of an inappropriate type of behaviour. It is this we are referring to when we talk about how valuable it is to let a child experience things for himself. (With experiences in this connection we often think of those of a

Punishment for a wrong move in traffic may be immediate and severe. But what about all the near misses? Do they teach us to be more careful, or just that we can get away with it?

negative type.) It is also of importance that the punishment is perceived as directed towards the behaviour and not towards the person as such. For both these reasons it is important that punishment is related to the errors that one has made, both as far as the type of punishment and its degree are concerned.

We are therefore not in the position of being able to tell how punishment would be received in a particular situation. The important thing is how the individual reacts to punishment and what it is that is going to be learnt. A typical reaction of punishment is to try to avoid the situation in which one has been punished. A burnt child avoids the fire, but the reactions to punishment may be different. Let us give an example from an experiment with animals performed by Miller.

A hungry rat is placed in a maze where the task is to learn which of the routes leads to the goal, that is the food. On the floor of one of the alleys in the maze an electric grid is placed and the rat may receive a slight shock on its way to the goal. If the current is put on as soon as the rat touches the grid with his foreleg it naturally follows that the animal would hesitate to move into this alley. In this case the punishment would lead to learning being delayed considerably. One could of course also say that the rat is learning to avoid this alley. If, on the other hand, the current is put on just a moment later, such as to make the animal receive the shock on its hind paws, then the result is that it increases its speed and on each new trial would use less time through the maze. The rat runs as fast as it can past the danger spot.

The experiment shows how a very similar punishment in two cases might have very different results. What we see here might have validity also for human beings.

What is important is not the punishment in itself, but what the punishment makes us do.

The transfer of learning

What is really being learnt?

Can it be necessary to ask such questions? A small child who after many forms of encouragements and after considerable repetition has started to shout "Daddy!" when his father is around surely has learnt what "Daddy" means? A student who has learnt Pythagoras' theorem surely should be able to find the length of sides in figures involving right-angled triangles or what has he learned?

Maybe the child surprises one by shouting a delighted "Daddy" to any man passing by, whilst the student turns out to be unable to utilise his knowledge if the triangle has the hypotenuse as its base, not to speak of the ability to find the length of the diagonal in a rectangle.

In a sense the child has learnt far more than his father had thought and believed and the student has learnt far less than what the teacher was hoping for. Both in addition may have learnt something else at the same time. The child, that it is possible to have people stop and smile, the student that mathematics is a difficult subject or perhaps that it contains a lot that one might use to impress younger students.

Much learning thus seems to be going on out of sight. We have difficulties in knowing what is really being learnt without having seen it in different circumstances. It will then usually turn out that we have learnt a great deal more than what the situation seems to offer. Little Albert, who became frightened by the sound Watson was making when the boy wanted to play with the white rat, later on seemed to be frightened also when other animals as for instance rabbits, were about. The dogs of Pavlov's classical conditioning who had learnt that a certain tone was always followed by food, reacted to tones they had never heard before as if they were signals for food as well. In such cases we talk about *generalisation,* where the individual reacts as if what holds true for one situation, also holds true for a series of similar situations. Very often this can save us from additional learning.

To what extent learning in one situation can be transferred to new situations is a question of great practical importance. In education and the bringing up of children one to a great extent builds upon the conception that what is learned in one connection has some influence on what we are doing under other circumstances. Formerly the teaching of Latin in schools was defended by the argument that the students thus were taught to think logically, to improve their memory and judgement etc. Nowadays we might find that a firm selling children's toys would claim that a colourful duck which can be taken apart and put together again, and which plays a tune when it is moved along the floor, will contribute to develop the two year olds sense of colour, musicality and love for animals!

In both cases we might wonder whether fantasy has been given too much of a free rein. What we are primarily learning is the activities in which we engage. We should therefore always practice as realistically as possible. If the goal is to write a good essay for the exam, the training must consist in writing essays, if a task is to get rid of one's timidity, one successful attempt at behaving in a natural way would perhaps be more effective than ten conversations about the subject.

The question of transfer of learning is a question of to what extent knowledge, habits and skills are something that we can be spoon-fed with or whether a more natural process of growth takes place. In this area we have two different psychological traditions which seem far apart.

The behaviouristic view is that what is learned is specific reactions to specific situations. Transfer would only occur to the extent that a new situation contains elements identical with (or very similar to) those of the old. A person who has been taught how to play a certain instrument would for instance, more easily learn to play another because there are common features to the two learning situations. A violinist, for example, could play the viola fairly easily, but would find it much more difficult to transfer to the trumpet.

The other point of view is in a sense connected with the concept of personality. Here it is stressed that an *internal connection* can be found between the various actions of a human being. It *is* really possible to change one's behaviour by talking about a problem, since a connection exists – if only in part – between what we think, believe or decide to do, and what we really will be doing. Within this view the important thing is what different types of experience come to mean for the individual's understanding, attitudes and emotional life. The more specific actions of the moment are believed to play a less important role.

The difference between the two views is not only of academic interest. Would a mother who takes up the infant each time it cries actually teach the child to scream by constantly rewarding the crying? Or is she teaching the child that mother is there to be trusted and that the world is not so bad afterall? And what about the father who punishes his son because the boy has beaten his little sister: is he making the boy refrain from future attempts or is he de-

Is this also a learning situation? If so what is being learned?

monstrating by his frightening example that adults too beat those who are smaller than themselves?

A compromise between the two views might perhaps be achieved through the point that learning can be both specific and general. It may also take place on several levels at the same time. When for instance, we are trying to learn a text by heart, we are also learning something about what is said in the text. Furthermore, we might learn something about the author and even more generally, about methods by which to learn material of this type. Experiments by the American psychologist Harry Harlow have very convincingly shown that animals such as rhesus monkeys (and many other species) can "learn how to learn", and thus transfer appropriate modes of behaviour to a wide range of similar situations.

Our memory for what has been learned

What happens to what is learned after the learning as such is over? Admittedly we cannot put a final end to learning because some learning is always going on. Neither do memory and forgetting start as new processes only after the learning is completed. Forgetting has been going on all the time even during the course of learning, that is partly why the learning has not gone as quickly as we might wish. It is however, possible to think of a turning point in the learning process, where the improvement stops and where a decline sets in. If we are going to draw a picture of this process it has to be something similar to what is shown in the figure (p. 48).

The left hand side of the figure is a typical learning curve showing how performance is improved with training. The

47

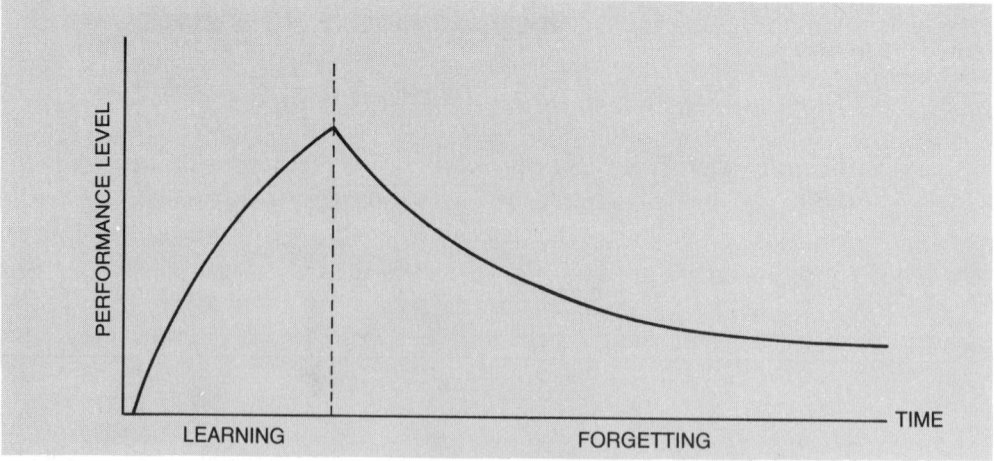

LEARNING   FORGETTING

learning curve in this case rises quickly to begin with, but more slowly later on. This is what we very often find when the learning situation is comparatively simple. In other cases it may take some time before learning is really under way in such a manner as to make the curve look different. The curve might also show a series of steps or levels. This might be the case when the learning of a more complex skill is involved, such as reading, typing etc. In these cases we may reach a point where it is difficult to achieve more progress without changing the method (by for instance a change from reading one letter at a time to reading word by word, or changing from reading aloud to reading to ourselves).

The right hand side of the figure is a curve of memory which shows how much is left after certain periods of time. This curve nearly always has the same shape. It goes more quickly to begin with, later on it levels out. It might be a comfort to know that if we have forgotten a lot during the first hour after having learnt something, we need not be afraid that we shall forget as much per hour thereafter. What we do remember after a few days we may remember just as well in the next couple of weeks. What may be worrying is of course the level of the curve which shows the total

amount of learning and material remembered.

A memory curve cannot be obtained by repeatedly asking the subject how much he remembers, because that would be the same as continuing the period of learning. Any test of memory is at the same time an opportunity to repeat the material and consolidate the learning. (This might be taken as an example of a very common methodological problem in psychology: when we try to observe or measure something, we influence what is going to be observed.) A curve therefore, must be drawn on the basis of observations with many subjects, where some are asked to recall what they remember after 5 minutes, others after 10 minutes and so on.

Whether something is remembered is seldom a question of either/or. Sometimes we say we feel it on the tip of our tongue without being able to get it out. At other times we remember very little but still feel sure what it was *not* about. We therefore will get different curves all depending on the method we use to take down what is remembered.

The most straightforward method, namely to ask a person simply to repeat or recall what is learned, is also the most demanding one. It is far more easy to

It may be difficult to re-member (recall) every-thing that is needed in the household when sitting down and trying to make a list. When going around the supermarket one usu-ally discovers a number of things one would otherwise have forgotten (recognition). But it is perhaps not so easy to remember what we had planned for our Sunday dinner when scanning the crowded cheese display (interference).

recognise the material of learning. Even if I am unable to imagine what Mrs. H. looks like – not to speak of making a drawing of her appearance – I have no difficulty in recognising her when I meet her in the street. If I can't remember at the moment her first name, I remember it immediately when someone reminds me of it and more often than not I am able to reject all wrong suggestions. Our capacity for recognising is often very impressive and that is something our ability to recall very seldom is. The problem of measuring recognition is natur-ally that some subjects very easily agree when something is suggested, perhaps in order to get the best results, whereas others would tend to hesitate until they are quite sure. Tasks of recognition therefore, are usually presented as a multiple choice task, where one has to decide which among a certain number of answers is the correct one. Also in this case are we faced with methodological problems, since the degree of difficulty is dependent on the number of alternatives and how unlikely the wrong proposals appear to be. Someone who is very experienced in answering multiple choice tasks knows that the method of elimination often proves the best one to reach the correct end result.

Re-learning has proved to be an even more sensitive method when we want to investigate if there is something left of what is seemingly forgotten material. If there are only a few traces left we are, with this method, able to prove that learning hasn't been totally wasted. This might be a comfort to students and teachers who are told that most of what is learnt through 12 years of schooling seems to be gone without any traces a couple of years later. If not in any other way one's previous efforts might turn out to make the time shorter if now we are going to re-learn the same material. After re-learning the forgetting would tend to be much less than the first time. Graphically we might demonstrate it in the way shown in the figure.

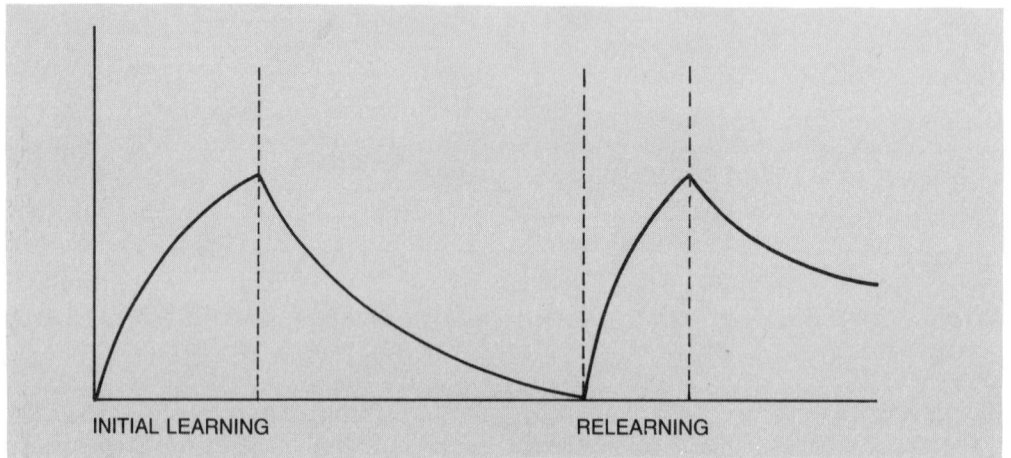

INITIAL LEARNING   RELEARNING

What determines the amount we will remember?

Whether at a certain point of time we are able to remember something we have learnt earlier is dependent on a number of factors.

1. To begin with it is a question of the learning material itself and the learning as such. How much will be remembered is chiefly dependent on how well it was learned. All that helps in bringing learning about would have a positive influence on memory. We might put it this way: how well something is learned will only show itself when after some time we try to recall it.

It is often argued that what is understood will usually be remembered better than what has been learnt without understanding. We might add that meaningful material would be better remembered than what is meaningless. Something to which we can find connections would be better remembered than something that stands quite alone. Even two lists of nonsense syllables (of the type Ebbinghaus constructed in his time) may have different associative values and thus be easier or more difficult to remember. Compare the time it takes to learn the following two lists by heart and how much is remembered after five minutes say:

a) KAL DEK MON TUP SYN POS RET KIP

b) GAJ XAP QYG LOZ XEG WLJ CEH BEX

Whereas the first list consists of syllables which to most people can be associated with something, it is very difficult to attach meaning to the syllables in the second list.

We further know that what we are interested in and motivated to learn will be better remembered than other material. This may be due to the fact that we have more associations that can be tied to the material and perhaps also that we repeat what we have learned to ourselves afterwards. We moreover remember well what is different and attracts our attention. What is unique is better remembered than the more common things. Of a series of similar experiences for observation, we might remember the first one and perhaps also the last one better than the ones in between. (Compare the list of syllables above. We might perhaps guess that the syllables you have already forgotten are among those in the middle of the list.)

The degree of system and order in the material will also be of great importance. When repetition helps us to remember, it is often, because by going through the material a number of times, we will have a better chance of sorting it out and systematising it.

2. The chances of remembering something are not only dependent upon the past. The present situation is also of great importance. The art of remembering can often be a question of finding out what we have in the store room. For this purpose we need all the clues and indications that the environment can give us. We might for instance have a very unclear picture of the story in a book we started to read some time ago, but if we now start reading again, it very easily comes back. If we return to some place we haven't seen for a number of years, previous incidents may come back to us, some of which we were quite unaware of. It is as if memories are stored in the surroundings.

An effective way of remembering something we have forgotten could be to return to the place where we last thought of it and hope that something there might remind us of it. Since ancient times speakers and memory experts have utilised the so-called method of loci. The method consists of first imagining a familiar room, and then placing each item of what we are to remember in a different place in the room. If we are to remember a list of syllables, the first may be placed behind the door, the next one on the table, the third in the table lamp etc. When recalling one looks, in imagination, around the room in the same sequence from one place to the other and then in turn is reminded of what one ought to remember. In this case the large capacity of our visual memory plays an important role.

A derivative of this method involves learning to associate a set of visual images with numbers. A well-known example begins "One is a bun, two is a shoe, three is a tree. . ." etc. Then when any list of items is to be learned, the first is visualised in connection with a bun, the next with a shoe, and so on. Recall of the over-learned list of images effectively aids recall of the new list of items.

3. Whether we are going to remember much or just a little is also dependent upon the time that has passed since the learning took place. It is not only a question of length of time, but also of what we have done in the period in between. It is often said that if this time had not been filled with anything, nothing might have been forgotten. We forget for instance less during the night than we do during a similar period when we are awake. There might have been a greater chance of remembering what one has read at 11 o'clock in the evening than what one finished at 6 o'clock, if only one hadn't been so tired.

To read just before one goes to bed may perhaps not be a good idea because it is our activity immediately after the learning that is most disturbing (compare the fall in the curve on memory). If what follows immediately after the learning receives our total attention, nearly everything that we ought to remember may disappear.

In particular if what is going on after learning has a great resemblance to the learning itself, without being mere repetition of the learning, there is a great chance that it will interfere with our memory. Our knowledge of George the First becomes more uncertain after having read about George the Second and George the Third.

The example might illustrate that the time *before* learning takes place is also of importance. Not only would the facts about George the Third disturb what we previously have read about the other two, but what we remember from the life of George the First and George the Second would probably be as disturbing when we try to concentrate on the deeds of George the Third. In this way our storage of previous experience will in effect make us less prepared to receive new information.

What is it to forget?

One usually looks at forgetting as a passive weakening of the traces of memory, where what we do remember steadily becomes weaker and where time eventually removes every trace. What we have said about the conditions influencing our memory should perhaps be enough to show that this must be an insufficient and partly wrong conception. The so-called *pro-active interference* (what we have learnt before disturbs the memory of what comes afterwards) and *retro-active interference* (what comes later has an influence on what we have already learned) show that forgetting cannot be conceived as a failing of traces. It is more correct to say that new things are written on top of the old ones on the same blackboard. The more we have written before, the less impression would a new thing make, and the more we write afterwards, the less are the chances of reading what was there before.

Forgetting is not always a process that runs as smoothly as we might think when we look at the curves of forgetting. In many ways our forgetting is selective. We only have to think of some people's tendencies to remember their childhood and youth in a rosy light while in reality it has been very much different. Psychoanalysts have given numerous examples to show that we are capable both of repressing unpleasant memories and of changing others in such a way that what we remember may be reconciled with our own wishes and conceptions of ourselves. Studies of how rumours come about show other sides to this process. We may see both a selective and a constructive component in the well-known parlour game where a story goes from mouth to mouth. In particular if the story is originally somewhat strange and special, we after only a

ORIGINAL

1st reproduction

2nd reproduction

3rd reproduction

8th reproduction

9th reproduction

10th reproduction

15th reproduction

18th reproduction

This shows how a drawing can change when each subject tries to remember what the previous one drew. The original Egyptian hieroglyph of an owl gradually lost its shape through poor memory or poor drawing until it looked something like a cat. Subject 10 seems to have identified it as such, and so it remains: the continuing reproductions confirm that a cat has nine lives. (After Bartlett, 1932).

few repetitions would have difficulties in recognising it. Sooner or later it would find its form, such as to make later repetitions lead to less changes. The changes do not only go in the direction of omitting some material, what is left also becomes edited such as to make the story more likely, understandable and coherent, while at the same time some special details might be focused upon and developed further.

Sir Frederic Bartlett (1886–1969) studied these processes in a series of experiments which were in some ways ahead of their time, and which are having a renewed in-

fluence today. He used two main methods: serial reproduction, in which what a first subject recalls is given to a second to remember, and so on; and repeated reproduction, in which the same subject is asked to recall something at intervals over a period of days, weeks, or even years.

In his book *Remembering* (1932) Bartlett stressed that memory is always an active process, striving to fit together what is retained into a coherent whole; but also to fit it into our whole existing framework of knowledge, which comes from our culture and from our individual life experience.

Over a long series of reproductions (as we might see in the transmission of folk tales or songs), an original can sometimes change out of all recognition, but this is a creative, not a random process.

Such examples of "creative memory" are nothing exceptional, even if what we remember usually gives a realistic picture of what we have in fact experienced. This does not mean that our memory is ordinarily lacking a creative aspect. The reconstruction of what we have experienced in the past can be more or less successful or correct. Studies of memory and forgetting clearly show that learning is not a passive recording sort of process, just as memory is not a simple playing back. The reason why we have such a good memory for well-organised material very likely is that it is so easy to reconstruct; to have good memory would often mean that on the basis of relatively small traces there is an ability to reconstruct what has previously been learned.

We have seen that memory might mean two different things: to have something in the store room (retention), and to get it out from there. In the same way we might think of two types of forgetting: forgetting that is caused by the material having disappeared from the store, and forgetting caused by the fact that it cannot be found or is difficult to bring into the open. While the fading out theory implies that forgetting is caused mainly by a failure in our retention, psychological research shows that the main cause of forgetting over a longer period of time is more a question of difficulty in retrieving what has been learned. By repression one means that access to the material is directly blocked, even if the material might continue to live its own life and perhaps contribute material to dreams or fantasies. Where interference is concerned, the problem is to find the right thing among a large variety of information and facts. Only in the time immediately after learning (the first few seconds or perhaps minutes) does it seem that the material may just fade out and disappear without any trace.

Some psychologists therefore have argued that we ought to talk of two different stores of memory: one in which we have possibilities of retaining material over a short period of time only and with a very limited capacity and another store with a greater, perhaps almost unlimited capacity, both when it comes to amount and duration. The first which we might call the short term memory functions as a sort of working memory, dealing with what we are able to deal with at a particular point in time. In the middle of a sentence we as a rule clearly remember what we started by saying, if not, it would be impossible to form sentences which are nearly always understandable, if not always grammatically totally correct. A telephone number of six or seven digits we may also remember long enough to be able to dial it, whereas shortly afterwards it may have been totally forgotten.

Contrary to what is the case with short term memory, long term memory is not based on a reproduction which is a direct copy of what we have experienced. To a much larger extent it is built upon some code. We would, for instance, for some time remember the meaning of what we have read even if we very quickly forget the actual words. The critical point in the process of memory then should be the transfer between short term and long term memory. If what we are going to remember survives the first few minutes, it has a chance of establishing traces, even if those traces are not very easily found later on. Some forms of failure of memory seem to indicate that this is a reasonable model.

We often find in cases of senility that neither the long term memory nor the short term memory as such seems to have failed. The person may remember detailed incidents of years back and may also be able to lead sensible conversations of what is happening at the moment. However the transfer of material from one type of memory to the other may seem to be affected. The person in question may for instance have difficulties in remembering what happened the day before and might ask the same question over and over again with an interval of only a few minutes.

We ought to be careful however not to conceive an all too concrete picture of storage of memory, as some kind of file with separate drawers, where something is put in and other things taken out. After all memory is the name for a *process*, namely the one of remembering, and not of a particular thing. The view that memory is of a certain size or is some particular ability that one might train, or which would be weakened in the same way as a muscle, belongs to the past, to phrenology and pseudo-science.

For some years now memory has been one of the most intensively studied of human activities. Until recently it has been the short-term processes that have attracted most interest from psychologists. There are mundane as well as scientific reasons for this. Experiments on how much is re- membered for a few seconds or minutes can be neatly controlled, they yield nice exact measurable results and fairly quickly produce a paper that can be published in a scientific journal, or a well-argued thesis for a higher degree. Studying memory over weeks or years, as Bartlett did, and as is now being done again, is obviously harder for all sorts of reasons: subjects have the annoying habit of not coming back to have their memories tested a year later, for ex- ample.

An outsider, leafing through some of the thousands of published experiments might think them among the most obscure and perhaps useless activities that scientists get up to. In fact they are a very good example of how it is impossible to say what research is going to prove useful and what is not. Older persons remember telephone dials that had letters as well as digits. The Bri- tish telephone system was based on local "exchanges", each with a local name, and one's telephone number was the first three letters of this name plus (in London) four digits, for example HACkney 1234. When in 1967 the British system was linked to the rest of the world, this was abandoned in favour of the present all-digit code. An obvious question, one might think, would be how users might cope with this; and the obvious thing, to a psychologist, would be to do some experiments. In fact the Go- vernment spokesman, announcing the change in Parliament added, "We have consulted a distinguished psychologist". Hansard reported: "Laughter".

The hilarity of MPs was misplaced, for the experiments were both elegant and relevant. Not surprisingly, seven digits are harder to remember, even in turning from the directory to the dial, than the old form which included a meaningful syllable. In fact, it is well established that the normal capacity for immediate memory lies bet- ween five and nine items. In a very famous paper, "The magical number seven, plus or minus two", George Miller (1956), one of the pioneers in this area, showed that it is not the items as such that count, but rather the number of meaningful "chunks" of in- formation. To a Londoner at least HAC would be one chunk. Thus it is easy to see that a great many more items can be re- tained if they are all packed into a mean- ingful chunk; and still more if the chunks themselves form a meaningful sequence; as they are, of course, in an ordinary sen- tence. Most people can repeat, say, "Now is the time for all good men to come to the aid of the party" or "The quick brown fox jumps over the lazy dog" at the first hear- ing, even though they contain nearly all the letters of the alphabet – and could write out the forty-nine or thirty-five letter sequ- ence correctly.

Obviously, the separate words of these sentences have been well learned long ago. This sort of interaction between short- and long-term effects leads some psychologists to think that memory is really only one process, not two after all. It is also the basis of many of the attempts to improve memory. One of the most famous and indeed reliable methods has already been mentioned, the "one is a bun" system, or method of loci as it is known. "Loci" is Latin for places, and the method was described by classical orators, who visualised a well-known place and associated each heading of a speech with a particular position, so as to recall the points in order later. The method indeed probably goes farther back still to the epic poets who were able to perform long sagas from memory in the days before writing. Later, at the time of the Renaissance, the method came to assume an almost mystical significance for the power it seemed to have of enhancing human capacity and encapsulating knowledge. The whole story is told by the great scholar Francis Yates in *The Art of Memory*. It is worth mentioning here to emphasize that human behaviour can be very different in other times and places, yet at the same time psychological problems are not new. What is new is the use of experiment in its widest sense.

It has been stressed that memory is an active process. An easy way to demonstrate this is to have a class write down as many as they can remember of the United States of America, then turn the paper over. After twenty minutes, they are asked to do the same thing again. The second attempt will almost always produce more correct answers. One practical application of this is that it pays to read through all the questions on an examination paper, and preferably decide which you are going to answer, before starting the first one. You will remember as you write.

It seems that some at least of the processes of memory must be «unconscious». The question arises whether we can get access to such memories. One way is simply to wait – or to sleep; one often recalls in the morning a fact that eluded one the night before. Another method is free association, as developed in psychoanalysis. And another way is by the use of hypnosis. Freud indeed originally used this method. Hypnosis has a very long history but its modern use begins with Franz Anton Mesmer (1734–1815). The term "mesmerism" is still seen, as are comic strips in which some kind of magnetic force (in which Mesmer believed) is issuing from the finger-tips of the mesmerist. Some followers of Mesmer held that in a trance state normal powers could be surpassed: subjects were supposed to be able to see at a distance or into the future.

The idea still persists that memory, at least, can be enhanced by hypnosis, and there are accounts of subjects being "regressed" to a very early age or even, more fancifully, to previous lives. A more practical application is to evidence in criminal cases. Several accounts have appeared of witnesses being hypnotised, with their consent, to see if they can remember more about the case than in a conscious state.

Even though we still do not fully understand how hypnosis works, this possibility is well worth investigating. A recent attempt (1983) to do so, was made by Glenn S. Sanders and William L. Simmons in the Department of Psychology in the State University of New York. They refer to several cases in which hypnotised witnesses provided useful clues or leads which were sucessfully followed up: for example, a hypnotically-recalled licence number helped to trace a car later found to contain stolen property. However, it is very well established that, even at the best of times, eyewitness testimony can be most unreliable. Is evidence given under hypnosis any better, or the same, or worse?

Sanders & Simmons used, as a very large number of experimenters do, undergraduate students, in their case 46 female and 54 male. They were seen twice, a week apart: thirteen however did not turn up for the second session. On the first occasion, all the subjects were shown a 20-second videotape in which a pickpocket stole a wallet. The victim was thumbing through a book on a street corner. When the last of several passers-by departed, he looked at his watch and turned to leave. As he was turning, the thief bumped into him, knocking his book to the ground. When the victim bent over to pick up the book, the thief snatched his wallet from his rear pocket. After the victim departed, the thief hurriedly looked in the wallet, pulled out money and credit cards, and quickly left in the direction opposite to that taken by the victim. Observers of the tape saw the thief for a total of 8 seconds but could see his face clearly for only 3 seconds. The thief wore a distinctive black jacket with large red stripes on the sleeves.

Half the subjects were given a practice hypnotic induction (half before seeing the tape and half after), so as to remove any apprehension about being hypnotised. The hypnotist was Dr Simmons, a clinical psychologist who has used the method for some twenty years, mainly in various forms of therapy. It is important to realise that hypnosis is not an all-or-nothing effect, rather individuals vary widely in their degree of suggestibility and depth of trance. Sanders & Simmons took care to take measures of these differences.

All the subjects were told to imagine that they simply saw the taped incident one evening on the university campus. After seeing it, they were told to behave as though they might be called on as witnesses, and to take some time to review the scene and fix it clearly in memory.

A week later when subjects returned, the hypnosis group were given the same induction procedure as before; the others were, of course, given no such induction. Both groups were asked to recall the incident, in a particular way. Essentially, they were asked to relax and to imagine they could "re-play" the incident on an internal, mental TV screen, complete with slow-down and speed-up features, stop-action and zoom-in for freezing action, and close-up inspection of important details. They were asked to practice this, and to use it to help focus their memory if they were unsure of anything.

They were then shown a second videotape which was essentially an identity parade. Six approximately similar males were shown for 20 seconds each, each holding an identifying number. Number four was in half the showings the thief, though without his distinctive jacket. Following this, subjects were then given two tests of memory: (a) they were asked whether the thief was present in the line-up; if so what number he was; and whether they would be confident enough to testify in court; (b) ten recall questions about the incident, five of which suggested an answer (eg "Did you notice it when the victim looked at his pocket-watch?"), and five did not (eg "Did the victim have a mustache?")

The statistical analysis of the data from this experiment was obviously quite complex. Essentially however the results were these. First of all, subjects in the hypnosis condition were significantly *less* accurate on both the tests of memory than those in the control condition. Second, the main factor contributing to this was that the hypnotised subjects were more susceptible to misleading implications in the recall questions. Thirdly, in neither group was there any relationship between accuracy and degree of confidence.

All these results are consistent with other previous experiments. They are important because there is a popular temptation to think that memory is like a kind of video-tape on which everything is accurately recorded, so that we could retrieve all the information if only we had a way to reach it. Hypnosis, with its still rather mysterious aura, might seem to be such a way. It is quite unlikely that this is the case. Even more seductive is the belief that a confident witness is a reliable one. A great deal of evidence shows that this too is not so.

As Sanders & Simmons point out, this does not mean that hypnosis must be abandoned as a detective tool. But it must be used properly and with caution, as a way of suggesting leads, for example, which can be investigated. It should not be thought a magic key to unlock memory. As far as we know, there is no such key.

Indeed, as we stress throughout this book, while psychology can give us a much greater understanding of how and why people behave, it does not give us laws that always apply to every case, like physics and chemistry. People are never like samples of some chemical. Each individual is different, and much depends on how she or he perceives the situation.

As with memory, so with learning. A "punishment" may be rewarding (reinforcing) to a child who is really seeking attention. Two Australian psychologists, Hilary Maitland and Alex Clarke, at the University of Wollongong, New South Wales, recently (1983) reported an experiment which showed some of the ways in which "punishment" depends both on the situation and on the person. Punishment in this case was rather mild, consisting of a tone heard through headphones or a flashing light. The task to be learned was pressing buttons in a certain order. Maitland & Clarke were interested in how this would be affected by several variables. One of these was what is known as "locus of control". It is fairly well established that people vary in the extent to which they feel their lives are controlled by external forces or by themselves. This trait can be measured by suitable scales. Maitland & Clarke found that subjects towards the external end of the scale tended to learn with less punishment than those towards the internal end. Furthermore, there was a general tendency to rate the aversive stimulation as less punishing when the subjects could control it themselves (by pressing the buttons correctly). There were other results, but these, which are consistent with other experiments, show some of the complexity of what at first sight might seem a quite simple situation.

CHAPTER THREE

Perceptual Experience

Introduction

In the previous chapter human beings were looked at "from the outside", in discussing how actual behaviour may be modified and how performance may be improved or weakened depending on the learning upon which it rests.

In the present chapter we shall focus on our *experience*. What a person will do in a given situation does not only depend on what he knows, remembers and has learned, but on how he generally experiences or perceives the situation.

Our world of perception may be said to have two opposing "poles"; on the one hand "*the world out there*" – as I see it, and on the other hand "*myself*" – the way I see myself.

Our reason for talking about two "poles" is that we may focus our attention, now in the one direction, now in the other, whilst normally it is difficult to picture both poles at the same time. If I direct my view outwards, towards the environment, I do not think of myself as more than a point of departure, at most. If, on the other hand, I direct the view towards myself, the environment becomes a sort of background only. The phenomenon may perhaps be illustrated by the story of the famous Danish fools, who were unable to count their number, because the one who did the counting always forgot to count himself. The problem was only solved when a passer-by suggested that they should each make a mark by making a print of their nose in the mud, thereby securing a full count.

Of the two perspectives, the former is the first to develop and that with which most people are most familiar. Many people will recall it as a unique event when as young children they "discovered" themselves as a separate individual for the first time.

This chapter first of all deals with our experience of *the environment,* which is also the part of our "field of experience" that is the more available to psychological research. In a later section some points from the psychology of self-experience will be dealt with.

The experience of the world around us: Perception

In our experience of the world we may make a distinction between two "layers" or levels: the concrete picture which our senses present of the things in our immediate surroundings, and the more abstract and more comprehensive picture we have formed of our total "life space". The first, more tangible one of the two levels of reality we might call our *perceptual field* (perception=knowing through sensory experience). Perception as a concept is used in psychology as a general expression for what is encompassed by hearing, sight, smell, taste etc. The other, more subjec-

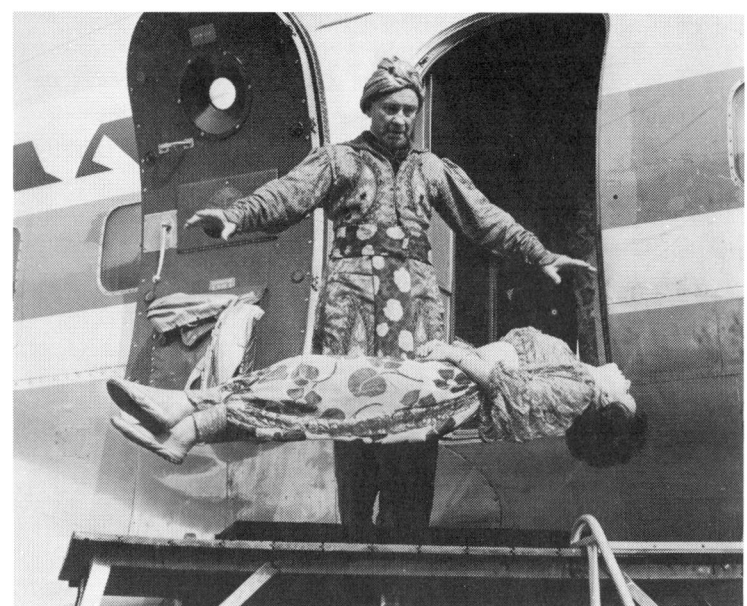

The art of the magician consists in showing us what we know is impossible. Here Alfredo Cantarelli and his subject realise the dream of miraculously floating in the air, before taking their ordinary seats in the aircraft.

tive reality, has to do with what is not necessarily present here and now, but what we can think of, believe, or simply feel we *know,* as opposed to what is seen or heard at the moment.

Sometimes we may experience the contrast between the two types of "reality", as when we go down the stairs into a dark cellar, and think we are down, only to discover the next second that there were two steps more; or when a magician leads us to see "with our own eyes" how he is sawing his lady assistant in two, while at the same time we *know* that she really is unharmed.

Contrasts as great as these admittedly are rare. As a rule perception and *cognition* (thinking, imagining) go together in such a way that each constitutes a supplement to the other. Looking around the room we find the different things where we expect them to be. The difference between the room, as we imagine it, and the room, as we in fact see it, is mainly that in the latter case it seems more "convincing". It has more details, brighter colours, a grea-

ter "reality". Our perception is in this case adding to and enriching the more schematic and fluctuating image. On the other hand, the perceptual picture of the room would become much poorer if what was directly seen or felt were not accompanied by our knowledge of a world existing outside our field of vision.

The interplay between the two levels normally gives us no reason to distinguish sharply between them. As a rule it would not even be profitable to insist on such a distinction. If someone asks me if I have seen the Telephone Directory and I answer: "I can see the back of it over there on the shelf, and I *imagine* that the cover and its content will be there too" – it most likely will be considered a not too good joke. I really don't have any doubt that in fact I "see" the Directory, even if, strictly speaking, only its back is visible. However, our tendency to let what we believe we have seen, or expect to see, equal that of which we have in fact received an actual sense impression, may sometimes lead us astray, which is something that the magician fully knows how to utilize. For the same reason we often find people perfectly willing to swear solemnly that they have seen something "with their own eyes" that might be proven not to have taken place.

In October 1983 Detective Constables Peter Finch and John Jardine were brought to trial accused of the attempted murder of Stephen Waldorf. Waldorf had been shot and clubbed, causing serious injury, in mistake for a wanted man, David Martin, who had actually shot a policeman. This terrible error was made in broad daylight. Waldorf had the misfortune not only to resemble Martin, whom he did not know, but to be travelling in a car with Martin's girl-friend. In the event, the policemen were acquitted.

The correspondence that is usually found between what we perceive and what we can imagine, is due to the fact that perception and cognition are mutually de-

Perception as a selective process. Only a few of the stimuli we are exposed to daily succeed in making an impression on us, even if they are not all water off a duck's back. Cartoon by Hans N. Dahl.

pendent processes. Our knowledge fits in with the perceptual picture because the knowledge is built upon previous sense impressions. And the way in which we come to perceive the world at a given moment in its turn is dependent on the conceptions we have already, (for example of the Telephone Directory). Still we sometimes find a disagreement between our immediate experience and the reality behind, which is something that is frequently demonstrated by the so-called visual *illusions*.

Since perception and reality usually make an excellent fit, we tend to believe that our sense organs function as some sort of window, through which we can see the world the way it really is (what philosophers call "naive realism"). In what follows some characteristic features of our way of conceiving of the world may be seen to show that this is far from the truth. We shall first look at perception as a *selective* process, and after that consider its *constructive* or *reconstructive* aspects.

Physical and biological limitations

Even if we have the impression that we have got an extensive and complete overview of the world around us, we will in fact never have access to more than a small portion of the totality. This is a fact that seems rather obvious, but one that is nevertheless often overlooked.

Our picture of the world is determined by what we might call "our place in existence". We find ourselves in a particular age in history, in a particular corner of the world, and with this particular view from our window. Any attempt to "break out" will only lead us to another corner – where

Our world of experience also includes the picture we have constructed of time. A moment, the hour, the day, the past and the future. Time is drawn here by Saul Steinberg rather in the way described by Francis Galton.

the view might be different, but not necessarily richer or larger.

Our ability to form ideas and concepts, and to retain a picture of what is no longer there, in front of us, naturally makes it possible to enlarge our "view" far beyond the horizon. But even so we will only get hold of fractions of the enormous possibilities that really exist. The "big world" which we know from newspapers, TV, books, movies and travels, rather seldom consists of more than some scattered glimpses and highly selected "spots". Were we to mark them as points on a map, we would most likely discover that there were fewer points as the distance from our local community increased. We know more places in England and Scotland, and more in Europe than in Africa. Moreover, the points would tend to be unevenly distributed and perhaps concentrated around certain centres, as for instance important capitals, places of warfare and popular holiday resorts. Washington might, in spite of the distance, seem nearer than Vienna, and Tenerife perhaps nearer than Norway. A "subjective" world map, where the size and position of the different countries is determined by the importance we place upon them, and of the *psychological* distance, would become very unreliable as a basis for navigating. During a journey we might suddenly realise the extent to which our picture of the world is incomplete, in particular if we make a stop at some small place that is hardly marked on the map, and find life going on here, as if the important world outside never existed.

The famous mediaeval map of the world, the Hereford *Mappa Mundi* preserved in the cathedral there, and the only one now in existence, has Jerusalem at the centre because it was the most important place. Before feeling too superior, we might recall a conversation between two young women in London, reported by Peter Gould and Rodney White in their Book *Mental Maps:*

"Where did you go for a holiday this year?"

"Oh, we went to Majorca."

"Was it nice?"

"Absoutely smashing."

"Where is Majorca?"

"I don't know exactly, I flew."

The limitations set upon our "picture of the world" may also be felt in other ways. If we take up the position on the other side of the counter, we will experience how different the world of the staff in the shop is from that of the customer; and by placing ourselves behind the teacher's desk we would certainly find that the teacher's classroom is very different from the one we experience ourselves, as pupils.

The world as seen by different animals will vary considerably more than among different people. A bird of prey that circles at a hundred yards up, from where it might rapidly swoop down on a rodent in the bushes, is familiar with a perspective that both with regard to width and to sharpness of details would greatly surpass what we as humans usually experience. A fly that bustles around the lamp and resists your attempts to wave it away until your hand is very close indeed, lives, in fact, within

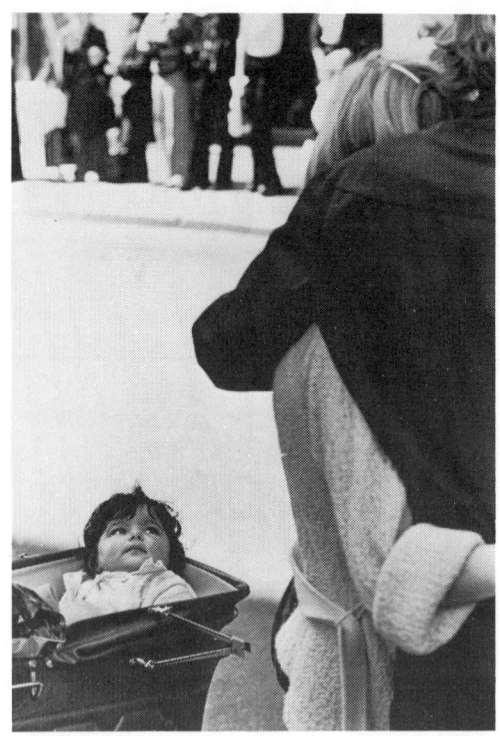

The child sees the world from another angle and with a different view from the grown-up.

"horizons" that are less than a yard apart.

To a human being the immediate life space is something that enlarges as one grows older. If we squat beside a 3-year old, we will soon realise that the child's perception of the world for pure physiological reasons is rather different from that of the grown up. Furthermore, the child's attention will tend to be directed towards the immediate surroundings. If we take the 3-year old for a walk, we shall have to stop constantly to examine flowers, pebbles, puddles and earth worms. The adult tries in vain to direct the attention of the child towards more distant objects: "Hurry up, we'll soon be there! Don't you see the house by the big tree?"

In the same way that our world of experience has its "upper threshold", it has also a "lower" one. Things that are under a certain size we will seldom notice; and if they are small enough, we will not detect them at all. The world of cells, bacterias, and other micro-organisms that reveals itself under the microscope, does not exist, for us, in our daily life – no more than a possible life on distant planets. The nearest we get to experience of such other worlds comes probably through the brilliant fantasies of science fiction – for example the trip through the human body in the film "Fantastic Voyage".

Not only our "here" but our "now" as well has its boundaries. We cannot see that the grass is growing – it grows too slowly, and our eyes do not detect the successions of frames on the film screen – they move too fast. The fly that does not discover our hand till it is very close, will still escape because of its ability to detect and react very quickly, once an object is near enough. If we imagine a sort of human fly, which we could take to the movies, we would have to prepare ourselves for its irritation by having to watch all the intervals between the frames. Not to mention how very boring the performance would become for someone, to whom it seemed to go on forever!

With the time perspective we would also find that there are changes during the growth period of a human being. To a child one hour may seem an eternity. The things that happened last year belong to a distant past – "when I was little". Grown ups seem to feel that the time runs faster each year, and much to the annoyance of their children tend to tell humiliating stories from stages passed ages ago "as if it were yesterday".

Limitations of the sense organs

The sensitivity of the sense organs will always set boundaries for what we will be able to perceive. For the different sensory fields there is a *threshold,* which the impressions have to surpass in order to be detected; the threshold varying from one sense organ to the other. Through smell we are e.g. able to detect a substance in a concentration 1 /10,000 part of that needed to taste the same substance. And this in spite of the fact that the sense of smell is less developed in humans than in animals such as the dog. Among the insects you would find the sense of smell even more developed. The gnat can smell its partner at a distance of more than a mile, if only the wind blows in the right direction.

Of greater importance for our experience is *the type of stimuli,* to which the sense organs are particularly sensitive. We might be liable to think that our eyes, ears, smell and taste organs and the skin's impression of temperature, pressure and pain, would present a fairly good and complete coverage of what we are facing of radiations, chemical substances and mechanical pressure. Still there are many "holes" in this coverage. The human ear is only able to detect soundwaves with a frequency from 20 to 20,000 Hz (vibrations per second). Sounds that fall outside this area do not exist for us or are in some cases only felt as vibration. A case was reported recently of an organist and choirmaster who, being deaf, relies entirely on vibrations. To the dog, on the other hand, the sounds may be audible, and also to the bat, who navigates in the dark by means of the echo from its own cry, of a pitch that equals a frequency of about 50,000 Hz. Our sense of vision, in a similar way, is only sensitive to electromagnetic waves with a wavelength of 380 to 720 nano metres (one-millionth of a mm), and rays that are either *shorter* (as ultra violet light and x-rays) or *longer* (as infra red light and radio waves) are totally invisible to us. We

When eyesight fails, the horizon of one's immediate experience is drastically reduced, even though hearing and touch can take over some of the functions of vision.

also find, with our senses of smell and taste, that they are only sensitive to a selected sample of chemical substances. With taste it is moreover necessary that the substances are in a dissolved state and for smell that it is a question of particles in gas form.

The localisation and the number of sense organs will also be of importance for what we will perceive. The cells or organs that receive the sense impressions – the so-called *receptors* – also are not as evenly distributed on the body as we might perhaps think. If we try to map them on a portion of our skin by carefully applying a pointed needle or a stiff hair, we would discover that the sensitivity for pressure and pain is distributed over a large number of more or less scattered spots. Between these spots we don't feel anything. Inside, under the skin, the body is even less equipped with receptors. We are able to feel pain in the tissue when it is stretched or contracts (e.g. belly pains), but we don't feel pain by cutting it. Brain surgery may

be performed without pain even if the patient is conscious because the cortex itself has no pain receptors.

Our senses also work in a selective fashion by being specially fit for detecting differences or changes in the surroundings rather than the constant and unchanging features. If one and the same stimulus is operating over a certain period of time, the sensitivity of the sense organ for this particular stimulus might be greatly reduced – a condition usually referred to as *adaptation*. The smell of food might be overwhelming the moment we enter into the kitchen, but after a while we are perhaps unable to sense it at all. When cautiously dipping our toes into the sea we might feel it to be freezing, whereas the others, who have been splashing around for some time, reassure us that the water is "terrific". Experiments on "the stabilised retinal image" have shown that if one succeeds in letting a beam of light constantly fall on the same spot on the retina of the eye, the visual experience will totally disappear after a short while. The phenomenon of adaptation does not, however, apply equally to all senses, stimuli leading to pain would seldom "cease to work".

The limits of attention

Even if only a small portion of the physical stimuli around us can set our sense organs in action, there are still more sense impressions than can ever be mastered or properly dealt with. If we watch carefully we can discover a whole series of impressions that obviously must have been there all the time, but some of which we have not noticed. They range from such things as the pressure of the body against the chair, the grip of the shoe around the foot, to the noise of the traffic outside and the sunshine coming through the parlour window. The number of noises that can be heard in a house at night you never realise until you have been lying in bed unable to fall asleep and believing a burglar to be around. And the number of places on the body in which one might start itching while one tries desperately to keep absolute still, is only known to someone who has himself tried to act as a burglar or a bird watcher.

That our attention is limited means that we are unable to notice everything that happens around us even if we try very hard. Especially when we really *try* to notice certain things do we discover how difficult it is to detect more than some parts of the total field. The more we concentrate on some definite impression, the greater is the chance that we will be ignoring others. If our thoughts are occupied with a difficult problem, or filled with a fascinating daydream, there is the chance that hardly any external stimuli will make an impression on us. Even with an attitude that is extremely "open" and extrovert, we can only attend to a few things at a time. A possible feeling of having "the full view" of a situation can only result from our ability to turn our attention quickly in the direction where something is likely to happen.

Psychologists have been interested in the "span of attention" – how many items one can perceive at once – for many years. Attention came to be of crucial importance, however, particularly with the development of jet aircraft having extremely complex information displays which the pilot must master. Horrific accidents can result from error especially on take-off, so consequently a great deal of work goes into both design of the displays and into pilot training.

With such a limited capacity for "intake" the basis on which the selection is done naturally becomes very important. What is it that determines our attention? Schematically we might say that on the one hand there are factors having to do with ourselves and our internal state, and on the other hand you have the conditions and qualities of the external stimuli. We are especially aware of things that fit with what we think, expect, need or fear perhaps, or what we simply have decided to look for. If we could not in this way direct our own attention, to some extent at least, we would run the risk of being completely a victim of environmental influences. On the other hand, if certain features of the environment could not attract us, or command our attention, there would perhaps be an equal risk of a person being absorbed in his "inner life" to such an extent that he might lose contact with reality. (This does seem to happen in some forms of severe mental illness.) The external stimuli that are especially able to attract our attention are those which are either intensive, large or colourful, or those which imply change and movement, and also surprise. All these appear to great effect in advertising.

There are innumerable demands for our attention – and our money.

However, to attract a person's attention is not the same as to keep it. Whereas strong and sudden impressions will alert us to look closer, constant attention will depend on the ability of the stimuli to engage us in some activity or other. Our attention is kept by the things which we can do something about, as when for instance a difficult puzzle will keep us occupied for hours, sometimes.

Perception as a reconstruction of the environment

When one considers the fact that the environment is only reflected through glimpses and scattered sense impressions, it may seem strange that the world does look as complete and stable as is in fact the case.

In part the reason for this is that it is not a *random* sample of the surroundings that presents itself through our senses. Obviously there is a close connection between what we *can* detect, and what is necessary or useful for survival. Were we inhabitants of a planet with a thinner atmosphere, for the protection of life it would have been useful to be equipped with receptors for cosmic radiation. On earth this need has not been felt so far. Also we probably don't lose too much by not being able to hear sounds of a very high frequency. It seems to be more important that our sense of hearing is most sensitive in the area within which the human voice belongs.

Furthermore, we are presented with a highly organised sample of stimuli. To begin with, the sense organ itself has a number of ways of organising the impressions, and what becomes conscious has already been placed within a certain context and has taken a certain form. It is in fact impossible to perceive the environment as a series of disconnected impressions. The things we touch belong to the same world as the one we see. What we do see is not some isolated spots of light, but objects, and what we see, hear and feel unmistakably is something external and objective. We may admit that when we put something in our mouth the taste is not part of the thing itself, but rather something that is located in the tongue. But that the visual picture is situated on the retina – and upside down as well – and not out there in the room, is something of which no textbook drawing will ever fully convince us.

Our ability to *reconstruct* reality through sensory experience in such a way that what is perceived looks objective, is illustrated below by the so-called "lens model" of *Egon Brunswick*.

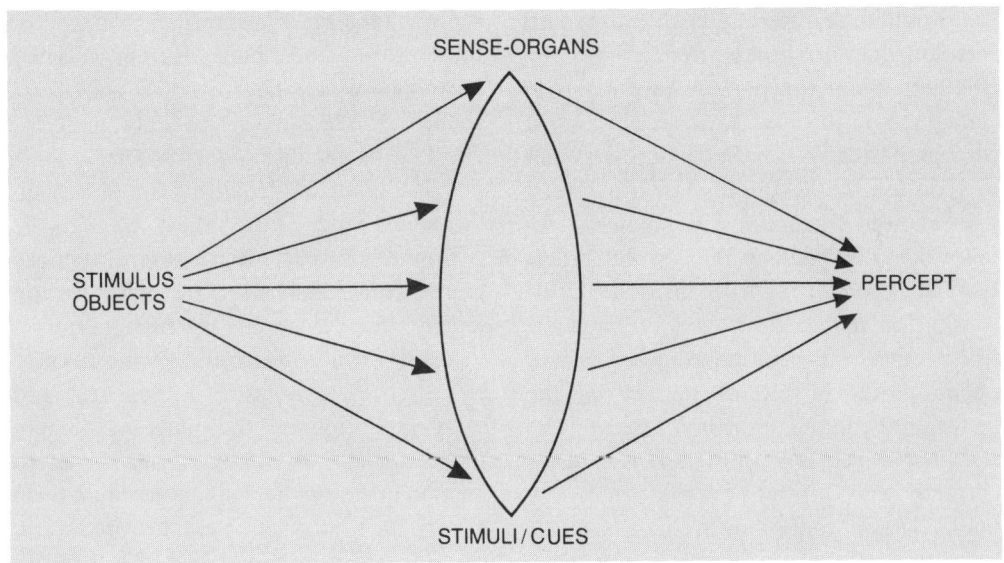

Egon Brunswik's lens model of perception.

The objects out there (the "stimulus objects") may influence our receptors in a number of ways. We can see the objects, get hold of them, view them from different angles, at various distances and in different lights. What is important is not the numerous impressions, but to get a realistic, stable and recognizable picture of the object (a "percept" as it is called). Rather than thinking of the sense organs as "windows" or "mirrors" through which we can see the world, we might regard them as a sort of lens, that works to bring together the scattered impressions into a full and realistic picture. There are a number of reasons for suggesting such a model for describing perception:

a. *Perceptual Constancy*
In perceiving objects we are to an astonishing degree unaware of the fact that one and the same object may give rise to a number of dissimilar sense impressions. We see the wall pretty much with an unchanging colour all over its surface, although by looking through a small hole in a piece of paper we would find that different parts of the wall would look different, both with regard to colour and brightness, depending upon whether or not the part in question is in sunlight, is in the shadow, or is perhaps lit by a lamp in the room. Such facts were put to vivid use by the Impressionist painters, who allowed themselves to paint the colours actually present in a scene rather than what "ought" to be there. Further we would find that a door stays rectangular, irrespective of its position as closed or half open, and this in spite of the fact that the image on the retina in the latter case has no right angles (cf. how difficult it is to draw correctly with different perspectives). The books right in front of me are seen as of the same size as those further along the shelf, although the former might occupy a space

in the field of vision three times as big as the latter. (Shut one eye and make a comparison with a pencil at a distance of the length of your arm.) What we have pointed to are the phenomena of *colour constancy, constancy of shape* and *size constancy*. They operate whenever there are enough cues in the field of vision to recognise an object and to judge the context within which it appears.

b. *The relationship between the objects and their perceptual qualities.*
Logically, the qualities of an object which are a possible source of stimulation for our senses are also the very basis for our perception of the object. If the book in front of me were not of a particular colour, shape, surface and weight, it would not have been perceived – and some philosophers would tend to suggest that the book *consists* of nothing more than qualities like these. From the point of view of our experience, the "thing" is nevertheless what is of primary importance, the different qualities come second to this. As an example we would not say: It is brown on the outside, white inside, it is square and thick – it must be a book. Rather we say: I see a book which is brown, thick and square shaped. The sensory qualities are perceived normally as qualities of the objects, not as a possible point of departure for judgments on the existence of the things.

However cases do occur where we more or less consciously work out what we are seeing, for example in recognising a stranger from a description: one says to oneself: "He's wearing a blue suit and carrying a briefcase, that must be the man I'm meeting." A similar thing seems to happen in cases where someone blind from a very early age has sight restored. The new visual impression has to be fitted in with the previously tactile or aural image.

In surrealistic art our usual perception of reality is stretched to breaking point. *Les Valeurs Personelles* by René Magritte shows among other things how constancy of size is dependent upon the objects having a normal relationship. Is the comb too big or is the bed too small?

A famous case is that of "S.B." described by Richard Gregory in "Eye and Brain".

c. Since our focus of attention is directed towards *what* we see and not *how* it is seen, we are in fact often unable to describe our sense impressions as such. In the example above I might quickly forget both the colour and the thickness of the book, but still feel sure that it was a book I had seen. In certain fields it may even be impossible to tell *why* we see the things we see. We might e.g. need complicated experiments to determine which impressions are decisive for judging how far away an object is located. What the senses give us is primarily *cues* for our orientation in the environment (compare also the example on blind people's abilities to orient themselves, Chapter 1).

d. We might think that many dissimilar sense impressions would make it difficult to form a picture of the things around us. The lens model indicates, however, that the more *comprehensive* the impressions are, the easier it is to locate the thing and the more complete the picture of it tends to be. In fact we know this from our own experience. We will become more familiar with the look of a particular person if we have a chance of seeing the person engaged in some activity, and not only have to judge from watching him when he is sitting still, or on the basis of some particular expression, as on a photograph. If we try to recognise an object by touching it, we prefer to actively manipulate it. The attentive spectator will move his eyes, look at things from different angles, etc.

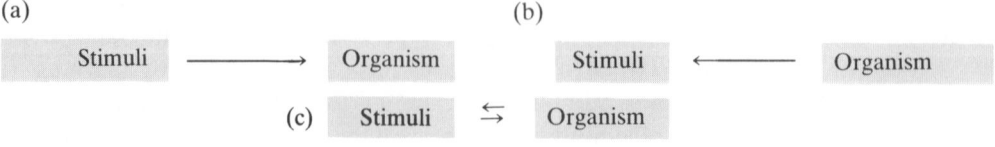

Perception as an activity. To be a spectator does not necessarily mean that one has to be a passive receiver of stimuli.

Perception as goal-directed activity

In the last point we touched upon a limitation of the model. The way the perceptual process has been described so far, we have – maybe logically enough – been drawing lines from the environment towards our sense organs, and from there further on to the brain, where the picture of the environment is built up. Psychologically seen this is, however, an unsatisfactory drawing. The attention is drawn towards the things in the environment and not towards some kind of an "inner picture". If we observe something, we feel that we ourselves are making an active contribution and are not merely passive receivers. (In antiquity it was actually believed that some power or light radiated from the eyes, which helped

(a)

| Stimuli | ⟶ | Organism |

(b)

| Stimuli | ⟵ | Organism |

(c) | Stimuli | ⇆ | Organism |

Different views on the process of perception.

72

in making the things visible.) It is not merely a coincidence that our most sensitive organs for touch, the hand and the tongue, at the same time are the most developed organs of movement. A drawing where the lines go *from* the organism *towards* the stimuli, may, therefore, give an even more correct picture of the process of perception. Or what? Perhaps we should draw lines in both directions?

On perceiving oneself

As is the case where our experience of the outer world is concerned, our self experience has two sides. Through the senses I get an impression of my body and its inner condition from moment to moment. But I have at the same time a more abstract self picture, which has been formed on the basis of actions, feelings and experiences, as well as other people's reaction to what I have been doing.

The immediate "feeling" I have of my own bodily condition, is also built upon impressions which are mediated by the "receivers" – the receptors – of the body. In part these are the same sense organs as those presenting information about the environment. The same receptors tell me that the room is hot and that I am hot myself. An impression of pain may tell me both that my finger is hurt and that the knife I cut with was a sharp one.

Moreover, in muscles and joints we have special receptors telling us about movements, resistance and the position of the limbs (often called the kinesthetic sense = sense of movement). In the inner ear there are the liquid-filled *semicircular canals* and the *utricle,* giving information about the position of the head and about movements (the sense of equilibrium). These senses are good examples of how we can utilise

Here both sense of balance and self-confidence seem to be first-rate.

sensory information without being aware of the sense impression as such. Under normal conditions we have no difficulty in remaining upright, but we experience nothing directly from the balancing mechanism in the ear. In fact the existence of these senses was not discovered till some 150 years ago.

We also experience bodily conditions such as nausea and fullness, hunger and thirst, and emotional states: gladness and disappointment, fear and anger – to a large extent without really knowing *how* these experiences came about. How can I know that I am frightened? *William James* once put forward a theory that caused debate and which implied that our emotional experiences mainly are an experience of the bodily *reactions* to different stimuli from the outside. If the body in some critical situation had not reacted with heartbeat, shivering, cold sweat and dryness of mouth and throat, we might not have experienced the fear! WE think ourselves that we shiver *because* we are afraid, but what if we turned it around to say that we are frightened because we shiver?

Among the experiments done to test this some of the most famous are those of Stanley Schachter. He told groups of subjects that he was testing a drug for its effects on eyesight. In fact what he gave them was epinephrine, a substance that produces effects like those of general emotional arousal – increases in blood pressure, heart rate, breathing and blood sugar. Subjects were joined by someone who acted either angrily or boisterously. Subjects' behaviour was noted and later their mood assessed by a questionnaire. Generally they tended to show the same emotion as the stooge. These experiments have been much criticised, however, for example they may have been subject to the "experimenter effect" mentioned in Chapter One. It is not certain that the physiological changes in real anger are merely those of general arousal.

Some recent evidence rather supports the James' view. Actors who followed instructions to put smiling, fearful or sad expressions on their faces produced bodily changes known to accompany those emotions. It is not clear if they also felt happy or afraid. This was reported recently by Professor Ekman at the University of California.

However, such experiments show that James' theory only tells half the truth. Correctly enough we are dependent on signals from the organism to be able to know "how we are", but it is at the same time necessary that we place these signals into a certain outer context. The signals from the body are far more ambiguous than those from the environment, and often systematic misinterpretations occur (cf. the compulsive eater who regards every sign of helplessness or distress as a need for food).

The boundaries of the "self"

Even our "self" has its extension and its horizon. Physically seen the boundaries are relatively clear. Impressions which I would consider to be information about "my self", as a rule are those that stem from my own body. Nevertheless we may think of a number of situations where a certain sense impression can be interpreted both as information about some external condition and about an inner one, dependent on how we decide to take it. A patient having fever may waver between thinking himself to be very hot and believing the room to be overheated. A heavy weight may be felt physically in such a way that one person exclaims: "What hard work", while another simply states that: "This was a heavy stone".

If we think of the more abstract "self experience" or "self picture" we have formed, the boundaries tend to be even more diffused. Sometimes we may feel that the body or some specific parts are less central to the experience. Under some other conditions the boundaries of the self picture might be widened out. We may for instance consider our favourite clothes to be as important as what can be found underneath. The rider who seems to have "grown together" with his horse and the

For bodybuilders the muscles of the body are of central importance to the self image.

proud car owner who feels a mark on the finish more painful than a scratch of his own skin, are examples of how the self perception may be dependent on some conditions in the environment, or on some values we come to find important. Feelings of pride and triumph or of shame and defeat give excellent examples of what the self-feeling – in its wider context – may comprise. The feeling of humiliation resulting from slanderous talk shows that our "name and reputation" can be as important a part of ourselves as "life and limbs". This is of course well recognised by the law, which can award damages for libel or slander just as much as for actual injury. If I feel ashamed by what has been done by a member of the family, I show – despite all my disassociation from the affair – that I consider the person in question to be an important contributor to my own value.

The question of *what is me* and *what is not me* can partly be turned into a matter of attitude or will. In times of hardship we try to make the self as restricted as possible to be better able to defend it. "Let people talk– they can't really hurt *me*", is a typical statement. The martyr remains steadfast by thinking: "If they mistreat my body – they still cannot destroy *me.*" At other times we do the opposite, we try to keep a positive balance by expanding the self in a favourable direction, by for instance "identifying ourselves" with a good cause, our own country, or sport and pop stars. We may experience a shifting between the two

There, piano, you've learned that tune now!

tendencies. If our national side has success, we feel each victory as a personal triumph we can "live on." In cases of failure on the other hand we try to avoid the feeling of defeat by saying to ourselves: "This England team is a joke. I couldn't care less." Such effects have been labelled reduction of cognitive dissonance; the tendency to make all our beliefs and attitudes consistent with each other. Probably everyone has had the experience of puzzling over which car or bicycle to buy. Once the money is committed, however, excellent reasons occur to us why our choice was the best one.

In situations where we are in some interplay with our environment it may be a question of definition whether we let ourselves or the external conditions have the honour of the result. When a task goes smoothly – is it because I am clever, or because the task is an easy one? When I felt bored the last time I went to the cinema – was that because the film was a bad one, or because I was indisposed?

We opened the chapter by stating that it may often be more difficult to notice ourselves than the surroundings. This may lead to the result that the environment must often "take the blame" in situations where an outside observer would consider

that the responsibility was our own. If we return to a place we have visited a long time ago, we may think that the place has undergone change, when it is in fact ourselves that have changed. Buildings and furniture that seemed huge to us as children commonly now appear quite small. We may say that the clothes "have become too small" when in reality *we* have grown bigger. In the sketch by Gulbransson above the boy is busy giving the *piano* a lesson!

The self picture as a construction

In prescientific psychology a sort of "inner sense" was supposed to furnish us with a direct and genuine picture of our inner world, in the same way as the "outer senses" tell us about the world around us.

What has been said above should show that the matter is far more complicated. When the question is to find out what our own "internal state" looks like, we are to a large extent dependent upon uncertain interpretations and conclusions, where the reactions of others towards us play an important part. To a large extent our self conception is a result of what others have told us about our strong and weak points. If during childhood we have been told a sufficient number of times that some of our dispositions are praiseworthy whereas others are absolutely objectionable, the natural result will be a picture of ourselves as a two-sided creature, with both a good and a bad nature.

Nevertheless a rather *stable* picture of ourselves may be developed – if only the reactions of those who are closest to us are consistent enough. We may fail to discover that the picture does not fit with reality by misinterpreting the situations we have to face and for instance explain away whatever would indicate that the self picture was incorrect. We may for instance feel that we are exposed to "bad luck" or "injustice" if our performances are not in agreement with what we think we can do. On the other hand a person might also come to reject a success as "a coincidence" if regularly he sees himself as a "failure". Within social psychology what is called *attribution theory* deals with the various ways in which we explain or interpret what happens in social situations.

Unrealistic or not, our self picture may profoundly influence our actions. It has been argued that to most people it is of the utmost importance to defend and strengthen their self picture – throughout their lives. This can be obtained by doing those things that fit with the conception of oneself and by refraining from things that will not fit. If we believe we shall succeed on a given task, we tend to do our utmost. If we look upon ourselves as useless within a certain context, we tend to avoid the challenging tasks which otherwise could have helped to qualify ourselves. In this way our self picture may become "confirmed" (self-confirmed) in such a way that gradually we come to develop abilities and skills and to gain experience and training according to the conception we already have regarding our possibilities.

For most people, one major factor in how they see themselves is the work they do. Even when work is quite boring and unsatisfying in itself, being employed, being paid and useful, is vital to one's self-perception. But in just what way, varies from one person to another.

Psychologists studied the effects of unemployment in the 1930s. Now in the 80s they are having to do so again. Here are two examples. Penny Swinburne (1981); of Nene College, Northampton, interviewed twenty men aged between 31 and 57, who were on courses for unemployed managers, run by the Training Services Division of the Manpower Services Commission. These were semi-structured depth interviews. That means that there were some questions usually asked in each case but not a strict questionnaire. Respondents were encouraged to talk about their individual feelings and relations, which was helped by the interviewer having worked as a counsellor with them the previous week.

Penny Swinburne focused on three broad areas: feelings about being made unemployed; the process of structuring time; and searching for a job. The studies of the 1930s found a fairly typical pattern, those losing jobs passing through shock, optimism, pessimism, and finally fatalism and adjustment to long-term unemployment. A very similar pattern appeared now, but taking longer and with more individual variations. Some of the interviews were dramatic, such as this from a 42-year-old European Sales Manager:

"The initial impact was absolute shock. A complete crushing of self-respect and imagination. It's not like losing a leg where it is obvious and you have a limp. Well, I feel I have a limp – like a mental illness. It's as bad and has to be respected as much as someone who's lost a leg. But we don't. You lose your self-respect. . . I couldn't articulate the problem. . . I lived in a mental shell, not talking about what the real problems are. . . the state of shock lasted from January until July and is still very much in the foreground. I was totally crushed by the whole thing."

Swinburne adds: "While all reactions were not this extreme and one person did react in a totally unconcerned way, this was the general trend." She concludes with the well-known cry, nearly always true, that "more research is needed".

One interesting piece of it comes from Sten-Oloff Brenner and Riva Bartell (1983) of the Karolinska Institute in Stockholm. They began with a report by S W Hepworth (1980) of interviews she had carried out with 77 unemployed men of a variety of ages and occupations. She was particularly interested in the extent to which these men were able to occupy their time, and *felt* they were able to do so, despite having no job; and their general state of mental health and sense of well-being. She found a clear relationship between two variables: the best single predictor of mental health was whether or not a man felt his time was occupied. This is a useful finding in itself, and one might jump to the conclusion that the best thing for the unemployed is to keep them occupied somehow. But Brenner & Bartell point out that we have here a classic example of the problem of correlation. We do not know which causes which. "Are those men who can fill their time with meaningful activities less likely to show a deterioriation in mental health? Or alternatively, does poor health, such as depression or anxiety, inhibit a man from engaging in positive activities in his free time?"

They set out to answer this, not by a new investigation, but by a more sophisticated analysis of Hepworth's data. They used what is called the Linear Structural Relations method or LISREL. Without attempting to explain the mathematics, essentially this method provides an estimate of what correlations would result if either of two alternative hypotheses were true, and then shows to which of these the real observed data are closest. The actual calculations, of course, are done by computer.

This is a good example of how modern statistical methods can help to unravel complex behavioural questions. But it also illustrates the fact that the answers to those questions are rarely simple. What the analysis showed was that both processes were at work. "The ability to reorganise one's life following job loss, so that a high proportion of time is experienced as occupied, can serve as a safeguard for psychological well-being and functioning." This was more strongly supported by the data, but at the same time: "Poor psychological functioning and well-being may hinder the individual in attempting to occupy his or her time with activities during unemployment." Furthermore, these processes may react on each other, producing a vicious circle. To understand this further, we really need studies extending over quite long periods, as Brenner & Bartell point out.

These interactions between perception and other aspects of mental functioning are in line with what we know from many other studies. For example, the famous "coffin" experiments (Bexton, Heron & Scott 1954) in which subjects lay in a soundproof room, wearing blindfolds and cardboard cuffs over their hands. Thus deprived of much normal stimulation the subjects, all volunteers, found the situation unpleasant, even intolerable, after only a short time. Some had hallucinations. It is clear that interaction with the environment is necessary. But a merely passive experience is not enough. Richard Held and Alan Hein have shown convincingly that motor activity (movement) is essential to normal perceptual development. In another famous experiment, two kittens were attached to the ends of a rotating arm within a circular cage. One kitten was free to walk; the other was merely carried round. The second kitten's perception became handicapped, for example it did not blink when an object approached its eyes, did not shy away from a steep drop, and so on. These difficulties disappeared when it was allowed to run about in a lighted environment.

Under normal conditions living things develop accurate powers of perception, as they must in order to survive. What is noticeable as one moves up the phylogenetic scale from simple organisms to more complex ones is that perception, like other behaviour, becomes more flexible, more finely attuned, more abstract. A very simple organism such as an amoeba, one-celled and without a nervous system, can avoid noxious stimuli such as heat or pressure. The stickleback and the herring-gull respond to simple stimuli of size, shape and colour as Niko Tinbergen has demonstrated. Human beings can at their best respond to meaning rather than simple stimuli. We fall in love with a person, not a set of stimuli. Yet most people would find it hard to say just why that person is so attractive. There is an automatic quality about our reactions that reminds us, as Freud did, that we are animals too. "I don't know what she sees in him," is a familiar saying; as indeed is "love is blind". "I like her with all her faults; nay, like her for her faults," Mirabell says about Millamant in *The Way of the World.*

Strong emotion can distort normally accurate perception. A common experience is to imagine one sees in a crowd the person one is eagerly waiting to greet. One might put it that the recognition response has been triggered by a few cues, such as the approximate height and colour. Unusual conditions can likewise interfere. The two come together in the case of a desert mirage, where a heat haze takes on the appearance of desperately-needed water.

As human beings progressively extend their environment – the ocean depths, the upper atmosphere, outer space – it becomes important to know whether they can continue to function normally. Not all the investigations get published, but some do. For example, I Y Yakovleva, G N Kornilova, I K Tarasov and V N Alekseev, of the USSR, reported in 1982 the results of studying spatial perception and sense of balance in 26 cosmonauts before and after 30 spaceflights. Both were disrupted to some extent, though with considerable individual differences. The typical reactions included, for example, a decline in accuracy of perception of spatial co-ordinates, and a decrease in the sensitivity of the semi-circular canals, the organs in the inner ear that control the sense of balance.

In another study Helen Ross, a British psychologist, and Millard F Reschke, an American, both working at the Neuroscience and Behaviour Laboratory, NASA, Johnson Space Center, Houston, Texas, examined some of the effects of zero gravity. Astronauts may have to carry out complex manipulations under altered gravity and so it is important to know whether their perceptions remain accurate. In these experiments, it was a question of the ability to judge weight and mass. It might be thought that weight could not be judged at all when there is no gravity, but this is not so. The mechanism of estimating weight is still not fully understood, although it has been investigated for 150 years. Physicists do not even agree on a definition of weight. If you are simply asked, however, to say which of two objects is heavier, all sorts of cues may be involved: size, shape, part of the body used and how it is used (eg arm moved from elbow or shoulder), sense of effort, muscular fatigue, adaptation to the range of weights involved. Discrimination of *mass,* which is the ratio of force to acceleration, also interacts with weight discrimination in a complex way.

The basis method of these experiments was simple. Indeed it was essentially a procedure, known as the "constant method", devised by Gustav Fechner in the 1850s. It involves systematically comparing a set of stimuli, such as weights, with one standard stimulus. In this case the blindfolded subject held a standard weight in one hand and compared it with a series of others in random order. The complicated part was doing this under conditions of altered gravity. This was achieved by the use of NASA's KC-135 aircraft, adapted for parabolic flight. In a parabola the aircraft flies steeply up and then steeply down again, the manoeuvre taking about 80 seconds. At the right speed, gravity is at zero for about 30 seconds, and at about 1.8G for 40 seconds. The aircraft normally does 40 parabolas per flight, and it was during these that experiments were carried out. Of course the experimenter had to accompany the sucject in the aircraft; they were strapped in side by side. Special apparatus was used, developed for weightless conditions, which has also been used on actual space-flights. For comparison, the experiments were repeated on the ground, both before and after flights. The subjects were scientists, technicians and secretaries working at the Space Centre, 20 men and 7 women, who had volunteered to help.

The results of this kind of experiment are less likely to be some dramatic breakthrough than the careful establishment of the parameters (or measurable limits) of behaviour. Judgments were indeed less accurate under the experimental conditions, as one might perhaps expect, and Ross & Reschke give detailed results. But just why, is much less clear. Low gravity had the effect of reducing apparent heaviness. But this may have involved the physical change in mass; the neurophysiological difference due to the physical conditions; or alterations in the judgment process itself. It must be remembered that in such short experiences of altered gravity there is very little chance to adapt to weightlessness, whereas astronauts in spaceflights do tend to do this, with the result that their own bodies and other objects come to have the same apparent heaviness as on earth. Thus their abilities may revert to normal. They have to re-adapt on return. It is also conceivable, the authors point out, that

performance might actually improve during prolonged spaceflight. It is possible, though as yet uncertain, that the earth's gravity acts as a kind of background noise, which tends to mask inertial cues (ie the effort to move an object), which may be inherently more accurate than weight cues. These experiments perhaps give some impression of the task of investigating even apparently straight-forward processes in novel conditions.

Our environment is, of course, cultural as well as physical and psychological, and cultural differences too can change perceptions. Many textbooks quote, for example, the inability to comprehend drawings using perspective cues by people unfamiliar with our conventions. Whereas we see two animals of different sizes as being at different distances, they see one as really smaller than the other.

Real space-craft may affect perception, as we have seen. Many perfectly normal people have been convinced they have seen UFOs, which later turned out to be weather balloons or reflections or cloud formations. Perhaps they did so, C G Jung has suggested, because alien visitors are today an acceptable belief or mythology, as angels were once. Dr Jerome Kroll and Dr Bernard Bachrach of the Departments of Psychiatry and History, respectively, of the University of Minnesota, made a comparison of the symptoms of 23 psychiatric patients who had hallucinations or delusions on a religious theme, with the contemporary accounts of 134 religious visionaries of the period 500–1500 AD. (Hallucinations are defined as false perceptions; delusions as false beliefs). There was considerable similarity, for example both groups often believed they had received messages from angels or devils. There were also differences, for example in mediaeval times the predominant theme was experiencing a tour through Heaven or Hell, whereas the Minnesota patients tended to describe possession by the devil or the Holy Spirit. Kroll & Bachrach argue that their patients would not have been classified as insane in the Middle Ages. Their altered perceptions would have been thought unusual, but not abnormal, consequently they themselves would not have been seen as "mad".

One might add that UFO watchers are not so classed today.

Of course this is not all there is to diagnosing mental illness, and a UFO-observer, even if mistaken, may have perfectly accurate perceptions apart from this. As we have mentioned, realistic perception is essential to survival. In the 1950s and 1960s the ancient idea was revived that our normal perception is limited, and can be transcended by suitable techniques of meditation or by drugs. Aldous Huxley (1954) wrote of *The Doors of Perception*. While this is partly a religious or metaphysical question beyond our scope here, many of the claimed benefits of "psychogenic" drugs can be, and have been, investigated experimentally. In general, there is very little to support them. No chemical substance known really makes one more creative, though it may seem so to the user. A useful summary of the evidence is given by Brian Wells (1973) in *Psychedelic Drugs* (Penguin Books).

Substances are somewhat arbitrarily classed as drugs, legal or illegal, by different societies. Indeed it is yet another example of social influences on perception that many people "see" marijuana as a drug, but not alcohol or tobacco. Many drugs clearly have useful purposes, medical, psychological, or social; our point here is simply that their effects, on perception or any other behaviour, are open to objective study, and need not remain a matter of belief or folklore.

CHAPTER FOUR

Thinking and Intelligence

Introduction

Sometimes we humans proudly describe ourselves as thinking creatures in contrast to what we assume is the case with animals. By this we refer to the ability to reflect: something implying a) that we are conscious of what we are doing ourselves and what is happening to us and b) that we utilise and work on the impressions we get in such a way that we don't have to be dependent on the environment at any particular moment.

In the early history of psychology great importance was placed on both aspects of thinking, but the modern schools of psychology, as for instance psychoanalysis and behaviourism, have placed less emphasis on human thought and consciousness.

A. For one thing we may question the extent of our consciousness. To what degree are we really aware of what is going on inside ourselves? Why did I for instance become angry this morning? Why am I so afraid when I see spiders when I know they are not dangerous? Why am I unable to concentrate on work today? Questions like these can be difficult to answer and even our best answers may turn out to be insufficient when we look closer. According to psycho-analytic theory it is fooling oneself to bclicvc that onc has a total view of one's own situation; and if someone insists that he knows everything about himself we then could ask the person to describe and explain his own dreams.

B. We might also question our ability to act independently of the situation. On this point it is behaviourism in particular that has spoken in protest, arguing that behaviour is best, indeed only explained when one finds the stimuli influencing the person and when one sees the reactions they usually elicit. This conception is in many ways a modern version of the old saying that habit is our second nature. Sometimes this is stressed to such an extent that one might almost believe it was our first, and that the automatic routine type of actions are the key to an understanding of behaviour. It is not difficult to find examples of behaviour where thinking plays a subordinate role. If one is asked whether the keyhole in one's front door is above or below the door knob it might be difficult to think about it, whilst the problem of acting in the correct way is a very small one. Maybe a number of what seem to be rational actions are of this unreflected automatic type. "Don't think, it only confuses you" says the Swedish character Kolingen – and Sam Goldwyn allegedly said "My mind's made up – don't confuse me with facts".

Psychoanalytic and behaviouristic psychology each in its way has contributed to reduce the importance of thinking – psychoanalysis by stressing the irrational side of human nature and behaviourism by studying the construction and maintenance of routine actions.

That man is irrational is not in itself an

Most people would agree that thinking is something unique, a strictly private sort of activity. Drawing by Saul Steinberg.

argument that thinking has nothing much to say. Irrational thoughts are thoughts in the same way as the more rational ones and a lack of logic is not the same as a lack of thinking. Not being able always to explain or describe one's inner life does not necessarily mean that there has been no reflection, and if a great many of our actions may be considered to be of a routine type, there may equally be some of the more important and more interesting ones which are not. Confronted with new and unknown situations it might be of the utmost importance what one thinks. This is so in particular if one's thinking is irrational.

The psychology of thinking during recent decades again has come into the fore-ground as a central theme for research. We shall, however, start this chapter with a section where the material is taken from one of the oldest and most traditional psychological fields of research, the study of consciousness.

Thinking as a process. The psychology of associations

Most people would agree that thinking more than anything else is a strictly private activity. To the extent that I prefer to keep my thoughts to myself no one else can know what I am thinking. If one is to study thinking directly one has therefore to turn to some kind of introspection.

Introspection in psychology means trying to observe the working of one's mind, it does not imply brooding on one's personal problems. This was the classical way of studying thinking from the time psychology was defined as the science of conscious life (see Chapter 1). The American psychologist and philosopher William James in the 1880's gave a brilliant analysis of the thought process as seen by this means.

1. Every thought is personal, it belongs to someone. My thought belongs with the rest of my thoughts, your thought belongs among yours. Between your thoughts and mine there is an insurmountable gulf. We might be thinking of the same thing but even so the thoughts are our own all the time. It is impossible to conceive an isolated thought that does not belong to anyone; and if it existed we would have no possible way of knowing it.

2. Thought is always changing. We often talk about one thought, the same thought etc., as if it has to do with some relatively simple and limited object that we could hold on to and eventually take a closer look at if we wanted to do so. Introspection ought nevertheless to convince us that thoughts are not particularly well suited for being held in view. This is one of the reasons why introspection is so difficult. Admittedly we may to some extent stick to one and the same subject for thought, but in this case what is constant is obviously what we are thinking of and not the thought itself. (And, we might add, even to hold the same object constantly in thought is incredibly difficult, as anyone who has tried seriously to practice meditation knows.)

3. Thoughts are connected with one another. Every thought comes out of previous thoughts and leads on to new ones. There is no absolute break. Even after sleep or unconsciousness one does not start totally from scratch. Our thoughts are always related to whatever we have been thinking previously. James used the expression "the stream of consciousness" and "the stream of thought" to stress the last

two qualities of thought: An ever changing and at the same time continuous process.

4. Thoughts are about something, they point to something beyond themselves. A thought is not only a thought the way a stone is only a stone, sufficient unto itself. A thought presupposes that there is something we are thinking of. Thoughts stand for something, there is an object for thought, we may say.

5. Thought is selective. We cannot think of many things at the same time. By thinking of something in particular we are prevented from thinking of something else, and looking at the matter from one point of view prevents us from seeing it from another angle, at least for the moment. Thus there is a great similarity between thinking and perception (compare last chapter).

Of the many qualities of thought which William James points to, it is perhaps the connections in thinking that generally have

Both the child who is following the teacher and the one who is day-dreaming are associating. What is different is the particular chain of associations and its direction.

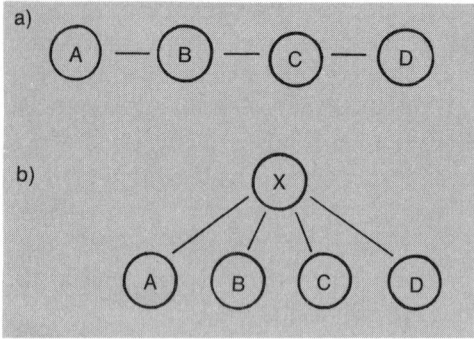

Two models of associative thinking.

been studied with the greatest interest. Why do one's thoughts go in one particular direction? Sometimes, it may seem as if thoughts come to us at random and it may seem to be in vain to search for order or logic. In psychology however, we work on the basis of the assumption that our thoughts have a cause in the same way as any other phenomenon of nature; and stand in a lawful relationship to each other. Associationistic psychology (compare Chapter 1) held that one thought gave the necessary impetus to the next one, all according to which thoughts had been previously associated. The thought of A naturally leads me to B if A and B have something in common. One possibility is that they have been experienced together in the past, the law of association by contiguity. Another possibility is that they have some common external or more likely, internal points of similarity: the law of association by similarity. In similar ways B might lead to C, C to D etc. We know the phenomenon from situations where we let our thoughts wander or, for that matter, let our tongue run freely until we stop, to ask how on earth did we come to talk about this. In such cases we can sometimes reconstruct the chain of associations, and find that each link of the chain is a natural one, but that there may be a very big difference between the first and last link of the chain.

Here we must however, stop to consider how common are such chains of association in human thought. Have we not previously in fact stressed the point that thought is always dealing with something and that it is active and selective?

In *The Psychopathology of Everyday Life*, 1904, Sigmund Freud extended his theory of the mind to show how, he believed, apparently accidental mistakes and lapses of memory are often, if not always, caused by chains of associations. He gave many examples, such as forgetting the Italian place-name *Nervi* because, he thought, it unconsciously reminded him of the *nerves* which were his daily business as a neurologist.

Similarly we in our daily life very often experience thoughts circling around one and the same topic. Perhaps it would be more correct to draw the connection between thoughts the way it is done in b) of the figure below.

The 19th century Scottish philosopher, William Hamilton stressed the fact that an idea A enters into a more general situation and that this more general theme called X in the figure would represent the point of departure for some further associations like B, C and D. We might find the same principle as a underlying precondition for the use of the so-called free association used in psychoanalytic treatment. The patient is here asked to tell about everything popping up in consciousness irrespective of how meaningless, unpleasant or seemingly unimportant the thoughts seem to be. It is assumed that the person in question, without necessarily knowing it himself, under such circumstances may come to circle round a deeper problem.

Thinking is often conceived of as what one does when doing nothing. But goal directed thinking is at its best when it is closely linked with behaviour, as when one actively tries to use one's previous knowledge to solve a concrete task.

Judgement and concepts

It is almost impossible to follow the stream of thought through its whole course. We can nevertheless be witness to the result of the thought process; in other words, what the person achieves by means of his thinking. For a long time psychologists have been less interested in what happens when the thought process is left to itself, so to speak, to concentrate more on what may be achieved by goal directed thinking. Goal directed thinking is what is going on when one has a problem or a task that has to be solved.

The simplest form of thinking is seen in cases where a question is put and we already know the answer. Not much thought has to be given to a question like "Who was William Shakespeare?" "Where is New York?" Assuming one has a certain background in literature and geography, in such cases we can use reaction time (the time between the question and the answer) as a way of telling how easy or difficult a question might be. In other words, how much thinking takes place. It may turn out that it needs more thinking to answer a question like, "give the name of an English author" or just "give the name of any of the big cities of the world". This is so even if in this case there are more correct answers to choose between; maybe it is because one has more than one possible answer to the question that it becomes difficult. It is in fact likely that someone who knows a great number of large cities would take longer to answer the last question than one who only knows a few, and that in the same way the question of suggesting the name of an author, irrespective of nationality, is more difficult than the more limited task of mentioning an English one.

Experiments show clearly that much depends not only on the amount of material but on how it has been processed. For example, different groups of subjects have been asked either to "estimate the number of letters in the words I shall present to you", or "give a rhyming word to each of the words I shall present to you" or thirdly "give me an association for each of the words I shall present to you".

In general, the last produces the best recall later: thus associations can both help and hinder memory in different circumstances.

In the examples mentioned so far the tasks have been very simple. It has only been a question of finding from memory certain information already there. It becomes somewhat more complicated if we are faced with a task which demands an assessment or evaluation of a topic or a situation. "Can I afford to buy such an expensive book?" "Was it a good film?" "How old do you think Peterson is?"

Judgement is relative

When we are asked to put our judgement in words we very often do it in absolute terms. I might for instance say that a book is expensive, when what I really mean is that compared to other books of the same type, this one is rather dear. I would probably not have described it as expensive if I had found out that most books on the same topic were twice as expensive. If I say that Peterson is old in a home for old people, it might mean that he is more than eighty, when at a discoteque it would probably mean that he is more than thirty. In cases like these the relativity of the judgement is clear and not much confusion would result. On the other hand it might be difficult to understand why one critic of films praises a film while another critic finds that the movie is worthless, if we are not at the same time told that the first person is comparing the film with what is generally produced when it comes to films of the same type, while the other critic has just come back from the film festival in Cannes.

We thus find that judgements always tend to have some frame of reference or a basis of comparison, even if sometimes we are very categorical when expressing ourselves. This also holds true about the judgement of oneself. When comparing my own behaviour with that of someone else, I might perhaps always succeed in finding someone for the comparison that would make me come out as a highly moral and intellectually superior type. On the other hand I may set up ideals of behaviour in such a way that I always come out as insufficient and unworthy.

Judgement is dependent on the concepts and the alternatives available

If the alternatives had been to call Peterson either old or young it is more likely that he would have been labelled old than if the question had been whether or not he was an old person. He would further, more easily have avoided being called an old person if there had been any opportunity for using other labels such as middle aged or older.

A judgement thus gives the full meaning if we know what has not been said: that is, the alternatives available. This is something we have to consider when we are going to interpret the results of an opinion poll. More people would state that they support a particular point of view if the only alternative is to say that they oppose this view, than if there is also a neutral category, like "don't know" or "undecided". One's vote in an election *may* mean that you fully support the candidate or the party, or it may mean merely that you dislike the alternatives even more. In a parallel way the chances of giving the correct answer in a test where you have a number of possibilities will vary both with the number of possibilities and with how close to one another the different alternatives are.

However we seldom have a number of ready made categories in answering the different questions of life. Life is not a series of opinion polls and multiple choice tasks. If I am going to evaluate the colour of the car of a neighbour or give my opinion of a certain pop group, no one hands me a questionnaire and asks me to tick off an appropriate answer. It is then more important to know what I myself see as alternatives, or in other words concepts it is natural to me to use. If I say about the colour of the car and about the pop group that they are "just top" it may sound as if I very seldom have come across anything as good as that. However, if anything that is not "top" in my vocabulary is called "lousy", the truth may be that the car of my neighbour or the pop group is not as excellent as all that.

Thinking as a way of structuring life

As long as all our thinking and indeed also our decisions, are dictated on the basis of the conceptual frame through which we see the world, it is not so strange that we put much energy into finding connections between the events happening around us. It is not only the scientist who tries to find order and system in the world. In this respect we might be called scientists, all of us. The child who places pebbles in a series according to size, or marbles according to colour, is behaving in a way as an astronomer, zoologist or historian does.

In our attempts to classify the phenomena around us we sometimes succeed in constructing classes which come close to what nature itself seems to provide. The dividing of heavenly bodies into planets, stars and other types, may be a good point of departure for studying the structure of the universe. But our search for order and system goes even further. Even where nature does not provide any grouping or boundaries, we seldom refrain from constructing the categories ourselves. Stars appear in all sorts of sizes and with all degrees of illumination. Still we divide them according to size in categories from one to six. Colours might be of any wavelength, still we divide the circle of colour into four or eight sectors and the rainbow since Newton's time (at least in text books) consists of seven main colours.

In different languages the categories of colour cannot always be matched one by one. What is in our society referred to as different colours, brown and blue, say, in another culture may be described as belonging to one and the same category of colour. Thus the spectrum of colours lexically has more than one way of being divided.

When it comes to time we all know that it passes steadily and evenly, although in order to keep records of greater and smaller intervals of time, we maintain a very complicated division into seconds, minutes, hours, days, weeks, months and years. Some of these, such as days, are natural. Others, such as seconds and minutes are arbitrary (our sixty-minute hour was invented by ancient Persian priests, to whom 60 was a sacred number). As children we thought it a great experience one day to wake up to a new birthday, feeling that overnight we had become one year older. Our way of structuring numbers also tends to make some years seem more important than others. We celebrate fifty and one hundred year anniversaries, whereas forty nine and two hundred and thirty seven years is nothing to take any notice of. Even historians are the victims of the magic of numbers of this kind, when they try to describe what is unique to the 1700's as opposed to the 1600's, even when they know how arbitrary and unhistoric such a division is.

In some ways we might say that our tendency to look for connections and relationships and to create categories, is a necessary precondition for being rational (and irrational as well).

Without some kind of grouping it would on the whole, be impossible to talk about a subject; language in many ways is essentially a sorting system. It would not be possible to collect experience in any systematic way, to see things in relation to each other, to predict the future, or find general laws. To understand means in many cases to have found where a phenomenon or an incident may be placed within our private system or view of life. Nothing tends to be more frightening than a phenomenon that does not fit in anywhere. What is uncertain and undecided, not being either living or totally dead, neither animal nor human, often supplies the horror in stories and films: for example Dracula (neither dead nor alive), and Frankenstein's monster (neither human nor animal). It sometimes helps to give a name to the fear, presumably because this makes it seem more familiar and more controllable.

At the same time, we can find examples of how concepts and categories lead to misunderstanding instead of understanding and can be a hindrance to knowledge instead of being helpful. History gives a number of examples of what the division of mankind into races, nationalities, social and religious groups etc., can lead to, when belonging to one particular group is seen as more important for a human being than his or her personal qualities.

A current joke concerns the Jew in Northern Ireland who, considering himself neutral, is asked "But are you a Protestant Jew or a Catholic Jew"?.

Prejudice is not so much the holding of an adverse opinion, to which one may be entitled. It is the application of that opinion to all members of a group, regardless of the facts. Peter Wason has shown in his ingenious experiments on making judgments that there is a very strong general tendency not to admit any negative evidence, any facts that might disprove what one has already decided is the case.

In the same way we can look at theories. We would need them in order to see clearly and at the same time, nothing can make one more blind than a theory when it becomes the master of a person.

Problem solving

When a task cannot be solved by routine behaviour or by thinking along well known routes, we are facing a problem, and indeed that a problem exists is something we very often do not know until we have tried to solve it. To get out of a room is no problem until we have found that the door cannot be opened. To get the contents out of a bottle is no problem until one discovers that the corkscrew is not where it used to be. In cases like these the obstacles may perhaps not make us stop to think, at least not to begin with. Perhaps we would start pulling and pushing the door or go through every drawer in a search for the corkscrew, but if this does not lead us anywhere, we probably sooner or later would come to a point where we have to admit that we are facing a problem. We see the goal but we don't see how we can get there.

Problem solving may consist of finding different routes to the goal and assessing if any of them is worth trying. In the first example we might for instance ask ourselves if getting out of the room necessarily

Children's problem solving can often be both original and elegant. Dr Edward de Bono, famous for his concept of «lateral thinking», asked a number of children to draw their solutions to the problems of weighing an elephant. The five-year-old who is the genius behind the left-hand drawing has solved the problem by letting the elephant distribute his weight on four bathroom scales. The six-year-old boy who produced the drawing on the right has been even more ingenious. If grown-up elephants are too heavy for the ordinary scales, one has to take precautions and weigh them when they are still small. (From Children Solve Problems by E de Bono 1972).

implies the opening of the door, maybe there are other ways of getting out, say through a window; and to get the contents out of a bottle one does not necessarily have to get the cork out, perhaps one could push it down into the bottle instead.

Problem solving thus is a very goal directed type of thinking, but this does not mean that it is a one-sided one. On the contrary we sometimes need to change our course several times. If the goal is too dominant as in cases where we are impatient or over-motivated, we run the risk of banging our head against the wall. The view that the best line between two points is the shortest one is not always correct when problem solving is concerned. Having a problem in fact often means that the most direct route is blocked and that we have to find a detour of some kind. The reason why solutions often do not come until after a break or a period of rest – the so-called incubation period – may be that the period has helped us to avoid or get out of a wrong track.

We might thus just as well say that our way of thinking sometimes *creates* problems almost to the same extent as we by thinking contribute to solving them. Try to solve the task of this figure before you go further in the text.

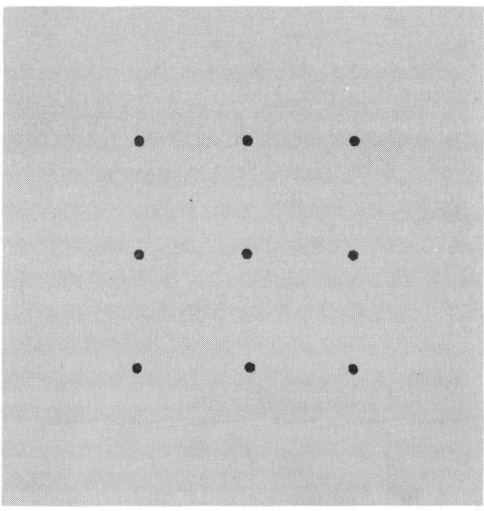

Can you, without lifting the pencil from the paper, join up all the dots with just four straight lines?

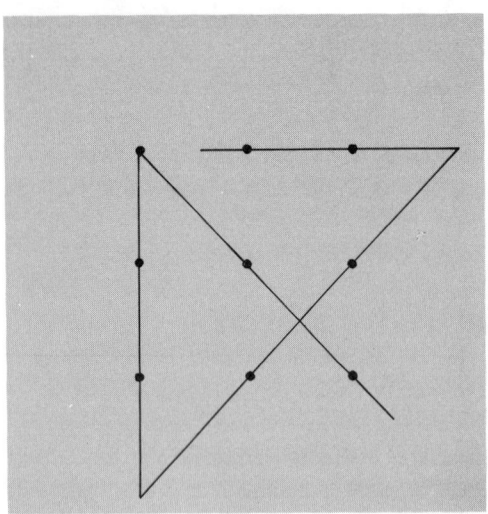

The solution to the problem of the four lines (see previous page).

As the solution shows it is necessary to go outside the invisible frame. Our tendency to see a square ("good form") is here inhibiting the attempts at solution. In other cases, a habitual way of thinking or a particular set can prevent us from finding a simple solution to a problem. Experience is not always a good thing.

One example is the so-called functional fixedness. We tend to think about objects according to their usual function. In an experiment where the task was to get hold of a ball in a small narrow cylinder and where the subjects have a bottle of water at their disposal, many subjects solved the task by pouring water down into the cylinder so as to make the ball float up. If the bottle contained coke hardly anyone solved the problem. Coke is something one drinks, not something one pours into jars for other purposes. (Some of the subjects in fact actually drank the coke in the course of the experiment and thus ruined any chance of getting the ball up.)

It would not be correct on the basis of these examples to draw the conclusion that the best problem solver is the one who has no experience beforehand. If the experience is sufficiently great, what to one person might appear as a new and unfamiliar situation, to the experienced person might be well known and not represent any problem. And the first step in the solution of a problem in any case is to compare the new situation with what one already knows. It then becomes possible to see what is lacking for a solution of the task.

This is what we refer to when we say that one first has to find out what is really the problem. The most difficult tasks of all are those where one has no idea where to begin. If we understand very little, we perhaps do not even know that we do not understand, and then, of course, it is not easy to continue. On the other hand, a question that is well formulated may sometimes represent half of the answer.

Most problems may however, be formulated in different ways. Perhaps that is what is difficult or problematic about them. Let us imagine that I am going to put up a poster on the wall without having any of the usual implements at hand. On the basis

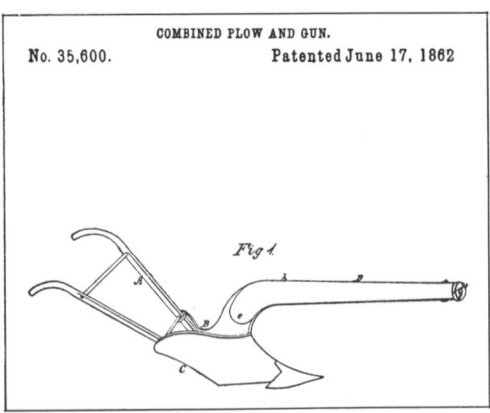

A combined plough and cannon for use in peace and war. According to the specification it is especially suited to cultivating the prairie in the Wild West, but it is uncertain whether it was used at any time. From A E Brown & H A Jeffcott: Absolutely Mad Inventions. (New York 1970).

92

of previous experience, I may come to define this as a situation where I am lacking drawing pins and consequently I would look for something else with which to nail the poster to the wall. Alternatively I could look upon the situation as one where I am lacking something with which to glue the poster, and thus start looking for something in that direction.

If we have formulated a problem in one way or other, the next step is to find out how to handle the unusual features of the situation or make up for whatever is missing. In the example above I might replace the drawing pins by needles or even nails. If I find some nails I might face another problem: if there is no hammer, how would I be able to get them into the wall? Is there perhaps a stone nearby or maybe I could use the heel of my shoe? If on the other hand I have looked upon the situation as a problem of glueing something to the wall, some plastic strips or perhaps even some chewing gum might do the trick.

We thus see that the difficulty of a problem can be of two different kinds. It is a question of both finding the best formulation of what is wrong and then handling or overcoming the hindrance when it is found. Many problems like the one above might be solved in more than one way. In some cases what is wrong or missing may be easy to discover, but very difficult to handle. In other cases the situation might be very easily handled when first one is aware of the hindrance or has been able to define the situation in an appropriate way. Those are the solutions sometimes called Columbi egg. Anyone could have done it if they had thought of it.

In most practical situations, the two phases of problem solving cannot be seen as entirely separate, and it would be a poor problem solver who worked solely on de-fining a situation before looking around for implements. Most probably he would then not find what he was looking for and have to start all over again. Sometimes it will pay off to start from the opposite angle with the implements at our disposal and see how they can be used. This is what happens when one wants to make something or paint a picture, there are two ways to proceed. One can start with an idea or one could start with the material. Very often the second point of departure is the better one. Of course in that case one at least has a chance of having *some* result.

The third phase in solving a problem is that of evaluating the results. Have I in fact reached the goal, is this really a successful solution? This part of problem solving has perhaps been less illustrated in the examples we have used so far. When a problem is set in the psychological laboratory or in school, the task very often is such that there is only one solution and it is usually easy to decide whether one has solved the problem. An example would be the so-called Hatrack problem used by the American psychologist Maier. Here the subjects have the task of constructing a coat hanger by means of two poles and a C-clamp. To most people this task is very difficult, but once you have succeeded in clamping the poles together and wedging them between the floor and the ceiling in the room, it is obvious that the clamp now can serve the function of a hook, on which to hang your coat. With less artificial problems, like those of medicine, it may take years to decide whether a particular treatment is really the solution where a certain illness is concerned.

In daily life most difficulties might be overcome in more than one way and with varying degree of success. The perfectionist who tries to achieve the perfect solution in a fault-free manner would find himself

For someone who can break free from the usual functions of the objects (functional fixedness) the paper punch is an ideal bottle opener and the sculpture a useful mirror.

in a different situation from someone who is satisfied with a less complete solution or who is not so particular about the means he is using. Some of the problems of daily life cannot be handled in an isolated way. What is in itself an excellent solution to a problem might create difficulties in some other ways. To use the bottle of coke to make the ball float is only brilliant until someone comes running asking "Who has emptied my coke!"

In daily life, we also have to decide whether the difficulties we face can on the whole be overcome on the basis of the experience we already have or with the implements at our hands. Sometimes the best way of proceeding would be to look for a new experience or other kinds of implement. Someone who insists on thinking about the solution might be less successful than someone who is good at asking others for advice or is most ingenious in looking for new sorts of equipment. Sometimes it would pay off simply to try at random. Quite a few creative solutions have come about after a period of trial and error. With the Hatrack problem, mentioned earlier, it has been clearly demonstrated that subjects who eventually solve the problem are not superior to non-solvers on tests of general intelligence or as far as other achievement scores are concerned. What seems to characterise the solvers is a higher activity in repeatedly trying out various (unsuccessful) attempts, prior to hitting upon the correct approach. Where one can no longer see one has to fumble about. In an experiment where the task was to use the bottom half of a box of drawing pins in a new and unusual way, more subjects solved the task blindfolded than when they could see. In looking at the box they immediately saw that it was a box for drawing-pins (functional fixedness); when blindfolded they had to feel the box,

When a problem cannot be solved by reasoning, one has to turn to a trial and error strategy. Sometimes there are more errors and even the most innocent-looking deck-chair turns out to be a real threat.

take out the little drawer and through active exploration get ideas of the uses it might be put to.

We find that problem solving, in the form of intelligently thinking about the task, is at its best in a situation which is only partly unknown or unfamiliar to the problem solver. If the situation is in all respects familiar, we may very well solve the task by some routine action. Reflection would then perhaps only lead to complications, just as a skill such as tying one's tie often breaks down if one thinks too closely about it. If on the other hand the situation is totally new and strange we would have to explore and use trial and error. In such cases, we cannot wait to act until we have found out how to do it. The creative personality in art as well as in science, has often the feeling of having found something or come across something by coincidence, rather than having got the new insight by systematic effort.

To think in problem situations is only one of the strategies we might use to overcome difficulties. Moreover, we sometimes do not aim at *solving* a difficult task. Often we simply deny that we have a problem, or in contrast, regard the task in front of us as a much too difficult problem to be worth a single try.

Differences in thinking. Intelligence and intelligence testing

With all forms of thinking we must reckon with great differences between people. In simple associative tasks where one is told to answer with what comes to mind, we might find great similarities between different subjects. If the experimenter says "table" four out of five subjects would answer "chair". If the situation is more open to free association, we would find far greater differences that would tell us that each of us has our favourite ways also in the world of thought. The differences do not become less pronounced when it is a question of goal directed thinking. As far as judgement is concerned we know that even experts have difficulties in agreeing. We have also seen examples of how the system of concepts with which we face the world can be different from one human being to the next. Sometimes the differences become so great that even with the best of will, we must give up the attempt at understanding one another.

The differences which have to the largest extent caught the interest of both researchers and the general public, are the differences in so-called "intelligence". This concept has probably caused more argument in psychology than any other. The argument has spread into politics with the attempts to show that whole races or groups of people are more or less "intelligent" than others. We are not going to add to these arguments here. We agree with those who hold that there is not a "thing" called intelligence that can be isolated and is the cause of what people do. Rather, irrespective of definition, the concept refers to the fact that individual humans are not only different in what we think about and how we think, but also when it is a question of how skilful and adaptive we are in using our thoughts in different areas.

If we try to find out the background of differences in skill in this case, we would perhaps make the following two observations: a. One who is among the clever ones in one field would perhaps also be among those who have most experience in that field. But, b. even if a number of people get the same training or experience they would not all become equally skilful.

To take an example, a skilful crossword

Chess is considered by many people to be a task typically requiring intelligence. But probably no IQ would enable a beginner to beat an experienced player. What is to one the most abstract thinking, may be mere routine to the other. Studies have also shown that chess masters do not necessarily score extremely highly on tests of intelligence or memory. What they do possess is a profound knowledge of moves and situations so that they are quickly aware of the implications of any position.

solver would probably have a long training on similar tasks. In the course of this time the subject in question has learnt a series of useful tricks about how to proceed. It is smart to shift between vertical and horizontal words, not sitting too long wondering about one single word; learn a number of more concrete things, like for instance that the "God, two letters" might be RA and that the bird of three letters is probably ARA, KEA or EMU (species which one never meets in nature but very frequently in crossword puzzles). It is at the same time clear that some people become more skilful and attain these types of knowledge much more easily than others, and can utilise them with greater art. It is this last difference we are referring to when we say that people have different abilities and aptitudes in some area.

To demonstrate that differences of ability exist in a number of fields, is however not the same as to have shown that there are differences in intelligence. It is possible to conceive the skilful crossword solver as having special talents for solving crossword puzzles and that this has very little to do with the ability to solve other intellectual tasks. An important question thus becomes the following: Will a person who has proved himself to have special abilities facing one type of task also be very good at mastering other tasks? Will the crossword solver also be good at essay writing, foreign languages or chess?

It is easy to find examples of people who are in fact brilliant in a series of different fields, but equally it is not difficult to find people who are very able in one field, but in another field are very helpless. An understanding of the connection or relationship between the achievements in two areas we might show by making a scattergram like the following.

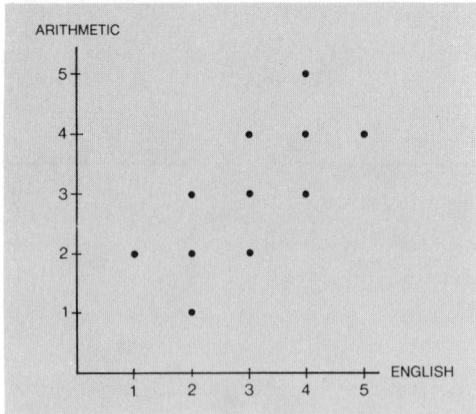

In this diagram each subject is marked as a point on the basis of two scores, one on a test of English and one on a test of arithmetic.

We see from the distribution, that there is a certain tendency for students doing well on one task also to do well on the other, and that someone who is below average on one test is probably also below average on the other. There is however no perfect relationship because in such a case all the points would have to be found on one line, as a diagonal from the bottom left to the upper right. By means of statistical methods we are able to give a numerical expression of the correlation in this example. A perfect positive relationship is given the value +1; a total lack of correlation gives a correlation coefficient of 0. In the example above the correlation coefficient is about .70.

But even with statistical calculations like the one above, we can find no absolute argument that there is such a thing as a general intellectual ability. Both very similar and different achievements in two separate fields might be due to differences in

experience, training and motivation. A student who is eager to do a good job at school would probably have good marks in a number of subjects, whereas one of equal ability at the outset, who couldn't care less about school work, might be equally unsuccessful throughout. A relationship between marks in different subjects might therefore be due to a general factor of motivation rather than to general ability. Differences in results from one field to another can also be due to differences in experience and interest. On top of that there is also such a thing as having talents in areas that are different from what is asked for in school.

In the course of the last 75 years psychologists have been engaged in constructing a series of tasks aiming at drawing a more reliable and general picture of the resources as far as human abilities are concerned, than what can be shown in school marks. The point of departure for the first so-called intelligence test was in reality to find a way of differentiating between the pupils of the elementary school other than by the usual marks. The French Secretary of Education in 1905 had appointed a committee to look at the question of mental retardation among school children. The committee asked the psychologist Alfred Binet to construct a series of tasks which would differentiate between the mentally retarded and the normal children.

Binet found that this could best be done by having a large selection of varied tasks, from counting to the interpretation of sayings, from memory for digits to the defining of words. He gave these tasks to children of different age levels, and kept the tasks that differentiated the best between the different age groups. This was done on the basis of the assumption that children's intelligence would increase with increase in age. Only tasks that are reflecting this tendency would then be considered to have something to do with intelligence.

In later revisions of the tests Binet's tasks were grouped according to age level, a child of ten who was unable to solve the tasks above the 7 year level, received a mental age of 7 years, which would mean 3 years of retardation in intellectual development. Later it was proposed that the relationship between the mental age and the chronological age would give the best picture of the intellectual skill of the child. To be 3 years behind one's age does not mean the same to a 10 year old as one who is 13, and would be more serious for a 7 year child. The intelligence quotient (I.Q. for short) is found according to the formula,

$$I.Q. = \frac{\text{Mental age}}{\text{Chron. age}} \times 100$$

A child functioning at the level of his own age would then receive an I.Q. of 100. A ten year old with a mental age of 7 would have an I.Q. of 70 and thus lie on the border of what in more recent times is called severe learning difficulty.

If we test a great number of children we would find that the results of most would lie in the neighbourhood of 100 (about 50% between 90 and 110) and that there are fewer and fewer the further we go up and down the scale. It has usually been believed that intelligence idea'ly seen ought to follow the normal distribution curve, a bell shaped curve which we often find in an approximate way when a larger number of independent factors lie behind some phenomenon. For instance graphical presentation of biological qualities, height, muscle power etc., would if drawn for a great number of people resemble the normal distribution curve.

The distribution is a mathematical abstraction, derived from the laws of chance. Measurements of the real world *tend* to fit it, they never do so exactly. And while height, for example, does tend to do so, there is no logical reason why psychological measurements must as well. This is an assumption based on theory. However it has generally turned out to be a useful one.

We are now better equipped to answer the question of whether there is a general ability that we might call intelligence. Instead of investigating the connection between school marks and other more or less randomly chosen measures of intellectual achievement, we might compare the results of different sub tasks of a test com-

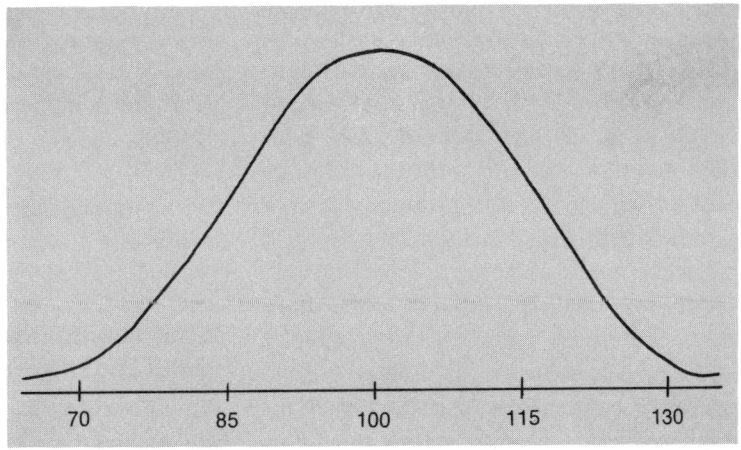

The theoretical pattern of results on an intelligence test according to the normal distributioncurve.

prising a large variety of intellectual tasks. It still depends, of course, on what tasks one chooses to have in the test, but the method of assessing the achievements is here highly standardised. We can now ask the question whether a person who is clever at solving numerical tasks will also be good at solving tasks with figures or in finding similarities and differences between concepts. The results of such comparison as a rule would be medium high positive correlations (.40–.70) between the different tasks. Such relationships might however be interpreted in two ways.

One may stress the fact that all our positive correlations are sufficiently high to suggest a general ability.

One may stress the fact that the relationships are far from perfect, pointing to the other fact that an underlying general ability cannot predict how far a person will reach in a particular field.

If one takes a closer look at the results, one finds that the tasks may be grouped in different ways. Some tasks obviously have more in common than others. It turns out for instance that tasks of a verbal nature are more related to each other than they are to other tasks like problems using figures. Some people are more intelligent in relationship to verbal theoretical tasks where others can be as intelligent when practical tasks are concerned.

To some extent we might also differentiate between tasks that imply an ability to handle relatively new and unknown situations and tasks that imply the use of previous knowledge. If for instance I ask a person where Brazil is situated or what a particular word of foreign origin means, the answer might be thought to be more dependent on his knowledge in geography and language than on his ability. If such questions nevertheless form part of an intelligence test, it is because they can tell us

something of whether the person has shown an attentive and intelligent attitude in previous learning tasks, and thus indirectly give us a hint of the person's level of ability. We might thus say that our intellectual capacity at any one time is the sum of how well we handle the things we have learnt plus how well we handle what we have not as yet learnt. Any intelligence test can only take a small sample of what the individual can do, rather as one race is only a sample of what an athlete can do.

A third and perhaps not less important division is between tasks of a traditional type that presuppose one correct answer, and tasks which to a greater extent appeal to fantasy and flexibility. In the last case the person giving the task has perhaps no particular answer in his mind, the point may on the contrary be to produce as many and as original answers as possible. A question of this type might be "What purpose can a paper clip serve?" "Mention as many ways as you can of using an ordinary brick." "What would happen if the sea level went down about 30 feet?"

Most intelligence tests contain few questions of this type and many people have looked upon the new type of tasks as tasks of creativity. This is, of course, to some extent a question of definition. The new tests surely demand inventiveness in using past experience. Still the basis for suggesting e.g. a variety of "uses for things" is to be found in some previous knowledge. A flexible use of past experience ought perhaps to be seen as something necessary for an intelligent adjustment to the demands of everyday life.

What can an intelligence test tell us about the individual?

A test comprises a large number of tasks which show a certain relationship to each other, but the relationship is not perfect and the results may vary from one test to the next, dependent on which tasks are used. A person who for instance achieves an I.Q. of 115 does not *have* this figure as something unchangeable as if given from nature. It is like taking someone's temperature, which varies somewhat according to conditions. And different tests use different scales, just as thermometers use centigrade or fahrenheit. To interpret a particular test result, we have to know the scale; and we have to know the reliability of the test and its validity.

By reliability (compare Chapter 1) is meant to what extent the difference we find in individuals are systematic ones, and not random variations which are due to the test itself. This can be investigated by comparing the results of two different assessments where we have used the same or comparable tests. In most cases we do find a high reliability between test scores. A score which means a result of 115 is not only due to pure luck, and 85 is not the result of sheer bad luck. On the other hand results may vary 4 or 5 points from time to time. If a number of years pass between the testings, one should not be surprised if the difference in points becomes even greater, 10 to 15 points range is often found, at least if the testing has been done with small children. We use intelligence tests with children down to the age of 2 and 3, but at this age level one ought to be very careful in trying to predict anything about the future. This does not only mean that the tests are unreliable, but the speed of intellectual development can be different from child to child and the environment and the conditions of development can play a role that is very difficult to predict.

There is a great deal of evidence that, on the whole, children in a lively intellectual environment tend to do better than those from deprived homes or in the old-fashioned sort of institution. But of course there are cases of geniuses coming from such backgrounds as well. Some of the complexity is suggested by studies of children in different cultures. These have led such psychologists as Jerome Bruner to stress the different *modes* of thinking that may develop in different circumstances. The fact is that human beings have a great capacity for variability and despite the psychologists, remain unpredictable.

The next important question is that of the validity of the tests. Does the test result say anything more about a person than that he has a certain ability to answer questions of this type? If one takes a closer look at the construction of the tests one may come to wonder, because so many different questions seem to be presented. Nevertheless it is this variety in the tasks that has made intelligence tests useful for practical purposes. Also in daily life the chances of success are dependent upon a large number of different factors; not just on ability in a particular field. In this way the tests may be seen as relatively valid, since they may tell us with some probability who will experience difficulties and who would have less difficulty in for instance, going for higher education. But they cannot predict who will in fact succeed, because success is dependent on the amount of work, on interests and many other factors which the tests do not measure. A more successful prediction is often possible if a variety of assessments can be made: tests of different kinds, interviews, life history so far, etc. Such a programme, taking a day or two, is often used in industrial career guidance.

It would be totally wrong to conceive the numerical result of an intelligence test as an exact measure of one single feature or quality about a person, like for instance his height or weight. Unfortunately, we have such respect for numbers that the use of them is sometimes taken as a proof that the psychologist has succeeded in revealing the inner sources of intellectual power in an individual or his hereditary equipment.

Psychological tests have many practical and research uses, and through them we know far more about human behaviour than we did a hundred years ago. But they remain tools, requiring skilled use and interpretation, just like the thermometer or the blood sample or the x-ray for the doctor. Those tools do not tell us how the patient caught a disease or whether he will be cured; they do enable him to be treated far more effectively.

"Decisions, decisions!" people often cry in comic despair, but of course we cannot avoid them. Some may be not very important but many are. Among the most formal and far-reaching in their effects are those of the law. Not many of our readers, we feel sure, are criminals, but such is the complexity of modern law that it is quite difficult to avoid minor infringements such as traffic offences. Once up against the law someone – judge, jury, police officer, magistrate – must decide what is to happen. It is important to understand how such judgements are made.

Andreas Kapardis (incidentally an ex-student of one of the present authors, JKR) and David Farrington reported (1981) an experimental study of sentencing by magistrates, done at the Institute of Criminology, University of Cambridge.

In England and Wales, magistrates' courts deal with about 98% of criminal cases. Magistrates are unpaid, serve part-time, and are not lawyers, though they do receive some training and are advised by legally qualified justices' clerks. They usually sit as a "bench" of three, the most experienced generally being chosen as chairman by the clerk. Their sentencing powers are limited to a maximum of six months' imprisonment or £1,000 fine (1981) for any one offence. More serious cases can be committed to the crown court for sentencing.

Investigations show that magistrates tend to be in professional and managerial occupations, older rather than younger, married and Conservative in voting intentions. There are slightly more men than women. It is well established that sentencing policy is not the same throughout the country, or between different benches, or between different types of offenders. For example, P Softley (1978) found in a national sample of convicted persons aged 17 or over that older people were more likely to be discharged; imprisonment was more likely if the offender was not living with spouse or parents, or was unemployed.

Kapardis and Farrington tried to isolate some of the factors leading to differential sentencing. Such real-life situations are hard to control experimentally. An ideal experiment might be to send simulated defendants, actors pretending to have committed offences, into real courts. At the other end of the scale, many experiments, especially those in North America, have had panels of subjects, such as first-year psychology students, read short descriptions of cases and give sentencing decisions. The problem for the experimenter is to decide between controlling conditions in the laboratory, or studying the real thing which may be very different.

Kapardis and Farrington took a middle course. They used real magistrates but simulated cases. These were based on real cases, but presented in transcript form. This included details of the defendant, the charge, the plea, statement by the prosecution, statement by defendant, social enquiry report and mitigating plea by defendant's solicitor. Four cases were dealt with by post, and another five by the magistrates sitting together as they would in real life. 56 groups of three completed the whole experiment. They were volunteers from different areas: Northampton, Peterborough, Southend, Poole, Nottingham.

It was first necessary to establish a scale of severity of sentencing, which was done by having a separate, pilot group of 23 magistrates rank 10 different sentences for severity.

The cases were prepared so as to vary the following variables: (1) seriousness of the offence; (2) criminal record of the offender; (3) age of offender; (4) sex of offender; (5) social status of offender; (6) plea – guilty or not guilty; (7) the prevalence of the offence in the area; (8) if the offence involved breach of trust; (9) race of the offender; (10) race of the victim. Each of these variables had two values, eg male or female, black or white, old (32) or young (22). The cases were presented in such a way as to balance the variables between the groups of magistrates.

The results showed that sentences were more severe when offences were more serious, when offenders had a more serious criminal record, when offenders were male, and when offenders were of higher social status. The other factors studied had no significant effect on sentence severity.

This is an example of the detailed establishment of what factors are involved, which may or may not accord with common belief. For example, many people might expect that higher social status helps the defendant to get a lighter sentence. This study does not, in itself, explain *why* decisions are made, and it needs to be correlated with real-life cases. Even taken alone, it does suggest something about improved training for magistrates.

Which of us by taking thought can add one cubit to his stature? asks the Bible. What we certainly can do, however, is add to performance. It is by no means clear even what the limits of physical capability are, for example the four-minute mile, now almost commonplace, was run first only in 1953. With the mind and behaviour, potential may be even greater.

One man who believes this strongly is Professor Reuven Feuerstein who directs a programme of child research in Jerusalem. Himself a refugee from Nazi-occupied Bucharest, Feuerstein was struck by the emotional disorders and low intellectual performance of Jewish children arriving in Israel in the 1950s. He became convinced that conventional intelligence tests could not show the potential of these children. Their low scores were the result, he thought, of the disordered lives they had led. They had failed to develop systematic ways of dealing with information. For example, they were unable to make systematic comparisons between objects and events, found it difficult to follow, or to give, directions, and often could not link causes with effects.

Feuerstein's answer was to develop a method of systematic training, called instrumental enrichment, to supply the deficiencies. This is not just any cultural experience. "You can take a child to a zoo and it might be very stimulating", he is quoted as saying, "but it can hardly teach him logic". (*The Guardian,* 3 August 1983). Exercises may be very simple, such as joining up dots to make geometric shapes. This, though, would be the basis for children discussing the best way to do it, to compare with each other, to distinguish what is relevant on the page from what is irrelevant. The intention is that children learn general strategies for thinking, which can be applied to any other situation.

These techniques are being applied, mainly to educationally backward children, not only in Israel but in the USA,

Canada, South America and Britain. Results are reported as encouraging and sometimes dramatic. However, while an improvement in performance is in itself good, helping retarded children to a fuller life, it does not follow that the effect depends on a particular method or theory. Very many methods have been tried, and quite a lot have worked. We do not always really know why.

Nor does it follow, as sometimes seems to be suggested, that if we can improve the abilities of the handicapped, we can therefore raise the general level of the average population. Here we almost enter the realm of science fiction, though one attempt to do just this has been reported. The government of Venezuela is said to be introducing the methods of Dr Edward de Bono throughout its schools with the specific aim of raising the average level of intellectual ability.

We have stressed in this book that psychology is not mainly concerned with abnormal or disturbed behaviour. Nevertheless psychologists in practice frequently have to deal with such problems. We also have tried to show that behaviour does not exist in the real world neatly divided into perception, learning, thinking, and so on.

Both these points are illustrated in the growing application of "cognitive" methods of treatment to emotional problems. For example, phobias, which are irrational fears.

"Cognitive therapies for phobia are based on the theory that faulty thinking causes phobic behaviour, and the corollary that if clients adopt more adaptive ways of thinking their fears will diminish. Cognitive therapists attempt to change what clients think primarily through dialogue in which the clients' problematic thoughts are examined and challenged, and alternative ways of thinking are encouraged."

With these words S Lloyd Williams and Alan Rappoport begin a report (1983) of an attempt to assess the effectiveness of the method. The study was part of Dr Rappoport's doctoral work, done at the Pacific Graduate School of Psychology in California. Some previous studies had found that, despite the optimistic claims for cognitive therapy, it was less effective than behavioural practice; thinking was less useful than doing. But this might have been because cognitive therapy is often done in a clinic or office, not in a real situation.

Williams and Rappoport selected 20 women, aged between 21 and 67, who were agoraphobics. They were irrationally afraid of open spaces, but in particular of driving a car when alone. Such situations as using buses or trains, heights, large open places, created severe anxiety, and they could not drive 10 blocks through a quiet residential neighbourhood. The cause of such disabling fears are complex, but this study was of treatment only. Subjects were randomly assigned to one of two treatment groups, cognitive and non-cognitive.

The treatment was carried out during 11 hours of supervised driving practice in 6 sessions over a 2-week period. "Treatment took place along 5 routes: a quiet residential street, a minor thoroughfare, a major thoroughfare, a scenic freeway, and an urban freeway. Each session consisted of a series of practice forays; on each foray the subject drove a designated distance along a route while the therapist waited at the starting point. When the subject returned, she indicated whether she had completed the assigned task and estimated how anxious she had become on a scale from 0 ("unafraid, not tense or anxious") to 10 ("extremely afraid, very tense and anxious"). A brief discussion was then held and the next foray planned and executed." The forays, and the routes, gradually became more difficult as long as anxiety remained low.

This procedure was the same for all subjects. The difference in treatment came in the discussions. "Between each driving foray, subjects in the cognitive group received instructions to use certain cognitive strategies for coping with fear on the next foray. The suggested coping strategies included attending to non-threatening aspects of the environment (eg trees and houses), self-distraction with engaging thoughts (eg planning a recreational activity), relabeling anxiety and other threatening aspects of driving (eg "These anxious feelings won't harm me, they're just uncomfortable"), substituting favourable anticipations for fearful ones (eg "I will be able to manage regardless of how I feel"), and engaging in task-relevant self-instructions (eg "Keep my mind on my driving")."

After each driving excursion, therapist and patient discussed the degree of success or otherwise and how to improve next time. Subjects used the coping strategies 83% of the times they were suggested, and found them helpful 79% of the times they used them. The other group of subjects were merely engaged in "general supportive conversation" with no mention of thoughts or of cognitive strategies.

The fears of all subjects were assessed on four occasions: at the beginning and end of a 2-week baseline period before any treatment started; at the end of the 2-week treatment period; and at a follow-up 3 to 5 months later. On each occasion five measures were taken: (1) a questionnaire to rate fear of various activities, including agoraphobia and driving; (2) the subjects' rating of confidence that they could carry out a number of driving tasks; (3) their anticipated anxiety over these; (4) actual driving tasks over five routes equivalent to those used in treatment; (5) their reported anxiety afterwards. Besides these, subjects' thoughts while driving were sampled by having a tape recorder in the car, which was switched on for 20 seconds, at 90-second intervals, when a bleeper sounded as a signal, at which the subject said whatever was passing through her mind at that moment. This was done before and after treatment.

Now for the results. Cognitive subjects used significantly more coping thoughts while driving. *But* they showed no greater improvement than the non-cognitive subjects on any measure. Indeed by the time of the follow-up they were slightly worse. Both groups showed significant improvement overall, and both groups had significantly fewer fearful thoughts while driving.

So much, it may be thought, for cognitive therapy, and Williams & Rappoport rather tend to this conclusion. It might be suggested that, as so often, it is not quite so simple. It might be that much longer treatment, or different strategies, would be effective. Possible not all phobias are alike in their response to treatment. Or perhaps, as the authors suggest, "fear is indeed rooted in thought, but . . . the best way to change thought is through performance-based treatments which give clients first-hand evidence that they can function effectively".

When Aristotle considered man as a rational animal he did not mean that we are rational all the time but that we are distinguished from other species by a capacity for rational thought. Nowadays we might not want to be so precise. It is certainly clear that the relationship between rational thinking, irrational and emotional thinking, and behaviour is quite complicated. As we began this chapter by remarking, thinking is hard to study. We can try to infer what people think from what they do or say; but thoughts can only be studied directly by introspection. Ideally the two approaches should go together.

Introspection does have the advantage that it does not need expensive apparatus, and some of the earliest investigations can still be illuminating if repeated. For example, Francis Galton, the pioneer of the study of individual differences, was surprised to find such great variations in powers of mental imagery. He asked friends, by questionnaire, to imagine a familiar scene, such as the breakfast table, and then to say, for example, how vivid and detailed was their mental picture. For some it was almost as clear as the real thing; for others non-existent. One might ask oneself or others similar questions. How do you find your way along a familiar route? Is it by a mental image, or a series of instructions, or what? Or consider some of the other features of imagery Galton found in some subjects: do you see the calendar – year, month, day – as an image? do days of the week have colours? can you control an image – visualise a car, make it turn left or right, or change colour? Galton's account of these and many other effects is still worth reading, in his *Enquiries into Human Faculty* (1907 repr). Galton found no connection between imagery and other intellectual activities: currently, as mentioned in Chapter 2, the role of imagery in memory is a prime topic of investigation.

CHAPTER FIVE

Motivation and Emotional Life. Personality

Motivation

If we are going to understand our own behaviour or the behaviour of others, it is not enough to know the abilities and skills we have got, we also have to know what we are trying to achieve by means of these abilities and skills. It is not enough to know what the person can do, we also have to know what he wants and what he does not want.

We thus assume, and as a rule with good reason, that a person has a meaning or purpose in what he does; or put in another way, that a goal exists for his behaviour. In most cases, it is clear what the goal or the purpose is and in fact we have difficulties in describing the behaviour without at the same time pointing to the things a person tries to achieve. John is struggling to open the door, we would say if we observe John with a determined expression in his face and the hand firmly around the knob. It is very likely that this is also the way John experiences the situation – he has not locked the door on purpose to do some isometric muscle training.

If we attempt to describe behaviour without mentioning its purpose, it may very easily sound peculiar. The famous Danish psychologist Edgar Rubin gives the following example.

There was a man who went to his doctor to complain: "When I put my right hand forward and then move it back, while at the same time I put my left hand towards

my right hand shoulder after which I lean a little backwards and put the left hand behind my back and finally straighten up while again putting my left hand forward I have a terrible pain in my back." The doctor, believing it was the head and not the back that needed treatment suggested, "Would it not be possible for you to stop doing these movements?" The poor man answered quietly, "Yes but then tell me how I should manage to get my coat on."

Our experience of the purpose of behaviour may come so spontaneously, that we have often no time to look for different types of interpretation. If for instance, we see a young boy and a policeman running full speed along the street, but with just a few yards between them, we might get the impression that the first one is trying to run away and the second one chasing the first. The truth may be that they are both running for the same bus.

If contrary to expectations, we are not immediately aware of the purpose of some behaviour, we seem to feel a strong urge to find one. Few things may seem more frightening than behaviour without any observable purpose. This is also part of the reason why madness is frightening and perhaps also why psychologists, wanting to "understand" their patients, try to explain even the most peculiar acts as being "meaningful" from the sick person's point of view. In children we will find numerous

108

The goal of a driver's activity is among other things to get through the traffic. That this can be a strong, dominant motive we see from the feelings that can arise when the activity is frustrated.

examples of this type of curiosity. A man who was constantly moving some stones in his garden, turning them round to see where they fitted, was observed by a small boy who was passing. After five minutes of silently wondering the question came, "Are you removing them or are you putting them there?"

With simple conceptions of the behaviour we see, it is not easy to give a good explanation or to show sufficient understanding for what our fellow human beings in effect are doing. The five year old in the example above showed true psychological interest but very little psychological insight in asking his question. But very often we

just draw a hasty conclusion without even asking ("That man does not know *what* he wants."). The task of psychology in this connection could be to suggest how rich and many sided human motivation really is.

Is all behaviour motivated?

To say that a person has a motive for whatever he is doing is similar to saying that he wants something, or that his behaviour from his point of view has a purpose or a goal. Most of what we do has such a purposive aspect. Even an absent minded looking through the window or playing with one's pencil and rubber at the desk (when really I ought to be doing some serious work) may have a clear enough goal, namely to postpone some tedious or tiring work as long as possible. That the behaviour has a purpose does not necessarily mean that it is adequate.

The example above also shows that behaviour might be governed by a purpose even when the person in question is not fully aware of it. To want something does not necessarily imply that one knows what one wants. We might be conscious of what we are doing, but still not know why we are doing it.

It is nevertheless of importance to know the purpose. If we are able to see through ourselves and recognise our motives behind our fumbling about, it is more easy to do something about it and to choose another way of acting. The motive thus might come to have greater importance for behaviour when it is not conscious than when it is fully recognised.

We often only ask for motives when we are facing some new or unexpected type of behaviour. The cashier who runs away with the company's funds after 20 years of faithful service, makes us speculate about the motives he might have had. We ask, why did he do that now? We do not ask, why didn't he do it before?

We might ask if what we have mentioned here implies that we only need motives to explain the irregularities of behaviour and that the more regular, daily behaviour is not motivated. The answer is both yes and no. If by a motive we mean a reason in addition to behaviour, or a goal that goes further than the behaviour itself, it may make sense only to talk of motives in situations where a person changes the

The motivation to work may be no more than simply getting the job done.

Motives for choosing an activity and for going through with it are seldom the same. A stunt man may appear to be motivated by a wish to face danger rather than avoid it. Nevertheless he mobilises all his skill and power to come safely through the task he has set himself. Perhaps this is not so very different from our own lives when we put a great deal of energy into getting out of situations we have put ourselves in.

direction of behaviour or starts on something new. Someone who usually has no interest in books but who one day starts reading a large three-volume novel has some purpose in doing it. It might be that there has been so much talk about just this novel that his curiosity has been awakened or that he has started to become interested in a topic which that particular book deals with. These are good reasons to start reading, but are not necessarily sufficient to explain why one continues reading volume 2 after having finished volume 1.

The behaviour is still motivated if by motivated we mean goal directed. The goal does not necessarily have to be something outside the behaviour itself. By the expression "intrinsic motivation" we usually refer to something we are doing "for its own sake" such as swimming. Contrary to this,

"extrinsic motivation" is a term used when something is done for some end. Irrespective of what was the type of motivation that made us start doing something, we might prove very eager to finish some activity we have started. That this is more than a human tendency of continuing something for want of something better we see from the reactions which are typical when we are disturbed or interrupted. Sometimes we take the interruption as a well needed break, but sometimes we react by becoming irritated and show a tendency to continue where we had to stop, even if what we were doing was not as exciting as all that.

Some cases of problem solving are good examples of this. We sometimes rather reluctantly start on a difficult task, but now that we have started, and with the possibility of solution within reach, the motivation to go through with the task might be so strong that for some time other more basic needs may be set aside. In such cases, it is not only our curiosity to find the solution that makes us motivated. A helpful friend who at the critical moment comes to tell us the answer to save us from further trouble might probably not get much gratitude from the problem solver. The helpfulness of people often is not well received when it is not well placed.

The motivation to choose some activity and the motivation to go through with it thus may be of different kinds. Luckily, we might add, because the motives which make us start on something new are seldom strong and consistent enough to carry us through a long and troublesome project. Gradually also it becomes less and less new. To start sailing around the world or taking part in an expedition to the Arctic, may be motivated by a need for adventure, but if we are snowbound somewhere on a very freezing day or are fighting a storm in the Sargasso Sea, it is perhaps not the taste for adventure that makes us continue.

Behaviour thus may be steered by a purpose, even if we are not always aware of the purpose it serves and even if what we wish to achieve may vary. But this does not mean that unmotivated, purposeless behaviour never occurs. It is unreasonable to argue that a person who is trying to hit a nail and hits the thumb instead must have a motive for doing so, as for instance an unconscious wish to harm or punish himself. Nor can we reasonably maintain that a child who is crying in despair when the mother has said goodnight and left the room, cries with the purpose of terrorising its parents. In both cases, it seems inappropriate to talk about motives. If we insist on finding motives behind all kinds of behaviour, we have a sort of "psychologis-ing" instead of psychology.

Nevertheless, the striking with a hammer was goal directed. Only one did not hit the goal but missed it. And the crying of the child was perhaps due to the fact that the child felt helpless and prevented from doing something that could change the situation (a goal directed cry for help or comfort is not the same as a crying out in despair). Both children and adults may be able to endure a lot of pain and discomfort as long as we are able to look upon it as part of a goal directed and meaningful event. Going through a series of very demanding physical exercises to become a successful athlete or going around "constantly hungry" as part of a slimming programme are examples of this.

The relationship between motive and behaviour

Even when we are dealing with intentional types of behaviour where some motive lies behind our actions, it may be difficult to know which purpose the behaviour is actually serving. There is more than one reason for this.

1. The same motive may lead to very different types of behaviour. In the section about problem solving we said that a particular goal can be reached by very different routes. If our aim is to gain attention, this can be done both by showing exceptionally good behaviour and by behaving very badly. If one aims at being accepted at any cost the result may be that one will listen silently to the accusations of others; or, alternatively, that one attacks these accusations vigorously and tries to disprove them.

2. The same behaviour can be the result of very different motives. Why do I try to give up smoking? Is it because I am afraid of the possibility of getting lung cancer in the end? Or is it because my friends are constantly trying to make me follow their example? Is it because people who don't smoke at times look down on me or is it because I would like to save the money that smoking costs me for other purposes?

3. Behaviour nearly always serves more than one purpose. Strictly speaking it is not correct to ask about the "real" reason for any particular behaviour. Nearly always there will be different reasons. If some friends suggest that we should go out to have a meal, I might say yes because I'm hungry, because it is close to the normal time for my meal, because I'm not tempted by what I have at home, because I do not like to reject the proposal, because I want to talk to someone and because I don't fancy them talking together without me, and perhaps for all these reasons at the same time. With so many good reasons we may feel that the answer is overdetermined. It would be "yes" irrespective of how the question is put.

The example illustrates why it may be very difficult to describe the background for one's own actions and so very easy to give explanations which are not sufficient. Very often we tend to stress the more acceptable reasons for behaviour and forget about the more dubious ones. In psychoanalysis one talks in this connection about rationalisation. This refers to our tendency to find rational-seeming reasons for whatever we do in order to avoid being put face to face with the more irrational sides of our personality. In some cases the acceptable reason certainly may be part of the explanation. It becomes different when it is of very little importance or perhaps even added afterwards. The reasons behind our behaviour may often turn out to be so complex that one feels it to be more difficult to find the background for one's own actions than those of other people. The explanations we tend to give might be something we have added afterwards.

With what is called "post-hypnotic suggestion" we can see an example of this. The procedure may be as follows. When under hypnosis a person is told: a) that he will open a window shortly after having been brought back to normal functioning, and b) that he will completely forget that he has been given that order. Then when the person, who is now fully awake, really opens a window in the room, we may ask why he is doing that. Not being able to recall the order given under hypnosis, the person will explain his action by claiming that it is very hot in the room, or that fresh air is needed because so many people are smoking.

4. The purpose of the behaviour might lie on different levels. We often get the impression that the same type of behaviour can be given more or less extensive explanations. The achievement of a student in his school work might have been motivated by a wish to do well at the examination. In the next round a good examination result might serve the purpose of securing some further education. In its turn this education is determined by a wish to enter into some definite profession – and why just this profession – is it for the sake of a well-paid job or out of consideration for others? And what makes one put so much importance on for instance a good income, is it the fear of poverty, a wish to be independent, the possibility of doing something for other people, or the dream of a sailing boat or a cottage by the sea? In a similar way we can always react to an answer with a new why? and discover that purpose lies behind purpose, motive behind motive, until one perhaps discovers that one is going round in circles or has to stop by simply stating "because I want to".

Theories of motivation

Through the ages psychologists and philosophers have speculated a lot as to whether by constantly posing new questions "why?" one might find fundamental rules that hold for all motivation. Is it possible that irrespective of the type of behaviour we would in the end, be led to a small number of basic motives?

Through the years a lot of such basic forces have been referred to. In ancient times the Epicureans maintained that the basic motive always was to achieve satisfaction and avoid pain, whereas the Stoics argued that man, in the last instance is always seeking happiness. In the 17th and 18th centuries thinkers with critical views of society tried to show that all human behaviour was determined by the fight for riches, power and honour, or, in one word, self-interest.

Since the last century, and in particular after Darwin put forward his theory of evolution, it has become popular to look upon human behaviour from a biological perspective. In his view we have needs that secure the survival of the individual and needs that secure the life of the species (sexuality). This view had important consequences for psychology through Freud's theories which have become well known and hotly debated because of the central role given to sexuality as a factor of motivation. Freud also pointed to sexuality as something behind activities that are not usually thought of as sexual ones and he later proposed an even more fundamental division of the factors of motivation. Both sexuality and the survival of the self he grouped together under the "life instinct"

seen in contrast to what he thought of as a death instinct. This was thought of as a fundamental drive to destroy and put an end to things, even oneself, and this was the basis of all human aggression. Freud considered that the natural state of the organism, to which it always seeks to return, is one of inactivity. The ultimate goal of this is death. He based this on his knowledge of the neurophysiology of the time. However he formulated the "death instinct" partly as a result of the insanely destructive slaughter of the 1914–18 war.

Existentialist thinkers have given these drives opposite denominations, talking about a fundamental fear of living and a similar fear of dying, as a constant source of conflict and a background for our actions, choices or lack of choices. More optimistic personality psychologists have pointed to a motive for self-development or self realisation (self actualisation) as the most important and most unique of all human forces.

Such a list of fundamental motives perhaps tells more about the theorist than about human nature. In any case these theories cannot tell us much about what a human being in fact would do in a given situation. Perhaps it is correct to say that everyone is looking for happiness, but we haven't come far when we do not know what happiness consists of. And if we are told that all our activities are motivated by a need to realise our possibility, we don't know much until we are told which possibilities we are talking about. The variation from theory to theory, where different motives have the place of honour and where the number of basic motives may vary a lot, tells us something about the complexity of human nature and about the difficulties of finding simple explanations for the behaviour we see. Instead of presenting more or less detailed lists of our basic motives, we might perhaps take a closer look to see which types of motives would appear on a number of lists. We would then perhaps find two types of explanation of mechanisms of motivation. We might call them deficiency motivation and abundancy motivation.

Deficiency motivation

Much of what people or animals are doing obviously is aimed at satisfying certain needs. By needs we mean here a condition where the organism is lacking something of fundamental importance for its normal functioning.[1]

It is not difficult to notice the organic (biological) needs such as the need for food, the need for oxygen, the need to maintain a certain body temperature, the need to get rid of waste products and the need for rest and sleep. A lot of these needs are vital, meaning that they must be satisfied if the organism is going to survive.

It is more difficult to establish the fundamental psychological needs of human beings because we do not clearly see what happens when the needs are not satisfied, and also because the needs may be satisfied in many different ways. They also tend to vary somewhat from one person to the

1) Compare the discussion of problem solving in the last chapter where a problem situation was defined as a situation where something was missing. A need might therefore be defined as an internal problem (and a problem might perhaps in a similar way be described as a situation with certain needs).

When basic physiological needs are denied they tend to dominate behaviour.

next and from one age group to another. We might perhaps differentiate between a group of emotional needs, ranging from the need of a child for safety, care and love, to the need to find an expression for one's emotions, and social needs, as for instance the need to identify with someone, belong in a group and become accepted and understood at least by someone. Further there are the needs for activity and achievement that is needs to do something, to see that what one does has some effect, that one is capable of some performance; and finally, perceptual and intellectual needs which would be anything from sensory stimulation[1] to understanding and finding meaning for what is going on inside oneself and around one.

When so much of what we are doing can be tied to a need of some kind or other we might get the impression that a) a need would always lead to action and b) that actions can always be found to stem from some need, but this is to draw too hasty a conclusion.

a) To begin with it is important to discriminate between what a person objectively speaking needs and what he subjectively feels a need for. A person who smokes heavily ought to cut down on his use of tobacco but actually feels a need to light one. Unfortunately, we have no guarantee that what we need basically will be felt as such and motivate us in the correct direction. Some needs might not even be noticed, at other times we are aware that there is something wrong but we perhaps misinterpret it. Sometimes we

need a very long process of learning before we come to know our own needs. An interesting example of this we have in the so-called "cafeteria feeding" experiments. Here small children have been left to themselves, but being all the time under observation, and allowed to choose their food freely from a large variety of dishes. It has been found that even small children – in the long run – would "compose a diet" that is remarkably healthy. But on the other hand one has also found that some minor illness, or other irregularities in the situation quickly upset the ability to choose food according to what is needed the most.

b) Do we only take action when there is something missing? What then would a human being do when he or she has everything needed? If need fulfilment was the only goal in life, it would be too bad; in that case the person in question would then not have anything left to live for. Perhaps this could be seen as the reason why it is said that money does not make you happy – though it allows you to be miserable in comfort?

To work to satisfy one's needs and nothing more would in a way be to work in order to make oneself unnecessary. To create a balance in this picture we have to take a closer look at the next group of motives.

Abundancy motivation

What happens to a child who has had its last food and drink and is secure and satisfied? Nothing? On the contrary we would probably in most cases describe the child as very keen and eager to explore his surroundings, ready to do something, wanting to play, and perhaps with both greater and more varied activity than if he is tired and hungry. Experiments with animals such as rats have indicated that it may

---

1) Such a need may be illustrated by the fact that one of the most terrible forms of torture is isolation, not only from other human beings, but also from sensory impressions. This is one of the basic techniques of so-called "brain-washing".

Children do not stop being active when their basic needs are satisfied.

make sense to talk about a "curiosity motive". In situations where the animal has to endure some pain in satisfying its needs, e.g. receiving a mild electric shock when crossing a grill to reach food, the rat will be seen to be willing to take this "punishment" in order simply to explore the place with no particular goal in sight.

Such abundancy motivation plays an important role for behaviour. Our lives are not only spent repairing something, avoiding distress, and ensuring that there is no deficiency. Just as often we seek excitement, change, challenges, and entertainment. We do not do things only out of necessity but also from pleasure. In fact we sometimes create needs and deficiencies for ourselves artificially or give ourselves perhaps unnecessary goals and then oblige ourselves to follow rules of play that make

it rather difficult to achieve those goals. Hence the success of Rubik's cube. One young child solved this by unsticking the coloured bits and re-sticking them to make each side the same colour. But most of us accept the rules of the game. This we do because goal directed behaviour and achieving a goal in itself are experienced as something positive (compare play and competitions). At other times the activity is more attractive than the goals which are nothing more than an excuse for doing something. If every type of behaviour is assessed on the basis of what we might achieve, we would perhaps find a lot of things not worth doing, but then we would be overlooking the value of the efforts as such.

It seems reasonable to assume that there is little time for abundancy-based activity

117

as long as the central needs are not satisfied. This might mean that deficiency motivation has to be looked upon as more basic. In spite of that we often see people who choose some behaviour other than what is physiologically necessary, setting aside important needs in their pursuit of more or less a clearly chosen goal. For example, cutting down on food for the sake of going to a concert. The value we are to place upon the different goals of human beings in the last instance becomes a personal question.

Emotions

Motivational and emotional life are strongly tied to each other. Our behaviour may aim at *achieving* positive emotions and avoiding unpleasant ones and feelings of satisfaction, joy or disappointment may arise as *reactions* to whether we have reached a goal or not. But before going further along this line, we might take a closer look at what we are referring to when we talk about emotions.

In daily life we use the expression "feelings" about a series of experiences. They vary from something very faint to the strongest excitement; from the wildest joy to the darkest despair and from a short and passing emotional outbreak to a continuous basic mood.

The philosopher Bertrand Russell begins his Autobiography by describing, in a passage of noble honesty, the dominant emotions of his life: "Three passions, simple but overwhelmingly strong, have governed my life: the longing for love, the search for knowledge, and unbearable pity for the suffering of mankind. These passions, like great winds, have blown me hither and thither, in a wayward course, over a deep ocean of anguish, reaching to

the very verge of despair."

It is not easy to characterise such varied phenomena and we also find that most theories of human emotional life have a tendency to restrict themselves to certain aspects or emotions or to a certain group of emotions instead of others. If we say for instance that emotions disturb rational thinking and behaviour and thus ought to be under control, it is the strong, uncontrolled type of passions we are referring to and not for instance a feeling of peace of mind and optimism. Those who argue that human life would be intolerable and boring without feelings, forget that boredom is also a feeling.

If we try to identify something common to all these types of experience, it could perhaps be that they all in some way express our reactions to what is happening around us and inside ourselves. The emotional experience becomes a kind of counterpart to the more objective side of our experiences. If I hear someone play the piano in the flat next door, I could direct my attention towards the more objective fact, who is it that is playing? Is that piece an étude by Chopin? There is a wrong note. Now it's going better, apart from the fact that the tempo is very uneven. At the same time I might experience how all this is influencing myself. For a while it sounded rather nice. There is something special about music coming to one in this way, privately through the wall. If only the pianist hadn't been playing so badly! And the experience might change into a growing irritation, since it is impossible to turn off the noise. Some people certainly have no consideration for their neighbours. Now, in passing over from describing the external facts to describing how the music is influencing me, I have directed my attention towards the emotional experiences.

From the fact that our emotions are our

118

What feelings are being expressed by these people? The objective situation is that the family is watching their home being destroyed by fire. When the picture was taken firemen were carrying two dead children out of the house. The grandmother in the foreground is holding back the children's mother.

private reactions to what is going on, some important points follow.

A. Our emotional life has a very important role in what we call our self or our personality. By drawing a map of a person's feelings, what he reacts to and what kind of reactions we find, we see the uniqueness of the person. In contrast Science Fiction often imagines alien beings who, lacking emotions, lack the uniqueness of human personality.

B. It is difficult to predict the emotional reactions on the basis of the external situation alone. It is easy to become aware of which objects everyone would see as red ones, it is far more difficult to point to what kind of situations would make a person "see red".

C. Our emotional life is not something we can put aside. As long as we are engaged in something and this means something to us, everything that happens will have some emotional undertone, sometimes weak and at other times perhaps too strong; even if, very often, we cannot say why. "I do not like thee, Dr. Fell, The reason why I cannot tell, But this I know I know fall well, I do not like thee, Dr. Fell."

However, our emotions do not exist merely as conscious experience. They have also a very concrete bodily side which can show itself both through actions and facial expressions. Many strong emotions such as fear, involve characteristic physiological changes such as sweating, heart beating faster, etc. In psychology, we often use the word emotions instead of the word feelings, in order to avoid looking only at the internal experience side.

The emotional experience (feelings in a more narrow sense)

As is the case with thoughts, emotions do have their private side which may be even more difficult to put into words than is the case with thoughts. Most people would agree that feelings can be more or less pleasant and more or less intense. We would as a rule, also find that the feeling has a meaning or some direction. We are very seldom just glad or angry. We are glad because of something, or for something and we are angry with someone or because of something. Modern researchers in the field of emotions have stressed that a feeling will always contain an impulse to action. For instance a tendency to approach or withdraw from something that has given rise to our feelings in the first place. This impulse plays an important role when the question is whether we are going to experience excitement or anger or fear.

The subjective side of emotional life has often been looked upon as inaccessible to observation and as something unnecessary when it comes to explain and predict behaviour. Emotions in this connection, are looked upon as a sort of mental luxury, but if we consider our own definition of emotions as expressions of our own reactions and of our own condition, the emotional experience has an important function, namely to tell us how we are doing ourselves. Anxiety may signal that we are facing an external or an internal threat. A feeling of guilt may tell us that we have fallen short of our ideals, and so have lost something of great importance to us. By putting aside such signals, perhaps also refusing to experience them (emotional blocking) we may come to create great problems for ourselves. The alternative is not that we should react on the basis of each single emotional reaction, that would probably not be a very steady course, but we should at least be able to experience our emotions in order to make our decisions accordingly. In psychotherapy the task of the therapist is often that of helping the client to "go back" to some previous emotional experience, which the client did not react to in a healthy way at the time, to now giving the feelings a normal outlet.

The physiological reactions

The stronger the emotional excitement, the more we become aware that something is going on inside our body. We feel the heart beat faster, shivering, cold sweating etc., these reactions can vary from one feeling to the next and also from one person to another. Yet there are some common features to the reactions.

a. To a very limited degree we are able to control the reaction. Even with the best of intentions to stay calm and cool it is very difficult to prevent the mouth going dry and the knees shaking when suddenly one faces an overwhelming danger. This is connected with the fact that our emotional reactions to a large extent are governed by the autonomic nervous system which has its special centres in the brain stem and influences the internal organs, glands and non-striped muscles. It consists of two parts, the sympathetic and the parasympathetic parts and these two often have an opposite type of effect. Parasympathetic activity thus contributes in starting the pro-

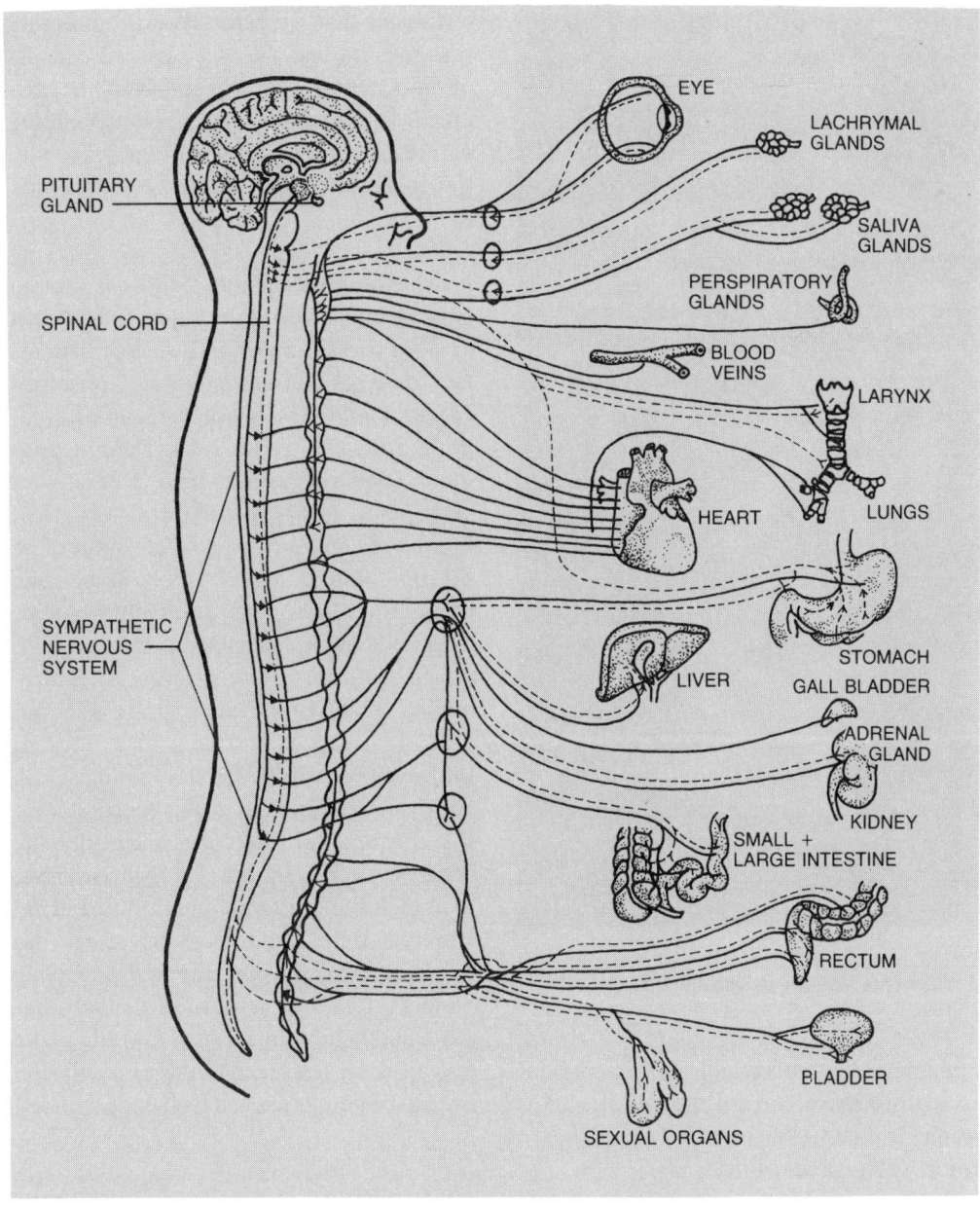

Schematic view of the organs connected with the autonomic nervous system, through which they will be affected by the person's emotional state. (The sympathetic nervous system is drawn with continuous lines whilst the parasympathetic system is drawn with dotted lines.)

cess of food consumption whereas sympathetic activity inhibits it. The sympathetic arousal increases the heart activity while the parasympathetic makes the heart beat more slowly. Emotional excitement also leads to hormones being fed into the blood stream and this may have similar effects.

When one's blood boils one may be ready for anything, but not always very constructively.

not mean that we can turn our emotional reactions on and off as we wish. Feelings, on the contrary, are very often experienced as something of an overwhelming nature, something of which one is the victim, something that is just carrying one along.

b. The bodily reactions follow a certain pattern and a certain sequence. To begin with the same organs and organic systems are part of most emotional reactions (heart, blood stream, the organs of breathing, stomach, glands etc.). The reactions often develop gradually, and interact with each other so as to lead to a very great excitement without any further input of an external kind. It may also take some time before the reaction has gradually stopped.

Thus there is truth in the old adage of counting to ten if one is trying to control oneself. If at first there is a strong reaction, we cannot expect it to be over as soon as the external situation has changed. A dangerous situation may be over so quickly that the fear is only felt afterwards, like the thunder after lightning. In such cases we tend to direct our excitement towards what has created the situation. A driver who has just escaped a collision may find his feeling of shock turn into rage towards the other party and behave in a way that would make one think he felt cheated out of a collision instead of being relieved by having avoided it.

Admittedly, we are able to some extent to learn how to control organic reactions by the technique of conditioning (compare the chapter on learning).

It has been claimed that various techniques of meditation, as for example in Transcendental Meditation (TM), can be used to lower blood pressure and heart rate, and there is indeed some evidence that this is so. But there is also evidence that purely psychological methods of relaxation are even more effective.

However effective they are, this does

c. The physiological changes prepare the body for certain reactions rather than others. A series of physiological changes that we find in anger and fear make the body capable of enduring more and performing more than before. The blood supply to the skeletal muscles increases; the heart beats quicker; the blood pressure increases; and the breathing becomes faster. Even the chemical composition of the blood is changed in order for the blood to coagulate more easily if some bodily harm should arise. The body thus is made ready for *fight* or *flight*. With a common name these reactions have been called reactions of crisis.

This is something which athletes among others know how to exploit. They speak of being "psyched up". If one is a little mad when entering the field, the chances are greater that the body will perform at its best, but at the same time the possibility of working in a very precise way is reduced. One would therefore be ill advised to ask a dentist to be a little hot blooded before working on his filling. Strong emotional reactions may also reduce one's attention. This might mean that we are less suited for tackling a situation where it is necessary to think well or to re-define the situation such as is often the case in problem solving.

The relationship between arousal and performance has been expressed systematically in what is called the Yerkes-Dodson Law. Increased arousal or tension gives better performance up to a certain point, after which any further arousal makes the performance worse.

The emotional expression

Emotional reactions do not only take place inside ourselves. As a rule we have no difficulty when looking at a person in discovering whether he or she is glad, angry or worried. On the contrary it sometimes is very difficult to hide one's feelings if that is felt to be necessary.

We may notice the person's feelings from his attitude, movement, the voice and not least the facial expressions. The basic forms of expression like laughter and crying, a mouth firmly closed or widely open, a raised eyebrow, a wrinkling of the fore-

head, do not have to be learned and may be understood across national groups.

But our external activities to a larger extent than the inner autonomic ones may be under some control. It is possible to develop this emotional language in different ways. We might for instance learn to stress or suppress certain reactions (a big boy does not cry), or simulate others (pretend to feel different from what we really do) and introduce special forms of expression (for instance movements of hands) that may vary from one culture to the next. In this way the smile for instance, in itself a

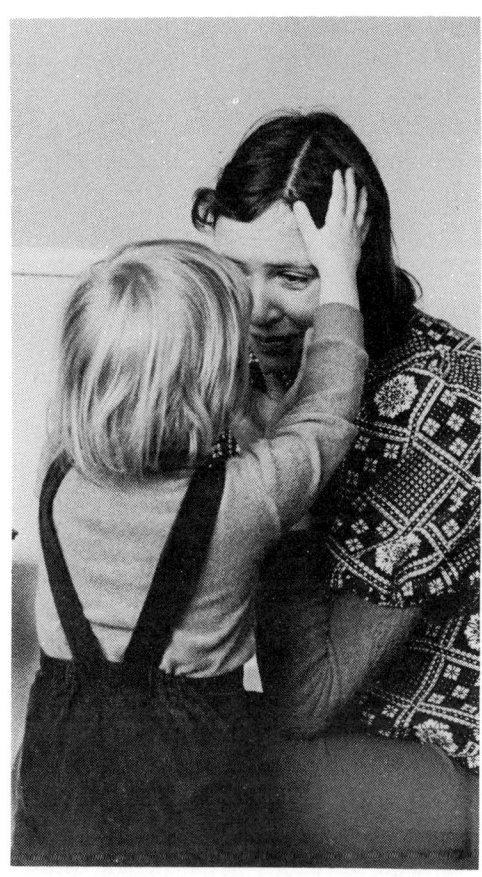

Emotional expression is often of great importance for how people relate to each other. The little girl can see that her mother is sad about something and also that it is of help to comfort her. Here neither smiles nor tears are in vain.

123

spontaneous expression of happiness and friendly feelings, may be used to portray feelings as different as pride and shame, mockery and politeness, stubbornness and encouragement, faith or doubts.

When despite all this we think we know what a smile is telling us, it is in part because we gradually have learned to recognise its many forms and are able to discriminate between an open and an artificial one, a bitter smile etc., and even more important is the fact that we are able to take the whole situation into consideration. Investigations have shown that when emotional expressions are taken out of context, as for instance in pictures where only the face is shown, our ability to judge others is greatly reduced. If we do not know the situation to which the facial expression is a reaction, we may have great difficulties in recognising anything but the more obvious emotional expression.

Emotional life and behaviour

A. Up until now we have described feelings as subjective reactions to stimuli which are closely connected to our motives. Schematically this might be shown in the following way.

Emotional stimulus → Emotional reaction
↑
Motivational condition

The figure shows that we cannot make conclusions about emotional reactions without taking the person's motivational condition into account. A push in the back which would normally be received in a friendly way, might elicit quite different emotional reactions if the person who is pushed is concentrating tensely before starting in the final of a 100 m race.

On the other hand emotional reactions may be used as cues to the motivational condition of the individual. They may signal both how strongly the person is motivated and which type of motivation is the dominant one. We would for instance find joy when a goal is reached, or, with deficiency motivation, perhaps a strong feeling of relief; whereas a blocking of goal directed behaviour may be experienced as a threat which would elicit anxiety.

B. But emotions are not only a type of reaction, they may also serve as stimuli and can lead to new activity. The emotions themselves may be motives for what we are going to do or not want to do because refraining from some action might also have its motives. We might draw this in the following way.

Emotional Activity → Behaviour

If we combine this figure with the last one, we might think of the following example. If I am motivated to reach a particular goal any obstacle becomes an emotional stimulus, it will trigger some emotional reaction like irritation, anger or despair. Anger, the emotional activity, in its turn may function as an impulse to continue with renewed force or produce actions not necessarily leading in the right direction. Often we will become more occupied with the obstacle than with the goal. Other emotional reactions as for instance an overwhelming feeling of lack of power, would have other behavioural consequences.

C. Emotions may also be described as a condition which does not in itself activate anything but which is part of the explanation of why we react in a different way to different influences. Many of the more quiet sort of feelings, bitterness, content etc are in themselves not strongly motivating ones but they partly influence our conception of a situation and the direction our reaction may take. The emotional condition has often been compared with a set of glasses, or coloured glasses, through which one sees the world: an optimistic person sees the world, as the saying has it, through rose-coloured spectacles.

The relationship might perhaps be illustrated like this.

Stimuli (Situation)	Reaction (Behaviour)
↓	↑
Emotional Condition	

Here we are assuming that the emotional condition determines the incoming and outgoing direction of the arrow. An example. A certain remark which in itself is completely neutral or innocent may be received in different ways acccording to the mood of the person who receives the remark.

Since a person's reactions also may be the emotional stimulus for other people we may easily set up a good or a bad circle, making a person's basic emotional attitude important to the relationship to other people and thus having an influence on his or her way of life.

Emotions and problems of adjustment

Some emotions may have greater and more serious consequences than others. As an example, we may mention anxiety.

Anxiety occurs when a person feels threatened, not only in the physical sense but just as often when our peace of mind or our self image is in danger. We may therefore react with anxiety in situations where we do not know what to do; in a strange and meaningless situation; when we run the risk of being overwhelmed by uncontrollable feelings or impulses or suddenly discover new and unknown sides to ourselves or our surroundings.

In its milder forms, anxiety acts like a signal of danger resulting in an increased potential for action. It may motivate to solve the problem or to handle the threat that was the basis of anxiety. In a negative direction, the feeling of anxiety may make it difficult for us to relax and in itself anxiety may become so unpleasant that we search for something to make us calm down and draw away our attention from anxiety. Some people have a tendency then to seek the company of others, while others wish to be alone. Some revert to a more childish or safer way of life or try to drown the internal unrest in hectic activity or entertainment, or drink.

It may become more serious if the anxiety is so great and persistent that the person has to build for himself different types of mental defence to get away from the threat without really having done anything about it. In its most primitive form, this may lead to some form of denial. A child who feels little and helpless, can state with great conviction "I am as strong as Daddy". To grown ups it may be more difficult to deny facts, we may nevertheless choose to ignore them, for instance by systematically forgetting things that may be embarrassing and unpleasant by suppression or by distorting the facts. Psychoanalytic theory describes such *mechanisms of defence* in detail. The basic mechanism is *repression* of unacceptable anxiety and what causes it. But though kept out of consciousness, it may be expressed in other ways.

The defence may take the form of reaction formation, where one tries to keep threatening and unacceptable feelings at a distance by going to the opposite extreme, as when someone who is not very brave, repeatedly tries to disprove this by some daring enterprise. Another mechanism is

125

Not all feelings stimulate to activity.

projection, that is to attribute to other people, tendencies one has difficulty accepting in oneself. A person who cannot recognise his own ambition may complain that other people are using their elbows to work their way. Such a twisting round of what is really the case is a means also suited to make one's own more dubious actions justified. In this case, we have an example of rationalisation, which we have previously mentioned as an effective form of defence. Some external threat may be brought under control by introjection, that is to accept its content as a part of oneself. Instead of feeling threatened by very strict parents one may start to become strict towards oneself. It is better to tell oneself "I wanted it" than having to admit "I had to do it". Not only anxiety but other unpleasant feelings as well, as for instance the feeling of guilt and feeling inferior, may lead to denial, repression and other forms of defence.

Personality

If we study processes like learning, memory, perception, thinking, motivation and emotional life each in their own turn, it is difficult to see the human being as a whole, but actually it is one and the same person who learns and remembers, thinks, senses and feels. A person has not in himself any feeling of being split into chapters the way a textbook necessarily has to be.

In the psychology of personality one seeks to collect these different threads into a whole. The concept of personality is meant to encompass the total pattern of the different psychological processes and the way they show themselves in the individual. In other words, the individual's characteristic ways of thinking, behaving and feeling. The psychology of personality thus deals with the connection between the different sides of mental life and the question of what is unique in one person compared to every other human being.

In both cases the motives and emotional reactions of the individual will play a central role. A theory of personality will often mean the same as a theory of human basic motives (compare the section on theories of motivation). A description of personality would often be one of the person's central needs and how these needs are formed and controlled (the character of the person). Not only which emotional attitude and types of reaction one would find (the temperament of the person) but also the person's abilities, ways of thinking, and the picture one has of oneself and one's surroundings are important components of personality.

Here we might pose a similar question to the one we posed in connection with intelligence. Would a person who is seen to have strong needs in one direction, also have strong needs in other fields? And will one who is seen to show certain emotional reactions in one situation behave in a similar way in other situations? Naturally, we cannot talk about a general personal factor in the same way as we can talk about "general intelligence". Personality is not something we can have much or little of. Rather what we might have a varying amount of is some trait of personality and because of the differences and partly also the contrasts between these traits it is not possible to have much of everything in this field. For example one cannot be both very arrogant and very humble. What we may ask is the question of whether there exist

certain connections or patterns in a way that would make us able to draw conclusions about certain qualities on the basis of the knowledge of one particular trait. Is it for instance, true that someone who does not talk much thinks more profoundly than others (still waters run deep); that someone who is fond of food and drink is extravert and that someone who very quickly becomes cross also very quickly returns to a good mood. Many attempts have been made to put together a number of personality traits into a picture and we then have what is called a psychological type theory.

Such attempts have been known from ancient times. Especially well known was the Greek-Roman division of human beings into the sanguine, phlegmatic, melancholic and choleric temperamental types. It was thought that the temperament was connected with a certain fluid of the body (as for instance blood, phlegm, black or yellow bile) which each could dominate the personality. Subsequent type theorists tried to find a connection between personality and different bodily traits, but as a rule without any great success.

One of the more popular has been that of W.H. Sheldon. This is based on measuring three aspects of physique: soft roundness, bone and muscle, and linearity and fragility. According to which is predominant, the individual can be classified as an endomorph, mesomorph, or ectomorph, and each of these is supposed to be associated with a certain sort of personality. Though this accords with folklore to a certain extent – the fat, jolly person, the thin scholarly person – it is not well supported by evidence.

A much more systematic theory is that of Hans Eysenck. This involves two basic dimensions: extroversion-introversion and stability-instability. These are founded, according to Eysenck, on basic properties

127

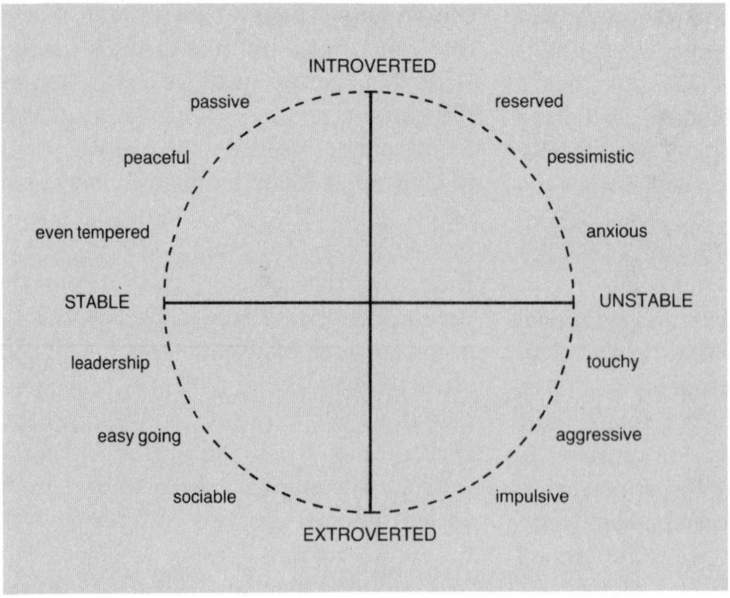

Hans Jürgen Eysenck's two-dimensional theory of personality, seen in relation to some typical traits of personality.

of the nervous system, which give rise to individual traits of personality and so to social behaviour. Taking the first dimension, the idea is that introverts condition more easily than extroverts. Thus they learn to be more careful, quiet, reserved; they learn the rules better, so to say. And thus they are less sociable, more law-abiding, less affected by alcohol, and many other characteristics.

This account, Eysenck claims, is not only supported by a mass of evidence but is consistent with the old Greek-Roman theory of the temperaments, which after all seemed plausible to many people for centuries. It is summarised in the figure above.

Much of what is more popular psychology is based on the assumption that human beings may be easily divided into a limited number of types. (In the more simple case this would be only two types: the bright ones and the stupid ones or the bad ones and the good ones. And perhaps also the abnormal ones and the normal people. Or

just us and them.) And one may think that if a person has been placed in a category one then automatically knows a great deal about that person. Easily noticeable traits, for instance how we dress ourselves, the interests we have, the way we greet other people or hold a cigarette, have been used as a point of departure for a comprehensive, but more or less fantasy based description of personality. Admittedly such descriptions which may appear in magazines or other forms of light literature are perhaps not taken seriously by most people. On the other hand, irrespective of how clearly done such analyses seem to be, they are doomed to fail for the simple reason that human personality has not been sent out into the market with a limited number of easily identifiable models.

In reality, it may be difficult enough to find out which traits of personality we can use in order to describe different persons, even if we do not count on each trait describing more than a limited part of be-

128

haviour and even if we do not believe that the traits have a firm connection to each other.

As an example we may consider a possible study of children's honesty where we want to test it in a number of ways. The first time such a study was performed by Hartshorne and May in 1928, the experimenters to their great surprise found that some children who were among the most honest in one situation, more easily fell for the temptation to cheat in another and vice versa. Even a trait as well defined as honesty may thus be found in more than one version. Similarly we would find for nearly any trait that it may vary with the situation. If for instance, we take shyness, we find that a child who barely dares to speak a word among strangers makes up

for it on its home ground and when it comes to the question of feeling sure of oneself, we naturally show more of it in a field where we feel at home than what is the case under circumstances where we are "all at sea". We also sometimes find that the person who is very dominating towards his subordinates is also one who is submissive towards his own superiors.

On the basis of such observations, some psychologists have been tempted to draw the conclusion that it is impossible to describe the personality of a human being. Or at least that it would involve a very long list of how the person would be likely to react in all thinkable and unthinkable situations.

Is the truth then that there are no connections between the different reactions of

On the football field it has become the custom for players to show delight by hugging and jumping on each other. It is most unlikely that these men, however joyful, would behave in the same way in any other circumstances.

Quite often we try systematically to build up our personality, even by physical means, though few go as far as this fellow, 5 feet 4 inches tall, who decided to add 16 inches to his height. Some would maintain that Napoleon, who was even smaller, was motivated by a similar need to become the greatest man in the world.

a human being? What we stressed in the beginning of this chapter was in effect that we had to look upon a human being as a whole. Much of what we do in our daily life is also based upon a conception of ourselves as one unique person with some particular qualities. Sometimes I would do things I don't really like only to be in accordance with the picture I have of myself, e.g. as being responsible, tough or original as the case may be.

To many people, and in particular in adolescence, it seems important to find this connection, in order to establish one's identity or type as it is called in more popular terms. The problem of the psychology of personality is that this connection very often is strictly private. One girl might think that it follows from her female identity that she has to be a little naive and helpless towards a person of the opposite sex, another thinks this is totally unnecessary; but the same girl who feels she should not take the initiative when with a boyfriend would perhaps at the same time feel that she ought to take the initiative when she is dealing with children.

We may thus talk about traits of personality without expecting a person to behave identically in all types of situations, and we may also try to find a connection between the different sides of a personality if only we are aware of the fact that the connection may vary from person to person. In a sense we are all good examples of personality types, if we are only willing to reckon with as many psychological types as there are human beings. In any case it is certain that in a new situation a) I would act differently from what I normally do and b) that I would act in my own way, different from what many others would do. Even if no one had seen me reacting like this before, someone who knew me well might be tempted to exclaim, how typical of you!

If after all this, we attempt to draw some general conclusions about human nature it must be something that suggests both possibilities and limitations.

1. We have at our disposal, a greater repertoire of ways of acting and behaving than we are aware of ourselves. These possibilities of actions are far greater than what we are able to show in a single situation and for that matter perhaps through a whole life.

130

This may be confirmed by noticing how quickly a person sometimes enters into new conditions of life, takes on new roles or changes his style according to the demands of the situation. An example is the rapid adaptation of people from less developed countries to Western ways once they are introduced. The thoughtless young girl we may meet again after a few years as a sensible mother, the kind and considerate father of the family we may meet in business life as a skilful and ruthless competitor. In particular it may sometimes be worth reflection when we see how differently a person behaves when he is alone with someone and when he is a member of some group (compare the chapter on social psychology).

2. But while our repertoire contains more possibilities than we are likely to imagine, we also can be sure that we cannot do just anything. Sometimes, we might be lacking qualities we thought we had. In some cases, we are not able to adjust to situations which in themselves seem simple enough. Our limitations might show themselves in areas and situations where we least of all expect it. It might be that sometimes we develop with the task we are engaging in (when the Lord appoints someone to some service he is endowed with wisdom as well). But this does not keep us from sooner or later having to face that there are certain tasks which we are not suited for. It may perhaps take little time before we discover that we literally were not cut out for the movements of a ballet dancer, but it may take months, or even years, to realise that we are lacking the stamina needed to become a top class long distance runner.

If we think that one condition of harmonious living is a fulfilment of the old saying, "know yourself", it would be wise to remember that this may also be taken to be a demand to know one's own limitations.

"At the same time, taking and passing a polygraph test could well become the spy's ticket to a successful Civil Service career."

With these words Mr Gerry Gillman, General Secretary of the Society of Civil and Public Servants, ended a letter to *The Times*, 6 December 1983. He was pointing out the difficulties in using the so-called lie detector in preventing threats to national security. There is, in fact, no machine that can detect lies and probably never will be. The polygraph records several physiological measures, such as heart rate and the galvanic skin response (an index of sweating) which are related to arousal. The theory is simply that someone trying to deceive a questioner will be more anxious, more aroused, than an honest man, and this will show up in the recording. The idea is not new. There is a very old story of a judge (sometimes a tribal chief) making those suspected of a crime chew a handful of dry grain. The guilty man cannot do it: anxiety inhibits saliva flow also.

As Mr Gillman points out in his letter, you can beat the lie detector. Training can enable someone to remain relaxed under questioning, or to pay little attention to the questions. (This would produce a false negative result, what psychologists know as a Type I error.) Alternatively, it is fairly obvious that even a perfectly innocent person may be quite anxious in such a situation, giving a false positive (Type II) error.

The lie detector is a current example in the news of the close interrelationship of emotion and physiology, and indeed of both with personality. Another that has caught the public interest is what has be-come known as Type A and Type B behaviour. In the 1960s two Californian scientists, Meyer Friedman and Ray Rosenman, reported that certain people typically showed a pattern of behaviour that was twice as likely to be associated with coronary heart disease as its converse. This pattern – Type A – involves a constant drive to compete and achieve, and continual sense of urgency to get things done, together with hostile and aggressive reactions towards those who get in the way. Those with this pattern characteristically speak loudly and fast, tend to interrupt others and are impatient of hesitations and delays. Type B is essentially the opposite, a more relaxed and accepting attitude. This was based on a study of 3,000 men in California who were studied over a period of eight years, and tested in a further study of 1,500 men in Framingham, Massachusetts. It is important to note that being Type A increases the risk of a heart attack independently of other known factors such as smoking, high blood pressure, and raised blood cholesterol. Thus it is not that Type A behaviour makes people smoke more, for example. What it does do, it seems, is to activate the sympathetic nervous system frequently and strongly; the well-known "Fight or Flight" syndrome. This has numerous effects. Heart rate and blood pressure increase; and the hormones adrenaline and noradrenaline are released into the blood stream. These in turn release fats into the blood which may help to clog the coronary arteries. Noradrenaline causes blood platelets to join together leading to blood clots which, if they occur in an artery which is already partly blocked, would constitute a thrombosis, with resulting heart failure. The evolutionary function of this, of course, is to ensure that external wounds stop bleeding rapidly. Noradrenaline also functions in causing the heart to beat regularly; an excess may disturb the rhythm dangerously.

Effects such as these are termed psychosomatic. It is the mind (psyche) that controls the stressed behaviour, but this directly controls bodily (soma) symptoms. Thus theoretically the matter can be tackled from both sides. Drugs can reduce the effects that the hormones have on the heart – in particular the now well-known "beta-blockers". But of course the question arises, can we change the behaviour, and thus perhaps remove the need for drugs?

There has been considerable advocacy of traditional body-mind techniques such as meditation, especially the variety known as transcendental meditation. There is indeed evidence that these can have a beneficial effect, but one must remember that they were not designed for the purpose. Their origin is religious or philosophical, and their basic purpose is to bring about certain spiritual experiences. It is likely that Type A behaviour will be more readily changed by modern psychological methods; and so it proves. For example, the Recurrent Coronary Prevention Programme, again in California, is designed to achieve behavioural change in Type A patients who have already had a heart attack. It has halved the rate of second attacks. The Programme works on multiple levels: Cognitive (What and How I Think) – this includes reflecting on what one is doing and why, is it really necessary, is what happens really a threat, remind oneself not to rush, etc; Behavioural (What I Do) – talk slower, interrupt less, listen more, relax physically, wait patiently; Environmental (Where I Live and With Whom) – discuss reactions with spouse, reduce over-exciting TV, do not take on additional burdens, talk to neighbours, etc; Physiological (How I Feel and What My Body is Doing) – cut down heavy meals and high-fat foods, avoid excessive alcohol, eat more often during the day rather than once at night, avoid physical exercise unless medically supervised, carry emergency medication (nitroglycerin). This summary merely indicates the nature of the Programme.

More generally, it is widely accepted that stress is a major factor in physical and mental illness. Type A people react to it more adversely. Stress came to general notice in 1956, when James Carter, a machine operator on the General Motors production line in Detroit, suffered a breakdown. He was later diagnosed as a paranoid schizophrenic. Unable to keep up with the flow of the line, he kept quarrelling with the foreman. Carter sued General Motors, arguing that management was responsible for an over-stressful job. The company replied that all work is stressful; but it was unable to say what it proposed to do about it. Michigan Supreme Court awarded damages to James Carter.

Stress control programmes have become an essential part of American management, and there has been a marked decline, in that country, of stress-related illnesses. In the UK, on the other hand, where there has been less emphasis on stress control, such illnesses have increased. Deaths from coronary heart disease at age 45–54, the vulnerable group, for example, show UK just ahead of USA at about 300 per 100,000 of the population (1978), Norway and the Netherlands are at about 200, Japan about 20 (yes 20). Other stress-related illnesses include ulcers, skin disorders, asthma, bowel complaints, back pain, sleeplessness. Of course stress is only *one* factor in *some* of these cases. Beyond this, however, "Neurosis" is the leading diagnosis by family doctors in the UK at 355 patient interviews a year per 1000 population (1983). About half the drug prescriptions in western countries, are for sleeping pills, tranquillizers and anti-depressants.

Of course life cannot be lived without stress. It is a matter of how it is managed and of the conditions that produce it; in other words, of human behaviour. We have mentioned the old established Yerkes-Dodson principle of the optimal relationship of arousal to performance. Michael Apter, a psychologist of University College Cardiff, and others, have recently taken a new look at this in developing what is termed Reversal Theory. He illustrates this with some everyday examples: "First of all reflect, if you will, on what it is like to be in a dentists' waiting room, about to have a filling. Focus in particular on the kind of arousal which you feel. Now imagine that you are soaking in a hot bath after a hard day's work, and again try to conjure up what the arousal which you experience in this situation feels like. Next, make believe that you are waiting for a bus which is taking a long time to come; you are not in a hurry so that there is no pressure of time, but you have nothing to read or take your attention. Finally, imagine yourself to be in a cinema watching a thriller film and this film has

reached a particularly tense point. I think you will agree that the arousal feels different in some important sense in each of these cases."

The differences can be expressed as values of two dimensions. Unpleasant high arousal we recognise as anxiety (or stress); pleasant high arousal as excitement. Unpleasant low arousal is boredom, and pleasant low arousal, relaxation. Now, Apter goes on, motivation can often be seen as an attempt to move along one of these dimensions: when bored we seek excitement, when anxious we seek to reduce anxiety. But if we go too far, we will switch back again from pleasant to unpleasant. These switches are the "reversals", which according to the theory typically happen very rapidly, and in many cases frequently, so that one's mood fluctuates. Apter gives as examples such things as receiving an unexpected telegram, or inviting an attractive person out to lunch. There are also the many rather puzzling cases where we do something, such as mountain climbing or parachuting which, looked at objectively, would seem to be quite unpleasant. There is real danger but, once mastered, this leaves a degree of arousal which is experienced as excitement.

Apter now goes further, and suggests that individuals tend to prefer one mode of reaction over the other: some of us are more inclined to seek excitement, some are more consistently motivated by avoiding anxiety. The theory next distinguishes between two sorts of activity: those where one is trying to achieve some goal or end, called *telic* activities (from the Greek "telos" end); and those done for enjoyment or "for their own sake", like games played for fun. These are termed *paratelic*.

People vary in their predisposition towards one or the other. One can see that this is somewhat like Type A and Type B. In the telic state, arousal is unpleasant (stressful); but in the paratelic state arousal is pleasant – the enjoyment of risky sports, for example.

Reversal Theory, only the main points of which have been described here, has applications in several ways. For example, in family therapy. It often happens that children are paratelic – enjoying play – while parents are telic – trying to get something done, such as cleaning the house or a DIY job. High arousal is then enjoyable for the children, but their noise and mess also create high arousal for mum or dad, which is stressful. Reversal theory can be used to assist if such situations become too frequent. It offers an *explanation* to parents of why the situation makes them anxious. It *reassures* them that the behaviour of both themselves and their children is perfectly normal. It helps them to *communicate* more effectively: for example shouting at the children may just increase the arousal which they are actually finding enjoyable. And it suggests that the best tactic may be to *re-direct* the child's energies rather than try to change from paratelic to telic; arrange for the child to join a sports club, say. Even watching TV or playing video games might serve. Such games do increase arousal, as has been found by Dr Douglas Carroll, a psychologist at the University of Birmingham. But, as we might expect, the effect is greater in some people than in others.

This applies too when we consider how people perceive violence on TV. There is a good deal of evidence that watching violence on TV can lead to increased levels of personal aggressiveness and social outbreaks of violence. But perhaps the first questions concern what is seen as violent, and by whom. Two researchers, Barrie Gunter (another former student of JKR) and Adrian Furnham, started with this question in a report published in 1983. Their subjects were forty ordinary members of the public from the Oxford area, not a representative sample but a fairly random selection by sex, age, and social class. They were shown a total of forty-five brief TV scenes in four sessions. Each scene was 30–70 seconds long and portrayed a complete violent action sequence. The scenes were taken from five categories of programmes: British crime-detective series (The Professionals, The Sweeney); American crime-detective (Kojak, Mannix, Starsky & Hutch); a Western film (Cannon for Cordoba); science fiction (Buck Rogers, Star Trek); and cartoon (Mighty Mouse). Subjects were asked to rate each scene on eight 7-point scales: Violent, Realistic, Exciting, Humorous, Likely to Disturb People in General, Suitable for Children, Frightening, and Personally Disturbing.

Subjects also completed the Eysenck Personality Questionnaire. This gives measures of several personality traits based on the work of H J Eysenck. In particular, Eysenck's theory of crime and personality suggests that criminals and delinquents tend to score highly on traits of Neuroticism, Extraversion, and Psychoticism. High scorers, the theory predicts, will also be less likely to perceive TV portrayals as violent, disturbing, or antisocial.

These subjects, of course, were not criminals but ordinary members of the viewing public. The results were statistically complex. In general, violence in contemporary drama settings was rated as more serious than when it was in a non-contemporary or cartoon setting. This effect was particularly marked with subjects who scored high on Neuroticism: effectively, more emotionally sensitive people. In other words they found violence more upsetting, especially when in a contemporary setting. Furthermore, they tended to see most of the settings as more realistic than did low scorers. Those who scored highly on both this trait and Psychoticism, however, tended to be more disturbed by most types of violence.

This is just one attempt to unravel the complexity of an important social question. It will not do simply to assert that TV does or does not have this or that effect. There is no substitute for patient investigation. What does seem clear is that we must look, not just at TV programmes themselves but at the viewers. "One man's meat is another man's poison" is one of the bits of traditional wisdom that can fairly confidently be said to have a good deal in it.

CHAPTER SIX

Social Processes

Introduction

Scarcely any human being or any human action can be understood without considering the other people present and the social situation in which the behaviour takes place. Even an objectively performed experiment in perception or memory is built upon a series of inter-personal conditions, as for instance that a person who is the subject will do what the experimenter tells him to do; that he will try to do his best and not ask irrelevant questions. In Chapter 1 we saw that such expectations may create problems in interpreting the results, since the subjects in some cases, perhaps without even being aware of it may come to answer in a certain way because they believe that these are the answers the experimenter wants them to give (the Rosenthal effect).

We have also seen that it may be difficult to explain behaviour completely on the basis of the uniqueness of a single human being. If the external social situation becomes different, habits and meanings which we thought were stable for the individual may undergo dramatic changes.

Some social psychologists would argue that even forms of behaviour which are constant over long periods, and which may seem to be typical for a certain person, to a large extent may have their roots in the social environment of this person. Maybe our surroundings from day to day are as responsible for our normal day to day behaviour as they are when we sometimes behave very differently from what we normally do. We might experience this particularly strongly if sometimes we feel a need to behave differently from what we usually do. It might be a case of really breaking loose and "doing one's own thing", or it might be pulling oneself together and trying to start a new and better life. In both cases, we may notice how the expectations of others and their reactions can hold us back, forcing us along the old trail.

The individual in the group

The influence other people have on the person is most easily seen when we compare the behaviour of someone who is alone or thinks himself to be alone with the way the same person behaves when there are more people present.

Many human activities are normally dependant on a number of people taking part. Nothing much in a normal case comes out of talking to oneself. The presence of others can also bring about emotional reactions, think for instance, of the roar at a football match. The more spectators there are and the closer together they stand, the louder each of them would shout. Laughter is also a typical socially determined reaction. If one is the only one watching a movie in a large auditorium one wouldn't laugh much even if the movie was a very

In some situations behaviour is dependent on the presence of many people, but this does not mean that everyone behaves in the same way.

funny one. With crying, we often find the opposite, at least in our culture, where one normally tries to be brave when other people are present. In small children however, we often see that crying also has an interpersonal function. They often cry more bitterly when mother or father appears.

In other cases, our reactions would be inhibited by the presence of others. Think for instance, of how patients behave in the waiting room of a doctor. Very few are brave enough to do more than take a few steps to pick up a magazine, and one has to be particularly brave to turn on the light or to open a window.

The task of behaving "properly" to a large extent consists of being able to discriminate between what one can do when alone and what would be suitable when other people are present. We are dealing here with a complicated pattern of un-

written rules which we sometimes have difficulty in passing on to the younger generation (and which we sometimes also have difficulty in explaining). Some of these rules of behaviour might in fact also create problems in situations demanding initiative and resolute behaviour, as for instance in the case of an accident where no one feels it as his or her task to take action.

Only in part will we be able to interpret the phenomena of social psychology if we build all our understanding upon differences between the behaviour of people when they are alone and when they are in the company of others. We belong to a social group even when we are alone. Both what we are doing and what we are thinking are influenced by our relationship to others: what we feel that other people would expect and what we wish to demonstrate. This will hold true for a writer who seeks loneliness to be able to work and to get away from the influence of others, and it also concerns someone who finds a quiet spot to write a letter. In both cases the expectations of what the reader may think, to a large extent forms or influences what is written down. Even a person writing a diary for himself may discover that it is difficult to escape the thought of someone reading it later on. It is for instance, difficult to put on paper thoughts that even an understanding friend would not be able to accept. Even behaviour that aims at cutting off the person from society, would be coloured by the thought of "the others". From this point of view, even suicide may be seen as a social act, that may express everything from protest and revenge (they had it coming) to a desperate and at worst unsuccessful cry for help.

Moreover, we cannot fully understand how we are influenced by others simply by observing how behaviour changes when there are people around one. We also have to take into consideration which types of people we are talking about and even more important, the type of social situation in which they find themselves. It is for instance, of great importance whether they make up a "group" or whether it is just a collection of people who happen to be in the same place.

Within social psychology, the concept of group is used where two or more persons have something in common as for instance a common goal or common needs. They would further have to feel a certain degree of togetherness and there must be some interaction between them. In a social group we would nearly always find a certain division of labour and it would be more or less clear who is going to take the initiative and who is keeping in the background to await further orders in each case.

The difference between what is only a number of people (often called an aggregate) and what is within social psychology referred to as a group, may be illustrated by a number of passengers standing at a bus stop. That they do not constitute a unit even if standing at the same spot, we can easily see from their behaviour: they are not talking to each other and they try to avoid looking at each other as well. It is typical that when two people accidentally chance to look into each others' eyes, they quickly look in another direction. Eye contact normally is an invitation to some interaction. The closer one is standing to someone else the more careful one is in looking around.

Despite this, the passengers have something in common. They are all standing at the bus stop for the purpose of making a short or a long trip on a bus. So perhaps we might take this collection of people as the point of departure when we want to illustrate how groups are formed and say something about the rules of group behaviour. Let us assume that the bus stop lies outside town and that there is only a bus connection a few times each day. The passengers standing there are people wanting to take the bus to work. Let us further assume that the bus for some reason does not appear at the usual time. What would then happen?

If we know our patient passengers, some time might elapse without anyone doing anything in particular. But as time goes by without the bus showing itself we would gradually see the building up of some connection between the persons. It may start by someone giving his expression to his anger over the delay. Others would nod agreement with his comments on the bad bus connections in this place. More people would say something and express their dissatisfaction with the service. Each indi-

To have nothing to do with each other is also an inter-personal relationship. It may show itself by people trying

vidual feels that here is a group of people badly treated. The passengers have in common that they are all suffering because of the other party, the bus company.

We see here an example of how people may be brought together when they feel they have the same enemy or opponent. Nothing contributes more to strengthen a group than some attack from outside. In our example, the passengers might have felt dissatisfaction with the company for some time. The long delay this time might lead to the forming of an action group with the purpose of negotiating with the bus company for better service.

If the bus is delayed for a sufficiently long period of time, we might see illu-

strated nearly all facets of group formation and group activity. A common goal or a common need may as we have seen, be the point of departure, but some organization of the work of the group is also needed. Someone is perhaps the natural leader who more or less spontaneously takes on the task of leading the action. Others are willing to do their part on the basis of decisions made by the group. A distribution of the tasks, where everyone does his or her job, is an important side of group behaviour. The next step is the development of norms and rules, both for the leaders and for the subordinate members of the group. We say that the different members of the group are taking on or are falling

not to look at each other and by keeping as far apart as the space allows.

into different roles and for each role we have a set of role prescriptions. There are not always written rules of how to organise the activity, even if often we do find examples of this (rules of procedure, instructions for certain jobs etc.). In our example it might be understood without so many words having been said that no one is going to do anything improper or that the leader must consult the others before anything important is done.

The example is meant to show how a social group is often formed on a spontaneous, informal basis and at the same time we have illustrated a number of the basic criteria of a social group, common aims, an organisational structure, rules of be-haviour, roles etc.

It is often said about social groups that they consist of people who have a connection that lasts for some time, but this is something that would vary from one case to the next. Some of the groups of which we are members have a more permanent character than others and it is also possible to talk about different types of social groups according to some other criteria.

The family is for most people the most important group and also the one of which one first becomes a member. In social psychology this is called a primary group. In a primary group each individual member has a close and personal relationship to the others and is often in daily

141

contact. This is not the case in more secondary groups as for instance the union we belong to. A union as for instance the association of teachers, is also a social group. In contrast to the more accidentally formed group of passengers the union can be described as a formal group.

We also sometimes differentiate between membership groups and reference groups. The first type refers to all the groups where we more or less directly are a member, whether it is a primary group or a secondary one, formal or a more informal group. A reference group on the other hand, is a group with which we identify ourselves without having to be a member. The reference group might for instance be the football team we support or the political faction representing our own point of view. To break out of a group in which we don't feel at home or to be able to have meanings and ideals which are different from the rest of the members, we usually need a strong identification with another group, which in this case would serve as the reference group.

The individual's dependence on the group. Conformity and group pressure

When groups are formed or when we enter into groups that already exist, it is often because of the practical use we have for the group membership. The group might for instance achieve results that are far beyond what is possible for the individual member. "United we stand". This holds true in particular for most secondary groups which are often working towards a concrete goal, as is for instance the case with unions taking care of the economic interests of the members among other things.

Group membership, particularly of primary groups, satisfies a number of fundamental emotional needs. Maybe the feeling of belonging somewhere and knowing that one is not alone is the most important one. Some would argue that this is a need that is biologically based and that it is part of nature to live in a group. Man is a social animal, Aristotle maintained more than 2000 years ago, but we can also

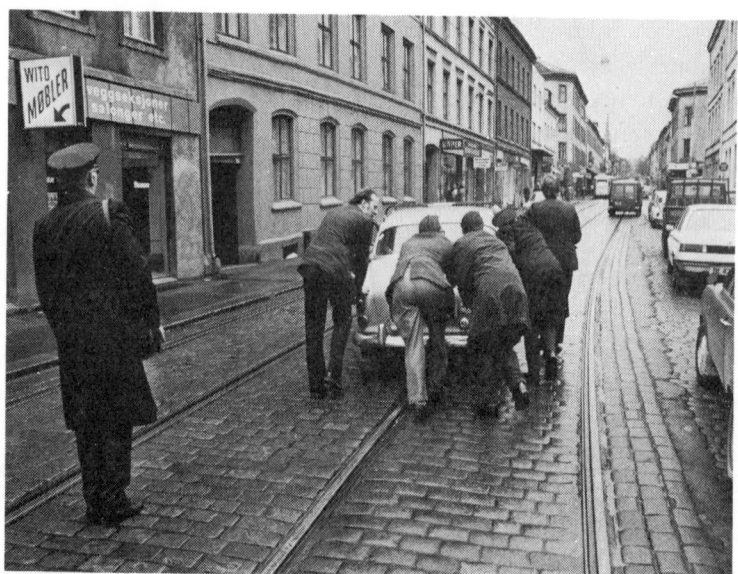

An unforeseen obstacle may lead to the formation of a group among people who otherwise have nothing to do with each other. Here the tram driver and the passengers are united in the struggle against a common enemy, a car on the tramlines.

Through supporter clubs, those who do not take part in the sport itself may participate in triumphs and defeats and at the same time give their team substantial and sometimes earsplitting emotional support.

point to the fact that the human being has a very long period of upbringing and dependency that might perhaps create the need to have people around one, someone to trust and to feel accepted by. The feeling of safety and that of acceptance are thus two important parts of the need of belonging. The group is also necessary for the picture we form of ourselves, for our self confidence and the feeling of being important. Sometimes we seek the membership of a group in a struggle for status or prestige.

But even if the need for belonging and the need for prestige are related they may come into conflict. It is not far from the individual's wish to be accepted, to a wish to be looked up to or to a hope of becoming popular. And similarly there is a short step from wanting to have something to say, to claiming to have much to decide. But to the group itself the need for prestige and status may represent a threat because

it means rivalry and competition. All may be accepted but everyone cannot become a leader.

One way of solving this problem is to look upon the group as a whole as something better or more important than anything with which one compares it. The members of a school class have very seldom chosen to be together but they nevertheless look upon themselves as a chosen group as compared to the pupils in the next room. In this way, one may be able to secure the feeling of togetherness and at the same time let everyone have the feeling of status.

Another way to regulate the need for prestige is to establish a status hierarchy within the group such as to make everyone know his place. Such a hierarchy we can observe among hens or chickens and we find it in a number of species living together in groups and, where it otherwise would very easily come to a fight about

143

who should have the first right to food, territory or the choosing of partners. The advantage of a more or less firmly established rank order is that one may reduce the open fights to a minimum. It is typical of a hierarchy that the greatest conflicts take place among members who find themselves on roughly the same level and who therefore easily see each other as rivals. Towards persons who are definitely below oneself one can afford to be gracious without risking misunderstanding; and towards the people who are further up one may act in a modest and subordinate way without feeling degraded. But such a system obviously can only work if it is accepted by everyone and not only by those who have got a place at the top.

What is the cost of group membership?

Since belonging to a group may provide both material advantages and satisfaction for each member and contribute to satisfying important needs like acceptance and prestige, it is not strange that participants can be willing to pay a lot for their membership. The price can be valued in time, money, and amount of work, but it may also be of purely psychological nature. We can agree to sacrifice previous friendship and sympathies and take on certain attitudes and meanings which are common in the group in which we seek membership.

How can it be for instance, that extreme groups of a religious, political or criminal nature, can come to achieve a complete control over their members without using any physical threats or force of any kind?

The secret seems to be a very simple one, even if the means might vary from one occasion to the next.

1. It is important to isolate the group members from the company of anyone who thinks otherwise and to portray others as enemies or as potential supporters whom the group may try to recruit or persuade to change their views.

2. Each single member of the group must experience a clear emotional profit in the form of acceptance, belongingness and a feeling of having some importance (in particular if she or he identifies wholeheartedly with the group).

3. It is also of great importance to have the members sacrifice much for the group. A member who spends much time and effort on group work is gradually more and more tied to the group. It is as if the person is telling himself: when I have done all this for the group, it has to be important. An experiment has shown that a group where the participants had to go through an ordeal to become members was afterwards evaluated as far more valuable than an equivalent group where one only had to register to become a member without having to go through any particular task.

Our need for group membership and group identification is so strong that we sometimes find that a form of sympathy develops between say hi-jackers and their hostages, if they have been together for some time isolated from the rest of society.

The power the group has over each individual member shows itself as a pressure to conform, that is a demand for common opinion and similar behaviour. The American social psychologist Solomon Asch is well known for a study that demonstrates this. The subjects, who thought they were taking part in an experiment on perception were asked to assess which of three different lines a, b, or c, was as long as a fourth one, a standard line s. To begin with Asch had demonstrated how easy it was to choose the right line if each single subject had the opportunity of answering without

What is seemingly a fight between two individuals may be dependent on the group behind them. The attacker also needs a friendly audience, and anti-social behaviour has a social context.

the influence of others, but in the experiment the participants were put together in a group and asked to answer in turn. Before starting the experimenter had instructed all except one to choose the same, wrong line. When the uninformed subject's turn came, it was found in most cases that he didn't believe his own eyes, but answered the way the others had done before him. Only about 20% of the participants managed to withstand the group pressure.

What was it that had really happened? Afterwards the whole affair was explained to the subjects. Many of them said that they felt sure the others were wrong but that they nevertheless had answered in the same way as the majority in order "not to make any trouble". Some of the subjects on the other hand had been convinced that

the others were right and a few even declared that they had themselves seen the lines in the way described by the others. Asch also studied whether the size of the group played any role and concluded that 2 against 1 could mean as strong a majority as a group with 9 participants. If the uninformed subject on the other hand was given some support if only by one of the other participants, it very soon became more easy for him to stick to his own original opinion even with a large number of subjects seemingly having another view.

The strongest man in the world is he who stands alone, says Dr. Stockmann in Ibsen's play "An Enemy of the People", but then one might perhaps notice that Dr. Stockmann feels sure that whatever happens his wife and children would be on his side.

Leadership

If the group is going to exist and achieve something for its members, it is not enough that the group participants share the same views and agree to what the majority decide. The group must also reach its goal and the participants have to feel satisfaction.

We may differentiate between groups which are mainly subject oriented where the goals and the activity are the most important things, and groups where the cause as such is of less importance and where the feeling of satisfaction and pleasantness on the part of the members is what really counts. This may be the case in groups where people come together to enjoy each others company, when playing cards, knitting or sewing etc. Most groups have elements of both kinds. Admittedly one may find subject oriented groups acting under some pressure such as to ignore the feelings of the participants (as for instance a rescue team or a company in battle) but if the group is to survive, one cannot one-sidedly be occupied with achieving results. It has been found that effectiveness is also reduced if the members are not enjoying themselves in the group. On the other hand, we may notice that as a rule people enjoy themselves more in groups where something has to be done. It is not always successful to come together simply to enjoy life.

To ensure that the group solves its tasks some leadership is necessary. Within social psychology leadership is not something that has to be taken care of by one single person; not even in groups having a more or less officially elected leader. It may be that the formal leaders are only taking care of the subject oriented matters whereas the other members of the group are looking after unity and satisfaction – perhaps sometimes with some opposition from the leader. Let us take a closer look at what the different aspects of leadership involve.

Subject-directed leadership consists in defining the tasks of the group and the goal to be achieved. This is something that may have been decided even before the group come together. It can also be one of the reasons why the group was formed (compare the example with the passengers at the bus stop).

This is also a question of planning what means the group is to use and in which order. Further, decisions have to be made, initiatives must be taken to implement the decisions, different tasks must be distributed among the members, and someone must oversee the work of the members. Sanctions must also be taken (distributing rewards and punishment) where this seems to be necessary. Sometimes some expertise is also needed, someone has to know in what particular way the tasks ought to be done and somebody must be prepared to handle the relationship to other groups. People outside the group must have someone to turn to who represents the group.

Here we have mentioned some important factors in leadership but we would naturally be able to find variations according to the nature of the group and the tasks that are to be solved. The different aspects of leadership are most clearly seen in large, formal organisations. Here they may be tied to special jobs or bodies. The different functions may be divided between a board, a general manager, a group of secretaries, consultants, inspectors, and representatives; and on the top of this co-ordinating, consultative and decision making bodies of different kinds. In smaller groups we will often find one single person who is appointed the leader of all the central functions of the group. The leader of a course may for instance be appointed because of his knowledge in the field and have as his primary task to give the participants professional support. It is also assumed that the leader must be the group's representative towards outsiders and take the initiative to get help if for instance one of the members of the course becomes ill. (We find here that group pressure does not only induce conformity; when a problem arises we immediately see a pressure on the leader that forces him or her to take the initiative.)

The emotional functions of leadership may be more difficult to define. Among the most important things is working to strengthen the unity of the group and give the participants a feeling of belonging together. For the group it is also important to find quick solutions to inner conflicts and tendencies to fight; and each individual participant must be encouraged and supported and be given possibilities to satisfy his own individual needs. It may often be very difficult for the former leader to combine his working with the subject with this type of leadership, but the leader may sometimes strongly contribute to the identification of the members with the group, in particular if the person in question has qualities that may make him or her into an ideal or symbol as we see it in some of the great leaders of history. The wise leader also knows how to contribute to the unity of the group by sometimes functioning as a scape-goat if no one else takes that particular job. A scape-goat is someone who may be given the blame when something goes wrong, in such a way that the other members will not let their disappointment and irritation destroy the internal relationship.

Sometimes it may be something of a

What sort of leadership tasks have to be undertaken by the staff in a nursery school? Are they different from those of a senior school-teacher or a parent?

Adolf Hitler making a speech. The Führer fulfilled a very special leadership role for his supporters.

dilemma for the leader to decide how much he is to concentrate on the task of the group as such and to what extent he must concern himself with the emotional needs of the members. In such cases the way the group perceive the leader is of importance. The popular teacher who places more importance on his pupils having a good time than on their mastering of the syllabus may in the end discover to his great surprise that his popularity has declined and that no one is really thanking him for his job. We often find therefore that two different persons take care of the two kinds of leadership. In an informal group, we often find one member who to a larger extent than the rest is eager to get things done (and who is also elected chairman or leader) whilst another member is much more clever at creating a good atmosphere, and putting into words what needs to be said when the atmosphere

becomes a little tense. If we look at the family group, we will find that the leadership roughly speaking is divided between the parents. It is part of the traditional role of the father to be concerned about the subject matter while the mother concentrates more on the emotional functioning, giving comfort and creating a feeling of safety. Of course in many cases these traditional roles are changing, but both functions are still necessary.

What is it that characterises the ideal leader? Is it possible to talk about the "born leader"? It is not very realistic to imagine that anyone can take on all the functions of leadership mentioned above. A more likely conclusion would be that the demands of the group towards the leader will vary considerably with the way the group is structured and with the tasks at hand. Sometimes it may be the ability to do administrative work, in other cases it is courage and the ability to make quick decisions and at other times understanding other people would constitute the most important qualifications.

Some features of leadership we would find in the majority of situations. Usually we find for instance that the leader must have the ability both to influence others and to be influenced himself by the view of others. In spite of this very few people would really argue that one who has the necessary skill to become a good officer will necessarily also be able to do a good job in a nursery school or host a teenage party.

To continue the old discussion whether the qualities of leadership are inborn or not is therefore of little use. As we have said it is a question of a long series of qualities some of which are very different from each other and even to some extent of a conflicting nature.

Roles and role conflict

A great deal of our behaviour seems to be governed by more or less clearly formulated rules and expectations. This holds true both when we are together with other people and when we are alone.

Rules may vary from those which are put down in the form of a law, to rules which are only accepted as common ways of behaving towards others. Usually everybody has some faith in people's keeping of the rules. For instance I may maintain my driving speed into a junction where I see the green light, trusting that the driver approaching from my left will respect the red light he sees (a quick look wouldn't harm anyone, though). We would also be surprised if when putting out our hand to greet someone, the other should refuse to shake it. These are examples of rules that are followed by everyone within a particular culture. It is expected from everyone that they answer questions, keep promises and don't drink directly from the soup bowl without using a spoon.

Other types of expectations are in connection with single individuals. It is for instance expected of Peter that he should hand in his homework in time whereas John might be looked upon with suspicion of being ill if suddenly he started to behave in a nice way. A number of expectations are however less firmly tied to the individual than to the position or place in which the person finds himself. We know what to expect of the behaviour of a priest for instance, in contrast to a rock musician without knowing the priest personally.

The system of norms and expectations which is tied to the position of an individual in social psychology is referred to as a role. By a person's role we thus refer to the ways in which the person ought to think and act in the particular social position.

Positions and their role prescriptions may be of many different kinds. As we have seen a person may take on different positions within a group. Positions may vary from being that of the officially appointed leader with the norms and expectations belonging to that role, to that of the ordinary loyal member of the group. Furthermore, positions would depend on the type of group to which we belong. Among friends one might expect that we

Both uniform and equipment make it easy to assess what role this man has and make us expect that he would act firmly and correctly irrespective of his personal feelings.

149

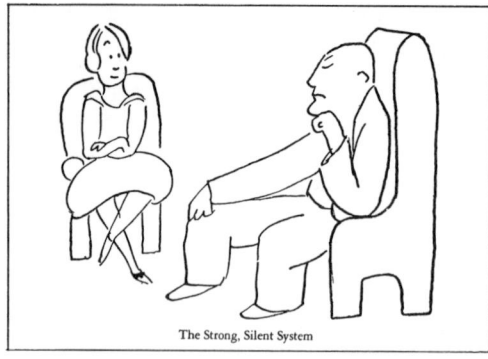 

The Strong, Silent System

.The Strange-Fascination Technique

The I'm-Not-Good-Enough-for-You Announcement

The Heroic, or Dangers-I-Have-Known, Method

The masculine role can be played in many different ways, especially when the object is to impress a woman! But what about the female role? From James Thurber: The Masculine Animal.

will be in good spirits and be able to enjoy life; as a family member it is expected that we should share the duties as for instance doing the dishes or cutting the grass. If we are members of a political group, it is expected that we demonstrate our points of view in a convincing way, that we would interest ourselves in certain topics and certain books, irrespective of whether other people might find them rather boring.

If we take a closer look at the role expectations of each of these positions we discover that it is not a question of one single way of behaviour but of a whole set of behavioural descriptions. It is part of the traditional masculine role to be tough and hard towards competitors, loyal and open towards friends, considerate and understanding in relation to a woman. Of a husband it is expected that his behaviour towards his wife should be different from that towards other women; of a mother that her behaviour towards her own children should be different from her attitudes towards other children. We can say with some truth that a role has as many sides to it as there are groups of people towards whom the role is being played. When on top of that each and every one of us each day enters into a whole series of different roles and sometimes also plays different roles at the same time, it is no wonder that we sometimes find ourselves in a role conflict.

Role conflicts

Role conflicts may arise on different levels.

1. Firstly, it may be a conflict between what a person wants to do himself or what

150

he is able to do and that which is demanded by the role. A person may discover that she or he is not able to fill the role (a common feeling when for the first time one starts on a job or is appointed to a position of some importance). It may also be the case that one feels it morally irresponsible to act the way the role demands. It is for instance part of the role of the subordinate to do what the leader asks, even if sometimes it may become a very heavy duty, as when for instance a soldier is given the order to launch an attack which he knows will imply the killing of a number of civilians.

2. Conflicts may arise between different sides of one and the same role as when one is confronted with persons above and below oneself in the hierarchy. A pupil being corrected in the presence of younger pupils would have problems in deciding whether he should play the role of a stubborn and somewhat naughty boy to satisfy the expectations of the other pupils or play the role of a more heart broken pupil to fulfil the expectations of the teacher.

3. The most common thing is perhaps that conflicts arise between different roles an individual is playing. Sometimes they might get in each other's way because one simply does not have the time or opportunity to play both the ways one expects. A commonly used example is that of the conflicting roles between mother and professional worker but we might equally well mention the role as father and football player. In some cases it might be the role of a friend coming into conflict with one's official position, where the latter demands that everyone should be treated in the same way (whereas the role of a friend presupposes that one treats people differently). If one belongs to two groups and each turns out to have a different view in a matter of some importance a conflict of loyalty may develop. In other cases the conflict can take the form of a choice of actions. As a somewhat funny but perhaps an illustrative example we might mention a personal and rather strange experience. As a guest speaker to a secondary school we wanted to pay a quick visit to the lavatory where one was faced with a choice between three different doors, marked Ladies, Gentlemen and Teachers. After a short internal struggle, we left the male identity and entered the third door.

Strangely enough role conflicts are not met with as often as we might believe from what has just been said. This is because after all there is a certain freedom in playing each role and we are left with the possibility of giving each particular role our special twist. We may also feel sure that our fellow human beings normally respect the roles we are playing at the moment by among other things entering into suitable roles themselves. Even if privately we know the bus driver rather well we seldom step outside the role of the passenger. We do not for instance expect to be given a free ride. In the same way we expect that a doctor will follow the rules of his position and not tell what he knows about different patients at a party even if the rest of the guests are contributing to the entertainment by telling stories about other people.

Attitudes

In daily life we come into contact with new people and new groups of people. We become acquainted with different institutions, we are confronted by news of many kinds and are directly or indirectly influenced by the different questions of society.

For each of us it becomes an important question how one ought to behave towards all these different questions of social nature. There is very seldom time and opportunity to go into details in every case and to assess each matter as it arises. If we were not to a certain extent prepared as to how to react in each case, we would soon become overwhelmed and lost in society. In particular it is important to be aware of the matters one ought to face in a friendly and positive way and those one ought to meet more negatively or to refuse.

The preconceived positive or negative tendencies of reaction in social psychology are referred to as *attitudes*. Attitudes may manifest themselves in different ways.

1. They may take the form of meanings as when one explains that one is positive to women's liberation or is against free abor-

	AP	SV	RV	NKP	H	KR.F	SP	DNF	V	FR.P	ANDRE
VALG 77	42,3	4,2	0,6	0,4	24,8	12,4	8,6	1,4	3,2	1,9	0,2
DES. 78	39,0	4,1	0,7	0,5	31,7	11,3	7,5	0,9	3,1	0,9	0,3
JAN. 79	39,4	4,0	0,5	0,3	34,4	10,4	5,6	0,9	3,3	1,2	–

Not all attitudes remain stable, something the political opinion polls show clearly.

tion. This is the side of attitudes that is more easy to assess by opinion polls or so-called Gallup studies (after the name of the man who was the first to launch such investigations on a large scale).

2. An attitude may also show itself in positive or negative emotional reactions. A person may for instance feel a little hostile towards foreigners without having anything in particular to point to as being wrong. Another person may seem to be happy with the progress of the Labour party without ever having made any statements about it or expressed any opinions of political parties.

3. Our attitudes may also show themselves in a tendency to act in a positive or negative way. A positive attitude to the Red Cross might be seen from the economic support we are willing to give, a negative attitude to armament might be expressed by taking part in demonstrations against nuclear weapons.

The cognitive, emotional and behavioural side of attitudes do not always fit very well. Very often people may express positive meanings about persons of another skin colour; nevertheless they feel distressed by the prospect of getting a son or a daughter in law who comes from another racial group. One's opinions do not necessarily lead to actions. One of the reasons why political polls have to be looked upon with some scepticism is that we cannot be sure that all who express their sympathy towards a certain party will turn this sympathy into action and actually vote for that party on the day.

The strength of the attitude is also of importance. Not only may a person take a more or less extreme position in a positive or negative direction. The person in question may also more or less strongly show

Demonstrations are a recognised way of expressing one's attitude to important social issues, but taking part is also dependent on the attitude one has to demonstrations.

his position or be more or less prepared to do something to really mark it. Some attitudes also will be more important and central to us than the rest. The different sides to attitude mentioned here will often go together. Those who are most strongly for or against some particular cause will often be those who also speak loudest and are the most eager when the cause is discussed. One very seldom finds a person who is fanatically neutral or a lukewarm extremist.

How are our attitudes formed?

If we are going to be honest we have to admit that our views, whether it is a question of women's liberation, politics or Christianity, are very seldom based upon extensive and mature considerations.

Some attitudes we have so to speak inherited from our parents and our family in such a way that we have not reflected upon the basis on which they are built. Other attitudes may be received in a more or less natural way from a group of companions and some seem to have followed more or less automatically with the roles we have taken on.

Naturally, we have also many attitudes based upon our own experience as for instance information received from newspapers and other media, or some other kind of personal experience, but the basis may also in this case be rather thin. How much information do we in fact seek before we make up our minds about some important question concerning foreign policy, and how representative are the personal experiences we are building upon? It

Stubborn attitudes are seldom weakened if they are attacked directly. The youthful rebel may get the feeling of banging his head against a brick wall. Cartoon by Rune J. Andersson.

may be that my positive attitude to Danes has its background in the parcels received during the last war, whereas my lack of interest in angling stems from a trip to the mountains when I got a fishing hook in my finger.

Despite the fact that many of our attitudes rest on a very insubstantial basis, they often show themselves to be very resistant to change. A large number of teenagers thus would be able to testify how a series of excellent arguments are totally wasted on the narrow minded, old fashioned views of the parents and likewise a number of parents have experienced how they may place all their authority and experience on the scale without being able to convince the younger ones that their attitudes are hopelessly immature and unrealistic.

There are a number of reasons why a change of attitude may meet great resistance. To begin with the attitudes are something of a guiding light in life, enabling us to discriminate between good and bad: what is worth thinking about and what one ought to forget. It therefore takes good reasons to change the attitudes. If they have served their purpose up to now they may be good enough in the future.

In many cases we also find an internal connection between different attitudes. Thus if one attitude is changed, a long series of other changes seems necessary. If for instance our view of sexual life is firmly tied to attitudes towards religion we might hesitate in changing one of these attitudes because then we would fear that it might have consequences for the others.

Attitudes resulting from a person's group membership will naturally also be difficult to change without changing at the same time the view of the whole group. This may be different if one succeeds in changing the person's connections with the group. In such cases one may astonishingly

154

easily see a change of points of view where a change previously seemed to be impossible (compare the section on group pressure).

Another reason why certain attitudes do not change despite attempts at persuasion, lies in their tendency to be self-fulfilling. A negative attitude to a subject at school will often lead to a lack of interest shown by a lack of homework, so that one in turn gets little encouragement and thus falls behind in such a way that one gradually has a greater reason to dislike the subject. A favourable attitude towards equal rights for men and women might lead to repeated discussions with others who share our opinion and to search for information through literature and newspaper articles that might support our own view.

It is this effect that Peter Wason, mentioned in Chapter 4, has investigated. In one of his first and best known experiments, subjects were shown four cards, with these symbols on them:

E K 4 7

They were told that each card had a letter on one of its sides and a number on the other. The task was to turn over those cards, and only those cards, necessary to decide if the following rule is true: "If a card has a vowel on one side, then it has an even number on the other side". Most subjects who do not know the task find it very difficult. Most choose either E and 4, or just E. The right answer is E and 7: because only these choices will allow you to *disprove* the rule.

We have an amazing ability to forget, explain away or misinterpret information that does not fit with our attitudes. If nothing more we might have great doubts of the truthfulness of the information pointing in the opposite direction, or conceive it as the exception which according to a very handy saying only proves the rule.

The conception of other people

Our conception of other people will also be coloured by our preconceived opinions.

As we have seen we expect different behaviour from different people depending on the group they belong to and the position they have in the group. This may of course in part be justified because the person in question normally would share his views with those of the group, and try

We all have stereotyped ideas about other cultures.

to behave in the way demanded by his role and the group. But very often our preconceptions would be of a too rigid and categorical kind, in particular when we are trying to assess people belonging to a group very different from our own. We may in such cases talk about *stereotypes*: as examples we might mention the conception of different nationalities. The Italian is thought to be lively and extravert, the Spaniard proud and temperamental, the Scotsman tough and careful with money, the Dane kind and good humoured.

Stereotypes and other preconceived meanings may play a role also after having become acquainted with someone belonging to the group in question. We can very easily notice the traits fitting into the picture, while to a large extent overlooking other qualities. As with all other kinds of assessment our judgement is dependent on the categories we use (compare the chapter on thinking). If we place human beings into just a few categorical types it will take a lot to discover what characterises the individual.

We might perhaps think that our judgement would be different when for the first time we meet somebody without any background information or as far as we know any preconceived attitudes. Let us take the case of Jim as our point of departure.

The American psychologist A. S. Luchins gave the following story taken from Jim's everyday life to a group of subjects.

Jim left the house to get some stationery. He walked out into the sun-filled street with two of his friends, basking in the sun as he walked. Jim entered the stationery store, which was full of people. Jim talked with an acquaintance while he waited for the clerk to catch his eye. On his way out, he stopped to chat with a school friend who was just coming into the store. Leaving the store, he walked toward school. On his way out he met the girl to whom he had been introduced the night before. They talked for a short while, and then Jim left for school.

What is your impression of Jim? The subjects of Luchins who were asked to present a description of personality on the basis of these few pieces of information were in no doubt. Jim was a rather extravert character. Let us compare with another sketch given to another group.

After school Jim left the classroom alone. Leaving the school, he started on his long walk home. The street was brilliantly filled with sunshine. Jim walked down the street on the shady side. Coming down the street toward him, he saw the pretty girl whom he had met on the previous evening. Jim crossed the street and entered a candy store. The store was crowded with students, and he noticed a few familiar faces. Jim waited quietly until the counterman caught his eye and then gave his order. Taking a drink, he sat down at a side table. When he had finished the drink he went home.

Here Jim does not seem to be himself or what?

Luchins now let two new groups assess both descriptions. One group received them in the same order as here while the other group got the descriptions in the opposite order. The first group seemed to have the first impression of Jim, describing him as a social, friendly, extravert, popular, sympathetic and satisfied person. Those who had listened to the descriptions in the opposite order on the other hand, had a strong tendency to assess Jim as shy, reserved, quiet, lonely, unpopular and unfriendly. They also made a quite different judgement on how Jim would react in a possible situation when for instance being invited to a party.

The experiment shows a number of important aspects about how we form a picture of another person. The most striking

What is your impression of the boy sitting talking to his mates? Is he popular? extravert? dominant? sure of himself? Can one judge correctly from the evidence available?

feature is how important the order of information is when the total impression is concerned. In this case the first impression had a dominating influence. The experiment also shows how quickly we draw conclusions about the personality of another human being on the basis of conditions that might just as well say something about the situation in which the person finds himself. If we meet Jim in the sunshine surrounded by friends we automatically form a different opinion of him to the view we may have if we meet him late at night in a foggy street with very few people. People we meet every day and whom we think we know well, we normally only meet in a particular situation. The actor we only know from the stage and the teacher from

the classroom. If we chance to meet the same persons in private life we are often surprised at the onesidedness of the picture we had before.

The possibilities of coming to the wrong conclusions are thus very great. On the other hand we often seem to have a good chance of pinning down the personality of a person very quickly. Here we might refer to our description of the psychology of perception, where we concluded that we sometimes have an impressive ability to form a trustworthy and correct picture of the surroundings, even if the cues may be very vague and ambiguous. The explanation may be that the task of observing and drawing conclusions about other people and their reactions is something we have been doing from early childhood. It has also been of great importance that we should succeed in this to a certain extent. If psychology is defined as the study of other people's and our own behaviour and experience, we thus all seem to be hard working psychologists.

The most important source of knowledge about others probably is the knowledge we have of ourselves. If we assess the emotional conditions of Jim or others correctly, it is perhaps because we know what it is to have such emotions. The better we know ourselves the better are the chances of drawing the right conclusions about others. A person who for different reasons is unfamiliar with certain aspects of his own personality, for instance because of neurotic blocking of emotions or anxiety towards his own impulses, would scarcely develop into a good psychologist.

In psychoanalysis one talks about projection, that is the tendency we have to attribute to others the unpleasant qualities we are unable to see in ourselves. At the same time the fact is that the knowledge of ourselves is best achieved by observing how other people are reacting to us. In a sense we are using other people as a mirror in which we see ourselves.

Our modern psychological knowledge is perhaps best summarised in the classical lines of Schiller:

"Willst du dich selber erkennen, so sieh', wie
die Andern es treiben.
Willst du die Andern verstehen, blick' in dein
eigenes Herz."

(To understand yourself, take a look at other
people –
to understand the others, look into your own
heart.)

"WOMYN FOR PEACE" reads a wall slogan near the home of one of the authors, the new spelling protesting against an implied view of "women" as a subdivision of the (male) race of men. Etymologically the word means "female person", but the use of "man" to mean both the human race and the male half of it seems to go far back into the history of Indo-European languages. Women, and many other groups and individuals, are currently concerned about the roles they find themselves in, however these arose. This is an example of the way in which the human sciences affect their own subject-matter. The psychological or sociological concept of a "role" has entered general knowledge and this in turn affects the way people behave.

How can one measure a role? One method is the questionnaire, and this was used in a study by two psychologists at Washington University, Elizabeth Jane Nettles and Jane Loevinger (1983). They were interested in causes of difficulties in marriage. In particular they hypothesised that in problem marriages the partners would tend to have differing views of the appropriate roles for men and women. Problem marriages were defined for this purpose as those where the couple had either split up or had been receiving professional counselling help for the past year. Attitudes to sex roles were measured by a questionnaire constructed specially and tested on a pilot sample. 52 "problem" couples were compared with 52 non-problem couples on this and several other measures. The hypothesis was supported: partners in problem marriages did tend to dis-agree over roles. But this investigation, while interesting, is a good example of one that leaves the important questions unanswered. Nettles and Loevinger do not tell us *how* the attitudes differed, only that they did. And even more crucial, we have no means of knowing what part, if any, this difference played in the problems of the marriage. Did one cause the other? If so, which? Or were both the result of other factors?

Roles are not as simple as they might seem. R K Unger has pointed out that there is a difference between a biological and a psychological sex role; and one cannot simply assume the second from the first. The psychological role may be the better predictor of behaviour. Physiologically, men and women are, normally, clearly differentiated: vive la différence, the French say. Even physiologically, however, there is some overlap of sexual characteristics, for example male nipples and female clitoris. Psychologically it is far more complex, and at least from Freud onwards it has been realised that there are degrees of masculinity/femininity: each person occupies a position somewhere on a continuum.

Roles are not simply a matter of behaviour, or even of attitudes, but also of inner experience. Jerome L Singer of Yale University has done a great deal of work on such experience in the form of fantasies and daydreams, something familiar, as far as we know, to everyone. He has found evidence for three characteristic styles of daydreaming, which are called Guilt/Fear of Failure; Poor Attentional Control (typically "woolgathering" fantasies); and Positive-Constructive (vivid and playful day-dreaming). These can be measured by rating scales. In a study reported in 1983 with Jacqueline M Golding, Singer tried to relate daydreaming both to sex roles and to mood, particularly depressive mood. These three – daydreams, or imaginal processes; moods; and roles – can be considered three ways of characterising inner experience. Are they all consistent with each other? 40 women and 33 men – predictably, introductory psychology students – were given questionnaires on each of the three. The results were factor analysed. This is a rather complex statistical technique, ultimately deriving from correlation, which enables us to discover consistencies across a range of behaviour.

In this case it was possible to conclude that inner experiences of the three different sorts fall broadly into a pattern of three orientations or perspectives. These were labelled Positive, Expressive, and Instrumental. A Positive orientation involves forward-looking, vivid daydreams, feeling competent and effective, describing oneself both as warm and supportive and as forceful and assertive. One's "cognitive structure" is based on assumptions emphasising the positive effects of life. In the Expressive perspective, one's assumptions emphasise interpersonal experience. One is likely to have difficulty concentrating, to feel dependent, to describe oneself as warm but lacking assertiveness.

The Instrumental assumptions emphasise achievement, and these tend to go with guilty daydreams and difficulty in concentrating. One tends to be self-critical and to describe oneself as lacking interpersonal warmth. Both the last two can be associated with depression, but of different ty-pes: one being more related to dependency and lack of support, the other with failure and fear of failure. From the point of view of sex roles, as had been expected the psychological role predicted both daydreaming style and depressive experience better than did biological sex. However, positive daydreaming, and feelings of personal effectiveness, were less closely associated with either an exclusively male or an exclusively female sex role, than with some mixture of them: with an *androgynous* sex role. Other investigators such as S L Bem have previously found androgyny associated with mental health. In this study it appeared: "that being simultaneously feminine and masculine is part of a general positive orientation. In contrast, lacking either femininity or masculinity is associated with unpleasant imaginal processes and depressive experiences."

While one should not base too much on a study of seventy American students, it is interesting that the concept of "unisex" has been part of popular culture for some time now. The singer and actor David Bowie has often been described as androgynous. At the moment of writing pop stars Marilyn and Boy George are the centre of attention. Time will tell if this is more than a fashion.

It is of course a commonplace that much of our culture is now transmitted through the mass media, perhaps above all television, with its recent derivative the video film. At the present time passions are raging over the censoring of "video nasties" which can be seen by children. The argument over censorship is essentially a moral and political one: is it right for some people to control what the rest can do or see or read? If so how should they be chosen, what rules should be followed, and so forth? Probably every society has faced this dilemma. Today, psychologists cannot avoid being drawn into the problem. For clearly if it could be definitely proved that "nasties", or any other presentation, do or do not have harmful effects, the moral question might look very different. Unfortunately despite a great deal of effort the evidence is not yet as conclusive.

Two questions that have been asked many times about television and films in particular are, do viewers model themselves on what they see? and does TV have harmful effects on children's development, education, etc? Here are two studies to illustrate the kind of investigation that is being done.

Edward Donnerstein and Leonard Berkowitz (1981), at the University of Wisconsin examined some of the interactions of sex and aggressions as affected by films. Berkowitz has become well known for his studies of how children copy aggressive behaviour. In this case however the subjects were adults. They were, once again, American college students, this time eighty men. It is quite common for students to be able to gain credit on their courses by volunteering to act as subjects, and this was the case here. It is just one more point to remember when considering how similar to real life are laboratory experiments. Indeed this whole study illustrates the lengths to which investigators go when tackling such contentious issues as these.

The procedure was somewhat involved. Essentially, however, subjects were shown one of four short films, made for the purpose. One was neutral (a chat show); the three others were erotic. One of these showed a young couple in various stages of

making love. In the other two, a young woman was the object of aggressive advances by two men. In one case she appeared to enjoy this, in the other she was shown as distressed and suffering.

However, this was all done in the context of a supposed experiment on learning, in which a real subject could both receive mild electric shocks from someone pretending to be a second subject, and (as he thought) administer such shocks. The object of this was that the subject could first of all be made angry (by either a male or a female) when he "failed" in his learning task and was punished for it; then be shown one of the films; and then have a chance to express his anger by, supposedly, shocking the person who had initially made him angry.

The upshot of this was that when the confederate was another man, the films had no effect. But when it was a woman, the aggressive erotic films, but not the other two, had the effect of increasing aggression. As the authors put it, the results "once again suggest that aggressive erotica can increase aggression against women under certain conditions". The last three words are crucial. It is obvious that the conditions of the experiment were highly artificial. An opportunity to give vent to aggression, quite legitimately, was provided by the experimenter. This is not usually the case in real life. Obviously one cannot go around providing men with opportunities to carry out real acts of aggression against women, in order to examine the effects of films. Yet the issue is an important one, for the balance between control and freedom is absolutely basic to any society. If we put together the results of experiments (of which this is only one out of many), and the investigations of other scholars such as historians, anthropologists and sociologists, we can only conclude that the relationship between pornography and behaviour is in no way a simple one, and is only a part of the whole cultural framework of our lives. (Two particularly revealing books on this wider context are *The Other Victorians* by Stephen Marcus and *The English Vice* by Ian Gibson).

Nevertheless patient empirical research does help us to make progress. The same issues apply in the second example. Each of the mass media as it has come into fashion has raised the question of what effect it will have on behaviour; particularly on children because they are presumed to be more impressionable. Television especially has been thought to have harmful effects on educational and intellectual development, because it has come to be almost universal in our society, and because watching is a particularly all-consuming activity.

Robyn Ridley-Johnson and others at the University of Missouri report (1983) another attempt to answer this question, which has been under investigation for at least thirty years. This was a relatively simple study although it required quite a lot of careful work. All the 322 children in a small mid-western town's middle school, Grades 5 through 8 (that is aged 10–13) were given a questionnaire. In part I of the questionnaire, children were asked whether (a) they watched television alone or with others; (b) they discussed the shows they watched with others; (c) their parents set rules concerning television watching. In part 2 they recorded all the programmes they had watched during one week. Part 3 assessed children's preferences for seven types of show: comedy, mystery/adventure, sport, family, game, police/detective, cartoon. School grades in mathematics and reading, and intelligence scores, were taken from school records. The average number of hours watched was 34.17, but there was a wide range, from 0 to 63.

The results analysed statistically showed several small relationships, but only one that looks important: children whose parents set rules for watching television had higher intelligence test scores and better school grades. What does this mean? Is it fewer hours of viewing that is important? Or do children from more orderly homes do better? Or are parents more likely to set rules if their children are bright and doing well at school? Or do more intelligent, or better-off, parents, have brighter, more hard-working children and also run more orderly homes? The mass media questions remain unresolved.

As with so many psychological matters, the technology, and the experimental approach, are new, but the underlying issues are very old. What is the best environment for children to learn in? How can information best be conveyed? How do social pressures operate to change behaviour?

In 1984 most people are aware of George Orwell's fictional state which achieved total control over its members. How possible is this? Stanley Milgram showed in some experiments that became famous that ordinary people will, on occasion, apparently be willing to administer harmful levels of punishment to others in the interests of science. This approached the limits to which experiment can go in our society. Perhaps the most ruthless reported attempt to control and change the minds of individuals in modern times was the Chinese "thought reform" programme of the 1950s. The primary feature seems to have been control of human communication – "milieu control". Within this, physical deprivation was used to lessen resistance and to reduce the individual to a child-like dependence. Later, psychological pressures were employed, such as confusion; creation of shame and guilt; confession; successive increase of demands; persistent exhortation and "help"; restriction of concepts through language (Orwell's Newspeak). These are the techniques of so-called "brain washing". Many of them would have been familiar to evil tyrants through the ages, and their effects are real, at least as long as the pressure is kept up. But when we add the modern technology not only of mass media but of behaviour modification, direct control of the nervous system, psychogenic drugs, genetic engineering, then there is indeed real fear that the advances of science may be perverted; even, as Orwell feared, irreversibly and for ever.

It is a relief to find subjects difficult and contrary and inconsistent even in simple experiments. Ray Cochrane at the University of Birmingham recently studied racial prejudices among teenagers in that city. Even such strong and irrational attitudes are by no means held consistently. He quotes remarks such as: "All the blacks ought to be sent home – but not Errol, he's our mate." Or this, on which we will end this chapter:

"I hate West Indians. They all smell of curry".

"No, that's Indians."

"No, it's West Indians. I live next to 'em, I know."

"No, it's Indians that eat curry."

"Look, anyone can eat curry. I eat curry. I like it. Why can't West Indians eat curry?"

CHAPTER SEVEN

Individual Development

Introduction

We have seen examples of how our behaviour and our way of thinking and feeling vary according to the social situation in which we find ourselves, but we also find variations according to the age level of the person. In particular this is so as far as reactions in social situations are concerned. It is not a coincidence that it is a child who withstands the group pressure in the story about the Emperor's new clothes and declares that he is in fact naked. Studies have shown that smaller children have a greater tendency to help each other than older ones and grown ups, but the child must have reached a certain age level to be able to understand that another person is suffering.

The developmental level of the individual is thus seen to be one of the factors that make it difficult to say something general about the behaviour of people and how they experience different types of situations. At the same time however, the changes that accompany growth make it possible to get a more complete picture of the psychological processes discussed before. Many would argue that we cannot get a full understanding of thinking without studying the development of thinking, or personality without having followed the individual through childhood. To study development is important if one wants to understand the adult, in the same way as the study of history is necessary to understand the social institutions, social movements and conflicts of our time.

The study of human development can be performed in different ways. Often the text books of child psychology and developmental psychology aim to give a picture of what is typical for the different age levels: in childhood, adolescence and among grown ups. Which phases does an infant go through? What are the typical problems of the two year old and what can one expect of a four year old, different from what one finds in the three year old?

To simplify the description one often speaks about a limited number of ages, "infancy", early childhood, later childhood, adolescence, adulthood and old age. These may again be divided into a number of sub-sections, but such divisions will always be arbitrary because development normally is a gradual and not a step-wise process. On the other hand it seems clear that some milestones exist in development. Some of them are biologically determined: it is chiefly a question of maturation when the child "learns" to walk at about 12–15 months of age or when sexual changes occur between 12 and 15 years of age. Other milestones are more socially determined as for instance when to start going to school, when to start working and when to become an old age pensioner.

Another way of looking at developmental psychology is to take a closer look at each psychological process and its special development. We may then ask questions like: what is the process of intellectual growth? How does emotional development

Maturation and learning in the pool. When do most children learn to swim? Is it possible to start learning too early or too late?

take place? How are our attitudes and social roles determined? Whilst a concentration on different age levels would make developmental psychology a more descriptive type of psychology (what is going on) the second type of view would invite a more theoretical or explanatory type of study (the questions of how and why). Why is development the way we observe it? Is it maturation or learning that is the chief factor behind the two year old starting to talk? What is the reason why some children are very similar to their parents when others are rather different?

We shall take as our points of departure a number of questions which may throw some light upon for example learning, perception, thinking and emotional life, that is the areas we have previously described in this book.

Some features of intellectual development

If we compare what children in different age groups achieve on intelligence tests we would be able to draw a curve describing mental development which increases quickly to begin with, but which gradually flattens out over the years. Previously psychologists were of the opinion that intellectual growth in the same way as biological growth had come to its peak when a person was 16–17 years of age. Modern research has shown that there is an increase in intellectual development much longer than this. The results however vary with the type of tasks in the tests. Tasks which demand quick reactions would favour younger people whilst tasks where no time limit is set would be solved equally well by grown ups. Where verbal understanding and general experience are of importance, older people would tend to do better than younger ones etc.

The picture we form of development is also dependent on the research strategy we are using. The quickest view is made by a cross sectional method where we compare the test results of groups of people on different age levels. Our problem with this method is that we cannot be sure that the groups we are studying are really comparable. If for instance a smaller percentage of the older persons have had some further education, this group might be less familiar with some of the questions asked. They may therefore achieve a poorer test result without this meaning that their intelligence is lower. This problem is avoided by using the longitudinal method where we study the same persons repeatedly over a period of time. We may let one particular group of children go through an intelligence test and then repeat the test each year until they are grown up. In a similar way we might follow development where other psychological functions are concerned. This method makes it necessary to keep contact with the same subjects year after year and we also have the disadvantage that it takes a long time to reach the final results.

Irrespective of method used, there are certain limits to the insight we can get into mental development if we restrict ourselves to results of intelligence tests. These

A child's development is reflected in drawings. Here the same child made a drawing of his father at three-year intervals. Father is first seen through the eyes of a four-year old, then by the seven-year-old (in pyjamas, the way he comes to wake me up in the morning), and finally with the ten-year-old's awareness of details.

tests only to a limited extent tell us how children at different age levels think and how they experience the world around them. It would be wrong to assume that differences between children and adults are only a question of degree. Some examples from development may perhaps show that the child has a long way to go before it can think in the adult way, and also that adults may have great problems in remembering or trying to understand how it is to be a child.

The world of the child

Naturally enough we know little about how the infant experiences the world. It is probably not able at first to differentiate clearly between self and the surroundings. Things happen, hunger and unpleasantness, warmth and pleasantness, light and darkness, tiredness and waking up just come and go without the child having any clear conception of what is due to the environment and what is due to something inside its own body. Only gradually would the child be able to discriminate between its own body and the surroundings though most of the sense organs work perfectly almost from birth. Very early on the infant prefers some impressions to others, as for instance showing more interest in a patterned surface than in one with only one colour. It will pay more attention to something resembling a face than to a meaningless figure. Still it takes some time before the child can see objects clearly separated from their background. When two months old a child will readily follow a toy train with its eyes and continue looking when it disappears behind a screen to reappear on the other side, but the child will start crying and look for the train when it stops. A train moving and a train standing still are not the same thing. And, surely

enough, a fascinating movement is no longer there.

Among the first things recognised by a child are faces, but to begin with all faces are equally good. The fear of strangers often shown by the 6–7 month old child may be due to the fact that the child is now able to discover that not all the faces approaching belong to mother or father.

Even with some knowledge of persons and objects, the child will for a long time have very imperfect concepts of the existence of objects. If we hide the toy of an 8 month old child under a pillow the child might start crying because the toy has disappeared, even if we have quite openly placed it behind the pillow. If it is gone it is gone; the greater is the joy when we remove the pillow and by some magic make the toy reappear. A somewhat older child may understand that the thing is hidden and learn to look for it, but perhaps the child will look in places where the toy was found last time rather than where it has just been hidden.

Only when about 1½ years of age does the child achieve a relatively stable concept of objects, but even in older children thinking can be influenced by what we would perhaps consider to be putting aside the laws of nature or of self evident logic. It is not uncommon for small children of a certain age to be afraid of the hole in the bath tub where the water disappears so quickly. The water is going out that way so there is a danger that the child may follow, the fact that the opening is very tiny and the child much bigger doesn't seem to be of any comfort for the two year old.

The boundaries between fantasy and reality are lacking in stability for a long time to come, not only because the child has a strong imagination (many are literally able to see what they are thinking of), but because reality has not yet emerged as the

A child might say about this situation, animals do like cuddling because they are so nice to feel.

stable, law abiding – and sometimes also trivial – place it gradually comes to be. The child may for instance believe that its dreams exist in a place somewhere "out there" and wonder why someone sleeping in the same place is unable to see the same things. To tell the three year old that the big lion in the book is not dangerous because it is only a picture is not a good way of trying to comfort the child. It would be much better to tell the child that the lion is a kind one.

Gradually, the child understands that the world comprises more than what it can see with its own eyes; that we have both a past to look back to and a future ahead of us; and that what happens must have a cause. It starts to become important to find out how things are arranged. Everything has to be looked into and everything may be asked about, even if the answer is something the child has no time to wait for; and if the grown up sometimes has difficulty in finding answers to the 1,000 questions maybe some other child will give the right reply. The Swiss developmental psychologist Jean Piaget tells how he once was asked by a six year old why two mountain tops in the neighbourhood, a big one and a small one, had the same name. Before Piaget was able to think of a reasonable answer, another six year old came up with the explanation: "It is because we shall have one mountain for longer walks, and another for shorter walks."

The answer not only shows how a six year old may have an imperfect understanding of reasons and explanations but is at the same time a good example of the child's tendency to put the human being in the centre of all things. Things are there for us and among all people there is one in an even more central position, namely the child itself. A three year old points to the letters on the front of the bus, and says "it says KIKI, doesn't it?" To her it is not unreasonable to assume that the bus would go through the streets of the city with her name in big letters. How could it otherwise be possible for daddy to recognise "their bus"?

We here see an example of the egocentric way of thinking in the child. By the word "egocentric" we in this case refer to the fact that the child is looking at things from its own perspective and has difficulties in understanding that other perspectives do exist. The child does not understand for instance how another person can fail to see what it is pointing at or to understand what is meant by what the child is saying. The feelings of others are also assessed on the basis of one's own feeling, which is something we all may be accused of at times. Even an 8–9 year old may argue that an animal likes the touch of the human hand *because* it has a soft fur.

The picture the child has of the world has been called magic or animistic, because the child does not draw any sharp line between living things and dead things and is prepared to see human qualities in everything. The doll hurts itself when it falls, a bulldozer looks angry and threatening and the stars wink in a friendly way. A 4 year old girl who is going along the street with her father explains, "I'm glad I'm not a car, they have to stand still nearly all of the time, just thinking and thinking. . ."

Almost anyone can be surprised by the language development of children. Drawing by Rune J. Andersson.

Only after having reached school age does thinking start becoming more logical and sensible. The world of the child is less volatile than before and has lost a lot of its more magic aspects, but logical reasoning is still tied to concrete matters. It is easy to show that when half a cake is divided in two, the result is a quarter, but far more difficult to explain that any half divided by two makes one quarter and almost impossible to get children to understand the general rule of how to go about dividing a fraction by a number. Concrete logic may result in the child finding it safest to go through the exercises of arithmetic twice, it might just be that 2×56 will come to a different number than 56×2. Some developmental psychologists, among them Piaget, argue that one first sees examples of real abstract reasoning when a child is about 12–14 years of age; a period of rapid growth, not only physical but also intellectual growth.

Language development

The greatest intellectual achievement in early childhood undoubtedly is the mastering of language. This makes it possible to communicate with other people, to get information oneself, and to be able to make assessments about things which are not present before one's eyes. Language development is closely tied to general intellectual growth. It mirrors that growth and contributes towards it.

The point of departure for language development, we find in the child's spontaneous babbling. Very early on a child is normally able to reproduce all the sounds of any known language in the world. Gradually there is a selection of noises such as to make the sounds more or less English or Norwegian sounding and then gradually to become English or Norwegian.

The first few words are normally heard around 12 months of age and usually are "mummy" and "daddy". The fact that the child says the words and uses them does not necessarily mean that it is employing them in the way a grown up would do. "Mummy" is used to begin with as a way of expressing oneself more than as a name of a person. It may mean anything from "I want food" to "come here" or "help".

When the child is around 2 language development increases rapidly, the 2 year old has already a vocabulary of a couple of hundred words and is soon seen to put the words together in incomplete sentences like "eat food" and "daddy car", the latter might mean either that it is daddy's car, that daddy is driving a car, or that I want to drive with daddy. The child is at this point of time, able to understand far more than it can explain in words. The passive or latent vocabulary throughout development is far greater than the active one (the words the child actually uses) and this remains true in adult life as well. The grammatical rules are discovered and used, something particularly noticeable when they are wrongly used.

D. McNeill gives this example:
Child: Nobody don't like me.
Mother: No, say "nobody likes me".
Child: Nobody don't like me.
Then after eight repetitions of this:
Mother: No, now listen carefully, say "nobody likes me.".
Child: Oh, nobody don't likes me.

Already as a four year old the child has learnt how to master the most important rules and a sufficiently large vocabulary to be able to talk about everything of interest. If we compare the child with the adult, we would naturally come to the conclusion that there is still a long way to go, but if on the other hand we compare the four year old with a new born baby we have to admit that the development has come a remarkably long way in these few years.

The development of personality

To many people the most obvious features of development are those connected with an older child being bigger and cleverer than a younger child, but development implies much more than this. While a child is growing in strength, wisdom and ability to master its surroundings, the personality is also under gradual change. The child goes through different stages in the "realm of childhood" which all have their special problems, and developmental possibilities.

Emotional development

It has been argued that we easily come to overestimate the intellectual level of the child whereas we often underestimate the emotional one. In any case, we know that the child very early experiences a great variety of feelings. Among the unlearned reactions of an infant the emotional ones are the most obvious. Whenever something is not to their liking children tell you very loudly and they are not many weeks old before they are able to give expression to joy and satisfaction through smiling and gurgling.

Further emotional development may be looked upon as a steadily differentiating of the basic emotions of excitement, pleasure and dissatisfaction. Already after the two or three first years we may notice a range of feelings from timidity to proudness, from love to jealousy. Freud in his time created much excitement and disagreement by arguing that not even a grown up

Even for a big boy it may be difficult to control the emotions when one fails and there is a great deal at stake. A child may be big enough to take part but not mature enough to lose.

feeling like sexuality was unfamiliar to the child, even if in the child we do not find it in the grown up way.

The changes in emotional life are perhaps basically that increasingly there are new things giving rise to emotions. It may be that there is not a great difference between the anger of a 5 year old and a 15 year old, but the reasons why they are angry are different, and when it comes to joy, the childishness of the joy of a small child playing with a lid of a saucepan does not lie in the joy or the emotional expression as such but in the fact that it is a lid of a saucepan that is the cause of joy.

What makes the emotional life of a child most different from that of an adult, is the strong and immediate way in which a child shows its feelings, and its lack of control. The child has difficulty both in mastering and hiding its feelings. Often it seems to be a helpless victim of its own emotional reactions. A fit of anger can easily lead to a child destroying his own things and joy can become so great that it ends in crying and despair. Needs and demands are also felt

as something that must be met at once. To wish is to want to see it done now and the demand follows. Mother's objections that there are no more cakes left in the bag or that we would have to buy more tomorrow are of little weight against the irresistible argument of the child: "But I want more!"

In such cases we see the close connection between thinking and emotional life. On the other hand emotions and needs influence the child's ability to think in a rational way. If the wish is strong enough as in the example above, the child is more than willing to deny facts. At the same time the decision to postpone something until tomorrow or to some other time, is naturally enough particularly difficult for someone who has but a vague idea of what tomorrow means.

With such an active emotional life, full of impulses, it is not strange that the child sometimes feels unsafe and needs someone to set boundaries. Therefore, children who are always allowed to do what they want are not always the happiest ones. Only after some time can the child learn to

171

understand its own feelings (that it is angry and also why it is angry) and then keep its reactions within reasonable bounds which sometimes also means that one has to keep one's feelings to oneself.

Socialisation

Through its growth the child develops from a mainly a-social being to one mainly social; from being a biological organism to becoming a member of society. Put in another way: the older the child is, the more necessary it is to know its environmental background in order to understand it. Infants are the same everywhere, young people from different cultures are not.

Development takes place in co-operation with other people, and something of great importance that has to be learned during childhood is precisely how to behave towards other people and to adjust and behave according to the rules and attitudes that are common to human interaction in the society in which one lives.

Somewhat simplified we may say that this process of socialisation has two different aspects.

1. The child gradually builds a better foundation for mixing and living together with other people, both when it comes to understanding and consideration for others, and when it is necessary to take

Each age has its task.

responsibility and to be independent. A central role is played by moral development (see later).

2. In addition to the general norms of human behaviour, the child also has to adopt the special rules, conventions and customs that are found within the particular culture.

A good example is the adoption of sex roles. A girl early on learns that there are certain things that she shouldn't do and other things it is nice for her to do, just because she is a girl. Gradually she chooses models among persons of her own sex. (In particular those she finds a reason to look up to and those who mean much to her, for instance mother or her big sister). In a similar way a boy tries to act like his models in his way of behaving, and he also, emotionally speaking, identifies with the models from which he learns to become a man, without necessarily anyone having consciously tried to teach him the role.

Moral development

Moral development comprises the child's evaluation of what is wrong and what is right and the ability to let such judgements influence behaviour.

In both these ways the infant is totally lacking morality. It does not show any constraints on action and has no understanding that all types of behaviour will not be acceptable. The first attempts to adjust behaviour show themselves when a one year old starts to become influenced by punishment and rewards.

The first adjustment of behaviour nevertheless has an opportunistic tone. The child learns that some activities have to be avoided because they lead to punishment or scolding talks, while other acts pay off better, at least when grown ups are present. If the child is left to itself both promises and threats may be forgotten.

Another step in the process of socialisation is taken when the child starts to behave nicely to achieve recognition and avoids doing the wrong things because it is embarrassing. This implies that the child has developed a certain self awareness or feeling of self esteem which it becomes important to sustain even if it is not yet strong enough to be independent of the reactions from the environment. Morality is still the outcome of what others want and what others know. The wrong things thus are not what one is doing, but what is discovered. It is the others who make one feel ashamed.

Sooner or later most children accept and internalise a good many of the commonly accepted norms for what is right or wrong, in such a way that there are some actions they will not perform even if there is no immediate danger of discovery or punishment. In fact now a child may have greater problems with bad behaviour which is *not* discovered or punished. We may now speak of a conscience developed by the child, a conscience one has to consider if one is to avoid the feeling of guilt and having problems with oneself.

Conscience as it develops in childhood is lacking in discriminatory power. To begin with the conscience does not discriminate between conventional rules of good behaviour and more general moral laws. In both cases the rules are more or less uncritically taken from the authorities in the world of the child, where mother and father to begin with have a central position, but where other children and other adults as for instance teachers, gradually may come to be of influence. We talk about a conventional morality (Kohlberg) and moral realism (Piaget) because the

173

rules are conceived as absolute and indisputable even if sometimes they may be somewhat inadequate. How wrong an action is seen to be is judged directly on the basis of its consequences and not on the basis of the motives behind it. One who breaks a number of things automatically is seen as someone acting more badly than one who only breaks a single object, even if the first one was the victim of an accident while the other was acting on purpose. The one who is beaten is more naughty than one who gets away with it.

As children we only gradually come to see that rules of play may be altered. It takes for instance a number of years before one is ready to accept that a friendly game can be played in more than one way and stops insisting that one's own way is the only "correct" one. The American psychologist Perry has even shown that in college years young people still believe that there is one correct answer to most problems (which one must try to find), and he has described several stages of intellectual development the students have to go through before they fully realise the implications of living in a relativistic world. On the other hand a child must also come to see that moral rules have their reasons and are not there simply because someone has said so. An older child will learn to accept that behaviour has to be assessed on a broader basis than that of its results (although the problems of morality, as we know, are among the most difficult ones, discussed intensely by thinkers of all times). Gradually a child will be able to reflect upon the question of what justifies a certain type of behaviour, but for some time most children feel that justice means that everyone gets the same, without considering that not everyone has the same needs.

Crises and conflicts

Each age level has its own tasks that need to be solved, on the basis of what the child is able to do and what a child wants to do on the one hand, and on the other hand what the environment demands and is able to offer.

Through the first few years the environmental demands vary especially because the child has only a limited mastery of its behaviour. On the other hand the child itself demands a lot. To many parents it may seem to be an age where most of the time is spent in satisfying the needs of the child. Already at an early stage these needs are more than the physiological ones as for instance food and sleep. It is not only important that the needs are satisfied but also that for instance a meal is of suitable length so that the child at the same time has bodily contact and is spoken to. Since the child is so dependent on his surroundings it is of great importance that those around him can be trusted and that they do not frequently disappoint or surprise the child. Between 6 months and 1½ years it is important that there is one or just a few persons who take care of the child all the time, in such a way as to make it possible for the child to be closely tied to someone and to use this person as a base for its exploration of the world. A long separation from the parents as for instance by being sent to hospital, can lead to special problems at this age. It is also of importance that there is a connection between the care for the child and the child's needs, in such a way that help is forthcoming when the need is great and not only when it suits the grown-ups.

Between 1–3 years of age the world of the child develops rapidly. The child learns to walk, to climb, open doors and get hold of things previously outside its reach. The

174

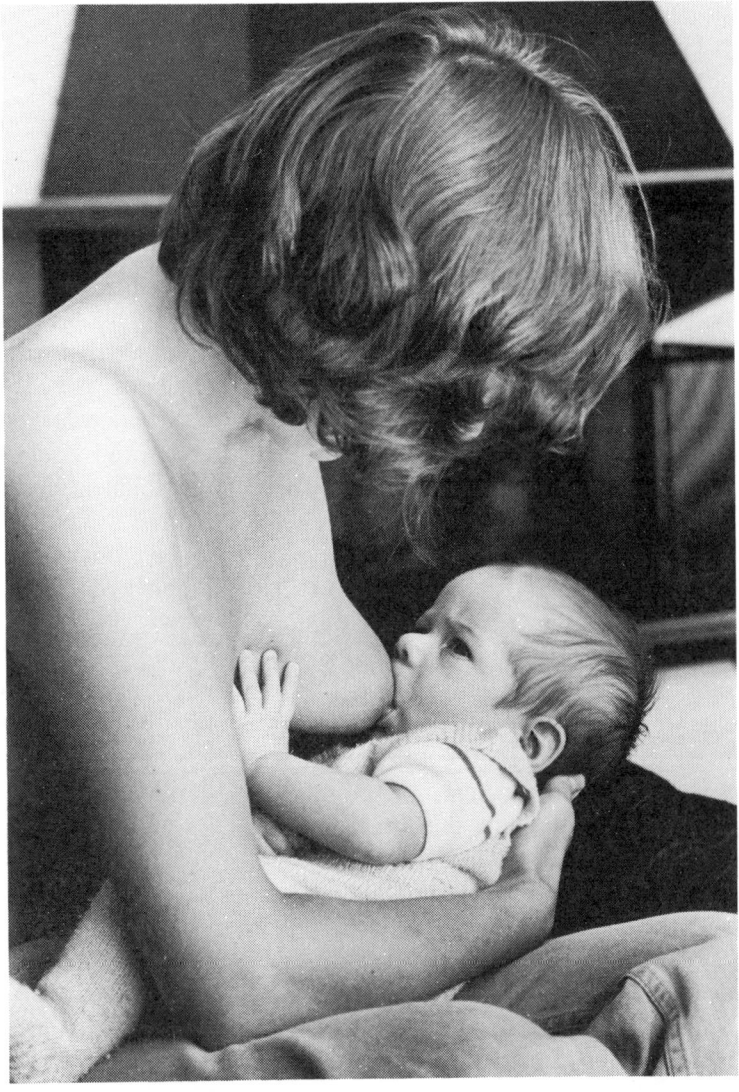

Breast feeding is not just a matter of satisfying the infant's need for nourishment. It also provides bodily contact and security.

child learns to talk, something also giving greater possibilities of influencing or resisting the environment. ("No" is a well understood word long before the child knows the meaning of "yes".) The child also gradually comes to master its own reactions and among other things toilet training is important. But with new skills new problems arise, especially at the start. One who is able to run also runs the risk of falling. Being able to say something implies the possibility of not being understood. By being able to get around more than before the child may enter into conflicts with the environment to a larger extent than before.

The child is in this period trying to give expression to its own independence. To the parents this sometimes looks like negativism and opposition and they may come to react in an unnecessarily strong way to show the child who really decides. It is better to look at this age of stubbornness as a phenomenon of development which does not necessarily mean that one is losing control over the child.

From 3 to 5 years of age the child spends much time in finding its place in the family and pays great attention to the emotional relations between its members. A new sister or brother can easily change the balance and create uncertainty and jealousy. The relationship between the parents also becomes important. A 4 year old might be very distressed if there is some sign that the parents are angry with one another but the child might also be provoked by signs of affection which may be taken to mean that the parents are more fond of each other than of the child. It is normal that the child goes through a phase where it feels more strongly attracted to the parent of the opposite sex (I'm going to marry mummy (daddy) when I grow up!). The other one may then be seen more or less as a threatening rival.[1] Feelings of aggressiveness, guilt and love may turn this into a stormy and difficult time, but most children are able to come out of this period with a stronger acceptance of their place in the world and with a certain identification with the parent of the same sex.

With the age of going to school, new demands and expectations emerge. A child is now expected to take its particular place in the social group, to show solidarity with its friends of the same age (at least those of the same sex) and no longer turn to mother or father in every difficult situation. From the adult world represented by the school the child meets strong demands for

achievement. There are problems of understanding, learning, and competence. The illusion of being the strongest or cleverest may now be mercilessly destroyed by friends and teachers. Now is the time when the child may feel the joy by discovering what it really can do or the disappointment of falling short of what is desired.

With adolescence a new life situation is again created with new joys and sorrows, triumphs and defeats. Biologically seen this period of development starts with rapid growth and sexual maturation. This development may in itself be experienced both as something desirable and as something problematic. In addition there are problems because this period of rapid growth does not start at the same time in every individual. A girl who has an early physical development may be forced into the role of a woman before she is emotionally mature enough. A boy who is slow in developing may for years struggle with feelings of inferiority, feelings which were not there before and which disappear later on when he has reached the level of his friends.

A problem faced by everyone is that one can no longer allow oneself to be a child, while at the same time one is not allowed to be an adult. In spite of all this adolescence in our culture is portrayed, through TV, pop music and adverts as the most glamorous period of life. From many quarters we are told that it is now that we must really enjoy life, but just how?

In this period, a new struggle for independence is seen (a new age of stubbornness many parents would say). One has to find out where one stands in relation to parents, to friends of both sexes and to society as a whole. Which job should I be preparing for? Is there going to be a job, or a place in society for me? What am I to think

---

[1]) Freud referred to this relationship as the Oedipus complex after the Greek myth about King Oedipus who grew up among strangers but who as determined by destiny later came to kill his father and marry his mother. When he learnt the truth he punished himself by blinding himself.

Nothing to do? Having finished with childhood but not yet ready to take on the tasks of adult life. For some young people the early years of adolescence are a time when one seems to be standing on a street corner waiting for something to happen.

about the important questions of society? – Adolescence is the time when one asks serious questions about one's own identity. To take on the responsibility for oneself becomes the central task.

What does it mean to become an adult? Does development come to an end? Probably we ought to look upon adult life as a further development with a series of developmental levels, each with their own crises and possibilities. New tasks are constantly entering the scene, one has to adjust to working life and partnership, take on the role of parents which also make different demands on the person when the next generation is growing up.

The modern psychoanalyst Erik Hom-

burger Erikson has put forward a theory in which the whole life is seen as a series of altogether eight stages, the first five belonging to the period we have already described. In the sixth stage, that of early adult life, a decisive task is that of developing the capacity for intimacy. Erikson is not only thinking of the relationship to the opposite sex but generally that of being able to open up towards other people and to share one's interests without having the feeling that this is done at the cost of one's own identity. Those who do not solve this task properly, may easily develop feelings of isolation and loneliness.

The next great challenge is the demand to go beyond oneself and to contribute something at work, towards one's family, and further to the whole of society. Erikson calls this *generativity*, a concept referring to the production of something creative, and doing something for others. If one fails here, one may end in stagnation and self preoccupation, concentrating on making life safe and pleasant for oneself.

Increasing age also has to be accepted in time, as well as the fact that one has to leave one's profession and perhaps also to face loneliness and illness. Sooner or later life itself must come to an end. A good solution according to Erikson is that of finding what he calls ego integrity: the acceptance of oneself and one's place in life. This is in contrast to despair, a feeling of the emptiness of life and that life has been in vain.

The demands are constantly changing but with them follow possibilities of continued development. When 86 years of age the philosopher F.C. Sibbern remarked that at that age one was perhaps unable to add much to one's growth, "but perhaps an inch if one stands up straight"!

Play

Are you doing anything or are you just playing? By asking this question daddy suggests that to the adult play is only to make time pass for want of other activities. From the point of view of the child the matter looks quite different. Play is something which one enters with enthusiasm and effort. Play is in effect a serious thing. The playing of children may more than any other activity tell us about the child, in

Children playing: a preparation for adulthood?

particular which developmental level it has reached both intellectually and emotionally.

There are many forms of play, so many that it is difficult to give a good definition of what play is really all about. It is perhaps correct to say that play is a name that is given to all the activities the child can turn to when it is not asked to fulfil a certain task or is dominated by some strong organic or psychological need. There is therefore more reason to worry about a child who seldom plays than a child who seems to be playing all the time. Common to all kinds of play is that it is voluntary, that it does not serve any particular external purpose and that it gives satisfaction.

The simplest and earliest form of play is called functional play. This is a form of playing without rules or any other purpose than to try out muscles and sensory organs, as well as the different things in the surroundings. Functional play may consist in exploring things in the neighbourhood as for instance when playing with water, playing around with cups and saucers etc. The play may also be concentrated around the body of the child and the way it may be used, a baby playing with its toes, later in crawling, climbing, balancing etc. In the older child such play takes the form of exercising more complex skills like riding bicycles or roller skating. Such exercises not only mirror the level of development but contribute to the development of knowledge of the world and of one's own skills.

Another type of play is activity aiming at creating or producing something: constructional play. In its simplest form we see this in the first drawings of the child and in building with building blocks. For constructional play it is more important that a child has some other material than ready-made toys. The joy is to see that the play leads to some results. Gradually it also becomes important for the child that the result is as good as possible and of some lasting value.

The fantasy type of play goes beyond what is actually present even if the point of departure may be some toy as for instance a car or a doll, something with which the child can do whatever it likes. The scissors may for instance take the place of a person, the top of the cardboard box may be a boat, the carpet may constitute a lake. From 4 to 6 years of age children themselves enter into play as persons who take on different roles.

The fantasies of children more than anything else give a direct view of their world of thinking and feeling. Through this type of play the child may satisfy wishes and solve problems which are more difficult to handle in reality. This does not necessarily mean that the use of fantasy is a way of running away from reality. We often see how the play helps prepare a child for a new situation, as for instance that of going to school, or that playing helps in working through a difficult experience as for instance that of having been examined by a doctor when ill, or having to stay in hospital.

At a later stage of development, the activity of play becomes dominated by rules. These are games and sports which have to be performed together with other children and where the co-operation and competition may be important features (hop-scotch, playing marbles, football and singing games etc.). This form of play gives little opportunity for individual ways of behaviour. It is on the contrary remarkable how similar the rules of such games are in different places and at different times. Many of these rules exist more or less as unwritten laws and the children seldom learn them from their parents. They represent a living tradition from one generation of children to the next.

As duties and work increasingly take more and more of the time of children there is less room for play. It is also often the case that the adolescent or the grown up dislikes play because it is seen as a childish or useless type of behaviour. This does not mean that the needs behind play are no longer there, but that the needs now might be satisfied through work, if only this gave room for self development, productivity and pleasure, in collaboration with other people.

More directly we see a continuation of the child's play in the later activities of grown ups. Functional play continues in sport and dancing which may also contain many rules, fantasy play is continued through interest in theatre, film and literature (many adults read comics), where ad-

mittedly we do not have to rely only on our own fantasies. The construction type of play gradually takes the form of hobbies, as model building, sewing or collecting things, often under the pretext of serving some useful purpose, but where the real cause may be the pleasure connected with creating something.

Playing is the most importance source of joy and satisfaction for a child, and it is at the same time an important form of stimulation for growth. It is therefore a question of whether it ought not to be accepted to a larger extent than today among adults, and not only to be expressed through a limited number of accepted forms of leisure activities. It is also often the case among adults that the core of play, the creative element, is lacking. In the few instances where play is really developed further in adult years we give it a new name: art.

Some traditional children's games go back hundreds of years, being passed on from one generation of children to the next. These girls are playing hopscotch using a pattern that can be traced back to the ground-plan of mediaeval cathedrals.

Development: Growth or a building process?

In our description of the intellectual, emotional and social development of the child we have not to any large extent touched upon the reasons why development takes the form it does. This is a question about which many different and conflicting views have been offered.

On the one hand we have the view that mental development is nothing but a process of maturation having its parallel in physical growth. If not too many obstacles are placed before the child, development will proceed by itself and the different facets of development will occur in a settled sequence.

As a contrast to this biological view, others would stress the learning process. They choose to look upon each new step in development as a result of experiences in the environment. The child learns to talk, it learns good or bad behaviour, it develops its traits of personality.

One's way of looking at the reasons for development in its turn will influence one's view on child rearing. If one looks upon development as a result of biological maturation, the task of those rearing the child is similar to that of a gardener who looks to see that the conditions are as adequate as possible. He would of course feed, prune and trim, but would in general make no attempts at directly influencing growth; a plant would grow by itself, stretching towards light, it is of no use to try to pull it up.

According to learning theory, this attitude is seen as an irresponsible one. Development should not be left to itself, it ought to be directed or perhaps even helped along by concrete actions in the form of reward and punishment. According to this view child-rearing practice is similar to that of a building contractor who has the task of checking that all parts of a building are in the right place. If the foundation is skewed there is little hope that the building will later come to an upright position by itself.

Both points of view may be seen to contain some truth and in many ways they give a good description of development. But both have their weaknesses. The growth model gives no explanation of the great differences we find if we compare children from different cultures and from different periods of history. For instance, we do not find the same crises and conflicts during development everywhere. In some parts of the world, the transition from childhood to adult life is a stormy and dramatic affair. In other places it seems to go smoothly and harmoniously. On the basis of biological maturation alone it is also difficult to explain how development sometimes goes wrong. If the tendency is for the development to run nicely by itself (you can't keep a good baby down) why then do so many people seem to develop in an antisocial or neurotic direction?

But the other view based on learning theory also has its limitations. The biggest problem is perhaps that of finding an explanation of why children normally make developmental progress from year to year without any systematic training and exercise. One might also wonder why development normally goes in a favourable direction even if the persons rearing the child do not have any feeling of having been doing the right things all along.

Children learn so much that it is unthinkable that everything can be learnt by way of spoon-feeding. It is therefore necessary to assume that some mechanism exists which would account for the natural course of development. Such mechanisms we find in the model learning and identifi-

Father is often taken as a model, especially if he is sometimes willing to come down to the level of the child.

cation concepts we have referred to when talking about the development of personality (the process of socialisation). As soon as the child starts to take parents and others as a model, a learning process is also started which is less dependent on special external measures but is more like a growth process. From this time on, therefore, what the parents *are* is more important to the development of the child than what they *do*. It is for instance more difficult to beat good behaviour into a child since then one is at the same time demonstrating one's own behaviour.

It is difficult to understand development if one looks at maturation and learning as two opposite types of explanation. In reality there is a close connection between the two factors. To be able to learn something one must have reached a certain level of development. Normally it is impossible to teach a two year old table tennis or a four year old bio-chemistry, but this is not the same as to argue that our achievements in table tennis or bio-chemistry are independent of learning. Maturation on the other hand, is dependent on the necessary conditions in the environment having been arranged for and often shows itself as an increased ability to make use of experiences.

Which factor we look upon as the most important is also dependent upon which aspects of development we want to explain.

If we are looking at language development, it is of course undoubtedly the case that a child learns to speak. The German emperor Frederick II of Sicily in the 13th century is supposed to have let a group of orphans develop in surroundings without speech, in an attempt to find out which language was the original one among human beings. (It is said that the Egyptian pharaoh Psammetik II made a similar experiment 1800 years earlier, coming to the conclusion that the original language was the Phrygian one.)

The children of the German emperor of course did not learn to speak at all. And what was even worse: no one survived the experiment. According to the mediaevel chronicler, the nurses who had strict orders not to talk to the children nor to talk among themselves, showed so little motherliness and care for the child that the physical and mental foundation for development was not there at all.

It ought not to have been necessary to repeat such an experiment, but, alas, both James IV of Scotland and Akbar the Great in India – the latter living in the 16th century – are reported to have done so. None of these experiments, even if they really took place, was at all conclusive. Twins do sometimes develop a "private language" of their own, but of course they are not isolated from others.

Natural observation shows that children who are handicapped when it comes to learning language (deaf children or children with deaf and dumb parents) do not automatically start to talk. Neither English, Phoenician nor Norwegian would come by itself. On the other hand many developmental psychologists and researchers of language have wondered why language development normally goes so quickly, in particular the adoption of the many complex and abstract grammatical rules is normally astonishingly easy, and takes place at about the same age with children from different cultures. The speculations of Ludvig Holberg about the mesopothamian language which according to him was so complex that even the natives were only able to talk it with the greatest of difficulty of course lack any scientific foundation. The remarkable ability to learn language showed by children 2–4 years of age has made some researchers assume that the learning of language has a specific biological base, that in other words we must reckon with some type of inborn language acquisition mechanism.

The development of individual personality traits shows perhaps even more clearly the interplay between the inborn biological factors and the learned environmentally determined ones.

Anyone who has had anything to do with infants can tell you that from the first few weeks of life there are great differences among the children in respect to activity and sensitivity. Some sleep very lightly while others are almost impossible to wake; some show much activity and react very strongly to external impressions whereas others take life very calmly.

It is not easy to predict whether these differences would lead to specific traits of personality later in life, even if in some cases we seem to see a connection. What we are able to say with greater assurance is

You can get parents
to see it all.
If you can have them
from when they're small.

Freely translated from Piet Hein.

that the behaviour of the child influences the way the environment and in particular the parents react to the child. A child who is almost not "noticeable" creates little disturbance and irritation in the family. On the other hand a very quiet child perhaps may get too little attention. A more restless and demanding child on the other hand comes into more frequent contact with the parents, who then sometimes as a result of this may come to react with anger and hostility towards something the child is doing.

The environment also naturally would seem a different place to a quiet child and to a child who is hyper-active. It is thus not only the environment that forms the child but also the child that forms its surroundings and thereby for better or worse takes part in the creation of its own environment.

A two-year old boy hit his mother, hard enough to make her cry. He "turned to me immediately and gazed intently, wide-eyed, a bit stunned, motionless", the mother wrote. He came to her, caressed her face and told her she was okay. "I'll take care of you, I take care of daddy, I be nice, you're okay", he said as he continued to caress her face "very gently and softly". This comes from some work by Carolyn Zahn-Wexler and Marian Radke-Yarrow, reported (1984) by John Bales, a staff writer on the APA Monitor, the house journal of the American Psychological Association.

These two psychologists and others at the US National Institute of Mental Health have studied the reactions of very small children to people in emotional or physical distress. They did so both in the children's homes, by training mothers to observe and record their children's behaviour, and also in the laboratory. The earliest reaction to signs of distress in other people is usually crying or other indication of sadness. This gradually lessens as infants become more capable of the beginnings of social behaviour. At about eighteen months there is "an explosion of prosocial behaviour". Children are seen to "help, share, protect, defend, comfort, console, give simple advice and mediate fights. . . Most of these different forms of prosocial responses have in common an apparent attempt to set things right for the victim."

This sort of concern is often referred to as altruism. Martin Hoffman of the University of Michigan suggests that the development of these feelings and behaviour goes through four broad stages. In the first few months of life, a child confuses distress in others with distress in itself. It is not able clearly to distinguish itself from other people. This is in line with many major theories of child development such as that of Piaget.

"In the second stage," in Bales's words, "beginning at about 10 or 12 months, the child can distinguish another's distress from its own, but its sense of the other's internal state is not fully developed. In this stage, the child will help others by giving them what it would want if it were in distress. For example, if child A were hurt, child B might seek out its own mother rather than child A's mother. By the third stage, at around three years, the child can distinguish the internal states of others from his or her own, and by the fourth stage, a six to eight-year-old is also aware of another's life apart from the immediate situation. In this stage, a child can feel sympathy for another child who, for example, has lost his or her mother."

The observations of Zahn-Wexler and her colleagues seem to support the second and third stages. Such work has practical implications, for example in the effects that distressed or depressed parents may have on even very young children, though there is no easy solution to how to deal with this situation. It also raises rather fundamental issues about human nature, suggesting that the capacity to develop altruism, concern for others, is very deeply rooted since its beginnings appear so early. This is in sharp contrast to the view held of children in at least some past ages, as more or less little animals that have to be disciplined into social behaviour.

It seems that human beings come into the world not with minds like blank slates, as the philosopher John Locke argued; nor, on the other hand, with instinctive patterns of behaviour which emerge regardless of experience. Rather, the human infant is a creature of varied potential, and can develop in many different ways according to the unique interaction of each individual with the environment. Even behaviour as apparently spontaneous and universal as affection between mothers and infants requires minimum conditions to flourish. The famous experiments of H F Harlow in which infant rhesus monkeys were given substitute mothers made of wire, sometimes covered with cloth and sometimes equipped with feeding bottles, showed the importance of physical contact. Dr Barry Keverne, of the Anatomy Department at Cambridge, and a French colleague, Dr Pascal Poindron, have discovered that a ewe can be induced to accept any lamb as her own by stimulation of the cervix. (*The Sunday Times*, 5 February 1984). This would normally occur naturally during birth. The possibility, at least, exists that the same mechanism might exist in other species including humans. If so, what would happen when mothers have babies by Caesarean section, or under epidural anaesthesia which blocks normal sensations? "Human maternal behaviour is affected by so many different things that we don't expect any long-term effects", Dr Keverne is quoted as saying, "but there might be some detectable differences early on."

The last twenty years or so have seen a great surge of interest in the study of very young children: it has become known as the "baby boom". In general, psychologists have become more aware of how complex is the world of the child, and less inclined to dismiss his behaviour as due merely to lack of maturity. The pioneer of this approach was Jean Piaget. Over the course of nearly sixty years of highly complex research and theorising Piaget stressed that any living thing functions as an organised whole at every stage of its development, evolving to the next stage through interaction with the environment. Exactly the same is true, he held, of the human mind.

While some psychologists have been describing the "competent infant", others have been interested in the other end of the life span. Possibly because of our peculiarly rigid social structure, in which for many people retirement is compulsory at 60 or 65, it is easy to assume that after this age abilities rapidly decline. We can all think of individual old people who are active and productive but perhaps consider them to be exceptions. Professor Paul Baltes, head of the Max Planck Institute of Education in Berlin, has recently (1983) shown experimentally that this need not be so. Two hundred and fifty Berliners, aged 60 to 80, were given systematic practice in "intelligence skills". This included practice in memory, inductive thought (logical reasoning) and problem solving: five or ten hour-long sessions over two or four weeks. They also took intelligence tests before and after, and follow-up tests after one and six months. The encouraging result was a clear and lasting improvement in performance for all participants "regardless of their initial prowess, education, age, and sex". "Most ageing people," Professor Baltes concluded, "retain either a latent ability or reserves that can be activated for intelligence accomplishments." Of course the physical changes of age produce some decline in abilities; but unless there is actual brain damage it is quite possible to maintain peak performance in selected fields.

A very similar conclusion comes from a quite different study by Seymour Giniger, Angelo Dispenzieri and Joseph Eisenberg of the City University of New York. They investigated a total of 455 workers in a factory in the New York garment industry. This industry has a wide variety of jobs within it, which differ in the extent to which they require speed and skill. Older theories of ageing have tended to assume that although skills may be maintained, speed of performance declines. In this investigation, jobs were first classified as mainly speed-oriented or mainly skill-oriented. Information was taken from the factory's records as to absenteeism and productivity, defined as average hourly piece-rate wages. "Older" and "younger" were taken as over or under forty-five.

It was supposed that older workers in speed jobs would do less than others. This was not so. Older workers fairly consistently did better than younger ones: they earned more, were absent less, had fewer accidents and had less turnover (leaving the factory), both on speed and skill jobs. However, there are several points to consider. It appeared that it was length of experience, rather than simply age as such, that was the important factor. Further, it may be that the demands of these particular jobs, in this industry, were not too great for the older workers; in another industry they might be. Again, it may be that as workers get older, those who find the job becoming too difficult tend to leave; the more able survivors remain. And it may

also be that older workers regard hard work as more of a virtue than do younger ones. Nevertheless this and other work suggests that the abilities of the old should not be belittled.

Nor, of course, should those of the opposite sex. Currently, it is women who tend to suffer in comparisons because, as would probably be fairly generally agreed, society, and education, tend to be male-dominated. Take mathematical ability. Pretty well all the evidence shows that boys score more highly than girls. Camilla Benbow and Julian Stanley, for example, work in a unit at Johns Hopkins University in the United States that is concerned with highly gifted young people: in the top 3% for mathematical, or verbal, or general intellectual ability. During 1980, 1981, and 1982, a total of 19,883 boys and 19,937 girls applied to be tested. Taking the average score of boys as a standard, boys exceeding this score outnumbered girls by three to two. The difference gets bigger as you go up the ability scale, so that when the standard is the best score in 10,000 the ratio of boys to girls is 13 to 1.

But why is this? It is sometimes argued that girls lack confidence. For example, some recent research by Barbara Licht and Carol Deveck (Florida State and Harvard Universities). They found that when girls do badly, they tend more than boys do to put this down to their own lack of ability; but when they do well, they are more likely to attribute it to other factors such as luck than boys are. In entering new situations, girls expect to fail more often than boys. Boys are more likely to choose difficult tasks over easy ones, and once they have chosen to begin a difficult task, they are more likely than girls to persist until it is completed. Of course this only pushes the question one stage back, for why should girls lack confidence?

It is not the case simply that boys do better than girls. Rather, there are two major sorts of differences. One is that boys and men are, so to speak, more variable than females: there are more geniuses, but also more at the bottom end, more mental deficients. The other is that the two sexes are good at different things: roughly speaking girls are better at verbal, boys at mathematical skills. Perhaps for this reason girls are often better at examinations, which often depend heavily on words.

The sex-role link with mathematics was shown convincingly twenty years ago by Lyn Carlsmith. Generally, one cannot of course bring children up in different conditions to see what will happen. Carlsmith, however, took advantage of the accident that World War II deprived many young families of their fathers for different periods of time. Taking a sample of 1,460 American college students born between 1941 and 1945, and alike in every respect except that some had had their fathers away on military service, it appeared quite clearly that early and long separation from the father resulted in relatively greater ability in verbal areas than in mathematics; while no separation resulted in relatively greater ability in mathematics.

Benbow and Stanley, however, also found that of the extremely gifted mathematicians – the one in 10,000 sort – 20% were left handed, roughly twice the US national average. It is also the case that boys are more often left-handed than girls; as well as more often dyslexic. This suggests that the right-hand half of the brain

tends to be more dominant in boys. The right half controls the left of the body; and it is believed that it deals with pattern and shape, important in art, music and mathematics, whereas the left deals with language. Dr Norman Geschwind of Harvard Medical School has even proposed a cause for this difference. He suggests it is due to the fact that boys, before they are born, are exposed in the womb to much more of the hormone testosterone. Some boys, on this theory, react more strongly than average, resulting in a right-dominant brain. The theory is still highly debatable.

Even investigating the causes of differences can be controversial, especially when such emotive issues as race are touched. *The Sunday Times*, 8 April 1984, reported fears that race relations could be damaged by official publication of a research project at Bradford University, involving 1500 children at nine schools in West Yorkshire. According to reporters Paul Flather and Peter Wilby, the research shows that only 44% of West Indian children say that their parents are helpful in getting them through their exams, compared with 60% of white and about 70% of Pakistani and Bangladeshi children. Asian children tend to get clear guidance about schooling and career options from well-educated relatives, while West Indian children do not. Interviews suggest that Asian youngsters have more positive attitudes to school and education than either white or West Indian pupils. And so on. Such findings may suggest why West Indians tend to under-achieve in school, at least in the sense of getting significantly fewer 'O' level passes than Whites or Asians.

Not to make public the results of research seems to most scientists to be directly contradictory to the nature of science itself. But while the principle may be clear, the consequences are not. Research, especially into human behaviour, has often turned out to be wrong or misleading, or it has been distorted by others than the original researchers. And what ought to be done as a result of research is often even more difficult to decide. William Labov, a leading American authority on language and changes in language, has argued that studies of relative achievement, in examinations for example, miss the point. It is not that races are potentially equal but some groups are handicapped; it is that achievement is essentially a relative matter, defined by the context in which it occurs. It is the context that, if anything, must change. Labov is quoted by Jeremy Campbell (*The Standard*, September 14, 1983) as greatly encouraged by the fact that the younger blacks in London are speaking almost pure Cockney. Tape recordings of blacks and whites are indistinguishable. "That means that blacks in London are being integrated into the local mainstream. . . In America, black and white dialects are usually quite different."

This may well be encouraging, as Labov claims, for race relations, but is the loss of a characteristic dialect an unmixed blessing? Some at least may feel that uniformity and conflict are equally undesirable, and that the task of research is to help us, if possible, to steer a difficult course between them.

Books mentioned

BARNES-GUTTERIDGE, W.:	*Psychology*	London, Hamlyn, 1974
COHEN, D.:	*All in the Head*	London, Peacock Books, 1979
COLMAN, A.:	*What is Psychology?*	London, Kogan Page, 1981
ATKINSON, R.C., ATKINSON, R.L., & HILGARD, E.R.:	*Introduction to Psychology*, 7th edn.	London, Methuen, 1979
RADFORD, J. & GOVIER, E. eds.:	*A Textbook of Psychology*	London, Sheldon, 1980
TAYLOR, A. et al eds.	*Introducing Psychology*, 2nd edn.	Harmondsworth, Penguin, 1984

In saying goodbye

We have made our introduction; we hope it has been interesting. Perhaps you would like to pursue the acquaintanceship. There are many ways to do so.

Textbooks, both general and on specialised topics, number many hundreds. Probably the most widely read of all is that of Hilgard, Atkinson & Atkinson, an American book, while among British efforts Taylor & David must be mentioned. One of us confesses to a certain partiality for that by Radford & Govier. Among smaller, paperback works we might suggest those by Barnes-Gutteridge, Cohen, and Colman; and two series covering a wide range of topics, Essential Psychology and New Essential Psychology, both edited by Peter Herriot, and published by Methuen. Probably the best plan is to visit an academic bookshop, if one is within reach, and browse.

Courses at all levels and for all purposes abound, from extramural, leisure type courses through GCE to degree level. We will not try to give information about these, which is available from local colleges, the careers service or the local education office. Many Departments of Psychology in Universities and Polytechnics, however, will try to answer enquiries even if not directly about their own courses. Some hold open days or have other opportunities to visit.

Information on many aspects of psychology and courses in it can be got from the British Psychological Society, St Andrews House, 48 Princess Road East, Leicester LE1 7DR.

We ourselves, your authors, will do our best to answer specific questions if you think we can help; or at least suggest where you may find the answer.

And so, at least for now, goodbye!

Kjell Raaheim
John Radford

London, December 1984